Radical Romantics

Edinburgh Critical Studies in Romanticism
Series Editors: Ian Duncan and Penny Fielding

Available Titles
A Feminine Enlightenment: British Women Writers and the Philosophy of Progress, 1759–1820
JoEllen DeLucia

Reinventing Liberty: Nation, Commerce and the British Historical Novel from Walpole to Scott
Fiona Price

The Politics of Romanticism: The Social Contract and Literature
Zoe Beenstock

Radical Romantics: Prophets, Pirates, and the Space Beyond Nation
Talissa J. Ford

Forthcoming Titles
Ornamental Gentlemen: Literary Antiquarianism and Queerness in British Literature and Culture, 1760–1890
Michael Robinson

Literature and Medicine in the Nineteenth-Century Periodical Press: Blackwood's Edinburgh Magazine, 1817–1858
Megan Coyer

Following the Footsteps of Deep Time: Geological Travel Writing in Scotland, 1750–1820
Tom Furniss

Radical Romantics

Prophets, Pirates, and the
Space Beyond Nation

Talissa J. Ford

EDINBURGH
University Press

for Fig
for every house is incomplete without him

Edinburgh University Press is one of the leading university presses in the UK. We publish academic books and journals in our selected subject areas across the humanities and social sciences, combining cutting-edge scholarship with high editorial and production values to produce academic works of lasting importance. For more information visit our website: edinburghuniversitypress.com

© Talissa J. Ford, 2016

Edinburgh University Press Ltd
The Tun – Holyrood Road, 12(2f) Jackson's Entry, Edinburgh EH8 8PJ

Typeset in 11/14 Adobe Sabon by
IDSUK (DataConnection) Ltd

A CIP record for this book is available from the British Library

ISBN 978 1 4744 0942 1 (hardback)
ISBN 978 1 4744 0943 8 (webready PDF)
ISBN 978 1 4744 0944 5 (epub)

The right of Talissa J. Ford to be identified as the author of this work has been asserted in accordance with the Copyright, Designs and Patents Act 1988, and the Copyright and Related Rights Regulations 2003 (SI No. 2498).

Contents

List of Illustrations	vi
Acknowledgements	vii
Introduction: Romanticism Off the Map	1
1. It is Not Amiss to Speak of His Beard	19
2. A Pirate or Anything	41
3. Coming Up From the Midst of the Sea	67
4. Jerusalem is Scattered Abroad	91
5. From Here to Timbuktu	123
Conclusion: Land Pirates and Republican Ragamuffins	149
Index	172

List of Illustrations

Frontispiece James Gillray, The plumb-pudding in danger: – or – state epicures taking un petit souper, 1805.   x

1.1 'Cap'n Teach commonly call'd Black Beard', *A General History of the Pyrates*. Attributed to J. Basire, 1724   20

4.1 'Negroland and Guinea. With the European settlements. Explaining what belongs to England, Holland, Denmark&c,' H. Moll, 1729   94

4.2 *Jerusalem: The Emanation of the Giant Albion*, frontispiece (proof), William Blake, 1804–1820   104

4.3 *Jerusalem: The Emanation of the Giant Albion*, frontispiece (copy E), William Blake, 1804–1820   105

5.1 'Mr. Caillié meditating upon the Koran and taking notes', *Travels Through Central Africa to Timbuctoo*, 1830   140

Acknowledgements

This book was first conceived in another place and time, in the company of Celeste Langan, Steve Goldsmith, and Kevis Goodman, all of whom were more generous than either the project or I deserved. Mai-Lin Cheng, Rae Greiner and Padma Rangarajan read more pages over more years than I can count. Joanna Picciotto, who has continued to read chapters in the years since, has been more present for me than she knows; her words, some a decade-old, resurface when I need them. And in a far different way, the words of Allan Pred remain present; Allan was a gift to the field of geography, and to me. All told, there are twenty-five years' worth of teachers to thank. Dorothy Bewick, Mary-Beth Morris, Judy Barrett, Rich Doyle, Jeff Nealon, and Paul Youngquist stand out among them. From Paul I learned not only that I wanted to be a romanticist, but what kind of romanticist I wanted to be.

The support of colleagues at Temple University has made my work possible: Eli Goldblatt, Kate Henry, Priya Joshi, Joyce Joyce, Michael Kaufmann, Peter Logan, Nichole Miller, Steve Newman, James Salazar, and Gabriel Wettach deserve special mention. The year I spent as a faculty fellow at CHAT (the Center for the Humanities at Temple) was crucial as the project made its transition from a dissertation to a book; I am lucky to have had feedback from faculty and graduate students across the humanities. I am fortunate, too, to have shared my work with humanities colleagues from around the area as a regional faculty fellow at the Penn Humanities Forum. The other fellows not only responded generously to my work, but inspired me with their own. One of my greatest joys in Philadelphia has been participating in P19, our regional nineteenth-century forum, organised by Rachel Buurma and Kate Thomas; the many scholars I have met through P19 remind me, again and again, the varied things that can be done with nineteenth-century texts. That Philly has its own star romanticist,

Michael Gamer, is a particular delight, and I was especially lucky that Michael was a fellow at the Penn Humanities Forum the same year as I was. Philadelphia's most surprising offering, though, was Eitan Bar-Yosef, whose work I had admired from 6,000 miles away; when he happened to turn up in Philadelphia, it did a world of good for my chapter on Richard Brothers and Joanna Southcott.

If this book has a point of origin, it's William Blake. But if it has three points of origin, they are William Blake, Peter Linebaugh, and Marcus Rediker. Two of these I am unlikely ever to meet. The third I was unlikely ever to meet, too, until I did. I had the good fortune of attending Marcus Rediker's "Scholarship and Activism" seminar at the University of Colorado Boulder in 2010 and found Marcus to be as inspiring in person as he is in print; in those few hours, my sense of what scholarly work can (and should) do was changed forever.

Radical Romantics cannot live up to all those who have inspired it, but whatever good it does is due almost entirely to the generosity of the brave souls who read the manuscript in its entirety. Padma Rangarajan and Paul Saint-Amour read this book at its very worst; nothing but their kindness could have saved it. Padma has probably spent as much time reading my work as I have over the past fifteen years, and her wisdom and good cheer have never faltered. The book's most recent reader, Ian Duncan, understood what I was trying to do and helped me find ways to do it better; the time I have spent working with him at EUP has made me wish I had known him better at Berkeley. I am honored that he and Penny Fielding saw potential in this project. I am grateful, too, to the two anonymous readers whose insights helped to reshape the work, and to Caroline Budge for her careful and patient copyediting.

My first writing partner, Michael Weisberg – besides keeping me company in what would otherwise have been an agonisingly solitary pursuit – helped me through the middle years of the writing process by cooking beautiful vegetarian lunches every day. He, Deena, and Brandon are a joy to know. So, too, are the Foley-Buurmas: Chris, Rachel, Frances Ruth, Prudence, Xerxes, and even April, who helped me through the last couple years of the project with banh mi, wine, love, and under-table *Hamlet*.

Being a Romanticist has a lot to recommend it, but the best part by far is Thora Brylowe. That she comes as a package deal with Dave, Duncan, Annabel, and David Boggess, and Libby, Jon, Devin, Liam, and Ian Carrier is an embarrassment of riches. Countless others too, at conferences and cafes, in person and in print, have sustained me and my writing over the years: Monica Ajer; Shane Barnard; Ron Broglio; Katie Cavicchio; Jeff Cox; Griffin, Kate, and Milly Henry; Karyn Leibovitz; Lital Levy; Margaret Szumski; Andrea Kneeland, and Daniel, Roxanne, Samantha, Sunset, and Luna Windler. Alison Dwyer, Jami Bartlett, and Austin Grossman have each, in their own way, been with me since the beginning.

When I moved to Philadelphia it was for a job; imagine my surprise when I found my family here. Amy, Olivier, Ella, and Blue Berton made Philly home. Ella has grown up alongside this book; I still have her toddler corrections on an early draft. Gabe Wettach was my first friend in Philly and has been putting up with me ever since. Huge love and gratitude, especially, to those people who don't have a choice about whether to put up with me: Nat Kessler, Sara Kessler, Joy Kessler, Steve Shostrom, Charles Kirkland, Anysa Kirkland, Andrew Kirkland, Heather Kirkland – and Margie Kessler, who deserves all the credit, really. I should also note that there would probably be no book if Fig, Satsuki, and Allegra had not sometimes decided to let me do something other than pay attention to them.

A conference paper that developed into Chapter 2 was published in *Romantic Border Crossings* (Ashgate 2008), edited by Jeffrey Cass and Larry Peer. An earlier version of Chapter 4 appeared in *Studies in Romanticism* (Winter 2008). I thank the Trustees of Boston University and Ashgate Publishing for allowing me to reproduce sections of them here.

James Gillray, *The plumb-pudding in danger: – or – state epicures taking un petit souper*, 1805. www.metmuseum.org

Introduction:
Romanticism Off the Map

For the Spaces reachd from the starry heighth, to the starry depth;
And they builded Golgonooza: terrible eternal labour!
What are these golden builders doing?
                                William Blake, *Jerusalem* 12: 22–4

Things *extra* and *other* insert themselves into the accepted framework, the imposed order. One thus has the very relationship between spatial practices and the constructed order. The surface of this order is everywhere punched and torn open by ellipses, drifts, and leaks of meaning: it is a sieve-order.
                        Michel de Certeau, *The Practice of Everyday Life*

This book begins with an ending: the historical moment in the eighteenth century when Britain succeeded in cleansing the Atlantic of its pirates. The argument that follows concerns a movement that, on the contrary, refused to end. It documents the pirate's persistence as a cultural memory of resistance to social, political, and economic oppression, and finds him to be just one instance of a revolutionary spirit that emerges in some surprising places during the Romantic period: in prophetic pamphlets, in travel narratives about Jerusalem and Africa, in William Blake's visionary poetry, and in Lord Byron's Eastern romances. The radicalism of these texts consists in their imagination of space beyond the terms of nationalism and territory; their power is that they force us to recognise the incongruence between mapped and lived space. I therefore move away from an account of radicalism that takes the nation as its primary point of contention and focus instead on figures who fall outside of the terms that nationalism imposes. Prophets and pirates are apt figures because they operate outside of the literal or figurative boundaries of the nation: prophets live in the nation of God, and pirates live in motion. Their particular and pervasive radicalisms are enabled by their status as outsiders to the nation; their practices of settling land and claiming ships in defiance of national authority become material interferences in a system of nationalised space. I trace these varied forms of geographical radicalism as well as the systems in which they are inscribed, thereby revealing the contours and limits of territorial sovereignty. And so, while varying in topic and form, my assembled texts share something crucial: their documentation of a radicalism that is mobile, informed by a conception of space as movement rather than containment, inscribed in an increasingly visible Atlantic network. The unified labour of sailing crews, the circulation of goods and information, the democratic ideals often cultivated on ships – all of these extended their influence far beyond the sea, provoking revolutionary movements that were felt everywhere. This book aims to make visible the network forged through practices of mobility, by rethinking the British Romantic period through such non-national conceptions of space: beyond territory, beyond borders, beyond maps.

The Cartographer's Mad Project

Maps fail. Or, at least, they fail if we imagine that their job is to represent space accurately: to be complete, objective, literally representative. Even if maps mean only to represent a place as it is experienced or idealised, they are necessarily inadequate to the task, limited by the page, by their two-dimensionality, by the mere fact of scale.[1] Maps are therefore exercises in choosing and excluding, exercises in futility: what Baudrillard calls 'the cartographer's mad project of an ideal coextensivity between the map and the territory'.[2] The cartographer's project is mad not only for the more obvious reasons I have already mentioned, but also because the map fundamentally misrepresents and misunderstands how space works. By insisting on the stability of spaces, it denies their fluidity and constructedness. This, therefore, is a book about what is beyond the map, and about what people can do when, literally or metaphorically, they rewrite maps. It is a book about those who move outside of the lines that delineate nation from other nation. It is about where those lines come from, what they tell us about people who believe in them, and what happens when those lines are contested or ignored. It is about how the map's failure to do the impossible might have things to teach us about what gets left out of national accounts of space, history and literature. It is, in other words, about what is off the map. But maps are where my subjects start, their point of departure, and so maps are where I will start, my own point of departure.

Geography began late. Just how late is of course subject to debate. There are several commonly cited possibilities: The increasing adoption of the Greenwich meridian in the eighteenth century; the 1750 publication of the *Carte de France*, the first comprehensive map of France; Cook's voyage into the Pacific in 1769;[3] Jesse Ramsden's 1787 improvements to the theodolite; the foundation of the British Hydrographic Office in 1795. What is clear is that *something* happened to geography in the second half of the eighteenth century, decades before the foundation of the Royal Geographical Society in 1830: not for nothing does Paul Laxton calls 1750–1800 a 'cartographic revolution'.[4] By the eighteenth century, technical advances had positioned cartography squarely in the scientific realm. Furthermore, the number of prominent map-selling houses had grown, placing map-makers in what Catherine Delano-Smith and Roger J. P. Kain call a 'well-defined professional sphere'; map-makers increasingly relied on the public market rather than on patronage.[5] But perhaps the greatest factor in the expansion and institutionalisation of cartography, and of geography more broadly, was war. The first map of agricultural use, for example, was drafted in 1801 in response to concerns about food supply during the Napoleonic Wars, and maps were crucial to the waging of war itself: 'Insofar as ... lands are claimed on paper before they are effectively occupied', writes J. B. Harley, 'maps anticipate empire'.[6] They are also the means of *imagining* empire, of understanding land and nations as spaces that might be conquered, subsumed, accumulated.

Take, for example, James Gillray's 1805 *The plumb-pudding in danger: – or – state epicures taking un petit souper* (frontispiece). The endangered plum pudding in question is the globe; Pitt helps himself to half of the world, while Napoleon carves out the small section that is Europe. Gillray's subtitle, '"the great Globe itself and all which it inherit" is too small to satisfy such insatiable appetites', is an allusion to *The Tempest* but also to Napoleon's 1805 letter to Britain, in which he declares that the war between them is 'purposeless' and 'can lead to no definite result'. His letter concludes by insisting that 'the world is big enough for both our peoples to live on'.[7] As Gillray's cartoon illustrates, the 'peace' that Napoleon proposes would require a violent division of the world into parts, and the danger is to the plum-pudding world as a whole, which is in fact not 'big enough at all'; as Shakespeare teaches us, that globe itself will dissolve, leaving 'not a rack behind'. The metaphor is almost too easy: the world is there for the taking, and maps allow it to be divided and consumed. 'There is no doubt,' writes Edward Said, 'that imaginative geography and history help the mind to intensify its own sense of itself by dramatising the distance and difference between what is close and what is far away.'[8]

Besides conspiring in the spatial imagination that enables colonisation, maps offer the material means to it, a blueprint for imperial projects of acquisition and so-called improvement. David Harvey writes that cartography 'opened up the possibility for the "rational" organisation of space for capital accumulation'; the 'facts' of geography, Harvey argues, are 'presented often as facts of nature' and can therefore 'be used to justify imperialism, neocolonial domination, and expansionism'.[9] The move towards cartography as a science in the eighteenth and nineteenth centuries meant that maps offered a scientific justification for the 'organisations' of space Harvey describes. Visual representations of unsettled land could be used to justify colonisation and the imposition of Western culture.[10] As Harvey writes:

> [T]he division of the world into spheres of influence by the main capitalist powers at the end of the nineteenth century raised serious geopolitical issues. The struggle for control over access to raw materials, labour supplies, and markets was a struggle for command over territories.[11]

It may seem obvious that the struggle over goods and markets is inseparable from a struggle for land, but more crucial here is the articulation of abstractions of power (financial and material) in territorial terms.

The danger of maps, in other words, is that we believe them – or at least believe *in* them, and depend on them for our basic conception of how space and territory work. We understand the state as land, as starting and stopping somewhere that can be identified and represented. Maps, we remain convinced, tell us something real: that a nation may own – or, in fact, may *be* – its geographical space. This belief that the state is a 'fixed unit of sovereign space' is, writes John Agnew, the '"rock-bottom" geographical assumption that underwrites the others'.[12] Though Agnew dates this phenomenon to the 1648 Treaty of Westphalia, critics more often argue that the association of state sovereignty with territory arose in the long eighteenth century.[13] Lauren Benton writes in *A Search for Sovereignty*:

> The association of bounded territory and empire became sharper over the course of the long eighteenth century. By the middle of the nineteenth century, geographic information was clearly established as one of an array of categories of knowledge that played a dual function of making strange landscapes subject to control and rendering them as property – one sense of *dominium*.[14]

In this account, cartographic knowledge is inseparable from legal sovereignty. Colonisation is academic as well as military and legal; the science of cartography produces the ideology of national territory. Henri Lefebvre, in his groundbreaking work *The Production of Space*, argues that the relationship between the nation and territory as we currently know it occurred as a result of the French Revolution. It was the Revolution, Lefebvre argues, that 'gave birth (contradictorily) to the nation, the state, law, rationality . . .' Post-French Revolution nationalisms fixed nations into territories, he suggests, by reorganising the symbolic power of space.[15] The French Revolution did not, in Lefebvre's account, merely make the map seem real; it actually made it *possible* by divorcing space from the practices that create it. As Napoleon and Pitt divided the world into portions, it became divisible in the common spatial imagination.

But such divisions are a fiction. Benton asks us to imagine a more accurate map of imperial power; as opposed to the 'standard, multicolored maps', she argues, it 'would show tangled and interrupted

European-claimed spaces and would represent, perhaps in colours of varying intensity, the changing and locally differentiated qualities of rule within geographic zones'.[16] This is cartography as mess, a map that would acknowledge the unwieldiness of space. Benton uses the sea as a means of conceptualising the ways in which empire is 'legally very lumpy', a disruption of the coherence of the territorial state. More recently, Siobhan Carroll has used the term 'atopia' to refer to resistant spaces: 'These are the uncolonizable spaces of imperial imagination, planetary spaces over which the metropole aims to extend its power but that recalcitrate their conversion into national property'. These are, Carroll writes, '"real" natural regions falling within the theoretical scope of contemporary human mobility, which, because of their intangibility, inhospitality, or inaccessibility, cannot be converted into the locations of affective habitation known as "place"'.[17] I therefore share with many geographers the belief that territorial definitions of nation and empire are inadequate to deal with the nuances, layerings, and excesses of space as it is lived.[18] As Gunnar Olsson writes:

> In the emerging world of globalization the fix-points are in fact so invisible and unstable that they are not at all . . . [T]he threads which once were woven into a set of longitudes and latitudes now form a hopelessly tangled skein; the screening mappa not a flat surface but a set of warped and rhizomatic napkins, culture-stained and with a scent distinctly their own.
>
> No wonder that people sometimes get lost. Not, however, because we are all mad (although that happens too), but because our navigational tools have become badly outdated, ordering directives designed for another time and another place . . .[19]

Our 'ordering directives' are 'designed for another time and another place', as Olsson puts it, precisely because they *are* ordering directives. They are designed for a time and place that never was, since space as it is practised (made and remade, moved through, lived, breathed) has never mapped easily onto that flat, ordered surface. Space is always social, always political, always imagined and imaginative. We learned this first from Lefebvre, who set a trajectory for David Harvey, Edward Soja, and countless other cultural geographers to come.[20] If Olsson's space is a 'culture-stained rhizomatic napkin', Lefebvre's is what leaves the stains: a space 'with a structure far more reminiscent of flaky *mille-feuille* pastry than of the homogeneous and isotropic space of classical (Euclidean/Cartesian) mathematics'.[21] For Lefebvre, the important point is that social spaces 'interpenetrate one another and/or superimpose themselves upon one another': this is space that produces and is produced by, organises and is organised by, social networks.[22]

To the extent that Lefebvre's theory is a response to both Hegel and Marx, the natural question might then be what a conception of space as 'interpenetrating' means for conceptualising the relationship between space and the state. For Lefebvre, it means that:

> the state and each of its constituent institutions call for spaces – but spaces which they can then organize according to their specific requirements; so there is no sense in which space can be treated solely as an a priori condition of these institutions and the state which presides over them.[23]

That we nevertheless continue to understand space as an a priori condition is evidence of what Agnew calls the 'territorial trap', a 'geographical unconscious' that continues to underlie most theories of the state.[24] As Neil Brenner et al. write in their introduction to *State/Space: A Reader*:

> [S]tates are not simply located 'upon' or 'within' a space. Rather, they are dynamically evolving spatial entities that continually mold and reshape the geographies of the very social relations they aspire to regulate, control, and/or restructure. This continual production and transformation of state space occurs not only through material-institutional practices of state spatial regulation but also through a range of representational and discursive strategies through which the terrain of sociopolitical struggle is mapped and remapped by actors who are directly involved in such struggles.[25]

Attempts to locate states backfire; states evolve, are produced – they are transformed from the bottom-up. The harder the state seeks to solidify its borders (parsing land to be settled in Palestine, declaring national waters), the more slippery space becomes. The figures in this book – prophets, pirates, maroons, and travellers – reveal the fragility of national identity and irrevocably complicate attempts to territorialise the state. Some outsiders pose a physical threat to the nation but, more crucially, they pose an ideological threat, disrupting a coherent territorial identity. They demonstrate that the territorial ideal upon which state power is predicated is a dangerous fiction: that, finally, space is made, is social, and is practised, and that anyone who moves through it has the power to transform it. This relationship between mobility and resistance has been most clearly articulated in Peter Linebaugh and Marcus Rediker's groundbreaking work *The Many-Headed Hydra: Sailors, Slaves, Commoners, and the Hidden History of the Revolutionary Atlantic*. Besides documenting the primacy of mobility in revolutionary movements – the power of a class that is (by necessity or choice) mobile – Linebaugh and Rediker illuminate the effects of that mobility, the ways in which it connects disparate instances of the revolutionary. *The Many-Headed Hydra* has given us a language for talking about a network of resistance that is not merely the sum of its parts: revolution is a hydra because, having been cut down in one place, it regenerates in another. I build on this account of revolution from below by also exploring another, less positive angle: the very real power structures under which such revolutions often collapse. I focus on state practices of repression in addition to resistance to such repression; it is only in acknowledging the messy relations between the two, I argue, that we can do justice to the radicalism of the period.

Because the sea is the most visible site of radical mobility, *Radical Romantics* is also deeply engaged with other work that, like *The Many-Headed Hydra*, takes the maritime world as its primary focus. There has been a recent surge of literary critical interest in the maritime; 2010 alone saw the publication of Margaret Cohen's *The Novel and the Sea* and Samuel Baker's *Written on the Water*, and *PMLA* dedicated its May 2010 'Theories and Methodologies' section to oceanic studies. *Radical Romantics* expands on these studies by articulating the inseparability of land and sea. Boats docked, sailors walked through cities, goods moved from land to sea and back again; and revolutionary movements travelled as well. Within the last decade, Romantic critics have paid increasing attention to such movements. Ashgate's *Nineteenth Century Transatlantic Studies* series, as well as the growing number of conference panels focusing on empire, colonialism, and cosmopolitanism, indicate the centrality of these debates in Romantic studies. Saree Makdisi, Kathleen Wilson, and Nigel Leask have published landmark treatments of imperialism; Kevin Hutchings, Alan Bewell, Srinivas Aravamudan, Debbie Lee, and Deirdre Coleman have focused critical attention on slavery and colonisation. I approach these issues from a different angle, however, by not taking the nation as the central fact of analysis: indeed, this notion of the primacy of the nation is precisely what I argue forcefully against. In this respect, my thinking is more in line with Paul Youngquist and Frances Botkin's new work on Black Romanticism. Against other narratives of the nation – Linda Colley's *Britons: Forging the Nation, 1701–1837*, Benedict Anderson's *Imagined Communities: Reflections on the Origin and Spread of Nationalism*, and Srinivas Aravamudan's *Tropicopolitans: Colonialism and Agency, 1688–1804* – Youngquist and Botkin shift their study to the 'restless revenants' of the Atlantic, the 'ancestors of the nation'. The accounts of Colley, Anderson, and Aravamudan, Youngquist and Botkin argue, 'share assumptions that get built into the study of national cultures such as British Romanticism': they are geographically, linguistically, and racially territorialised. Black Romanticism, however, 'deterritorializes British national identity and the culture of the Romantic era, reimagining them as the *effect* of myriad economic and cultural exchanges circulating throughout the Atlantic'.[26]

In my own attempt to deterritorialise identity, I treat texts which might seem, on the surface, quite extraneous to revolutionary movements, but which position themselves explicitly or incidentally outside the nation and national identity. This leads me to consider a wide range of genres and authors; I place texts by canonical writers alongside travel and slave narratives, prophecies, letters, journals, and inexpensive pirated texts. To read these texts together is to see in distinct acts of resistance – resistance to force in all its manifestations – a shared geographical imagination produced by mobility and maintained by a collectivity. Piracy, prophecy, exile, and wandering are forms of radical movement in which the traversals of outsiders (intersections between travellers and spaces where they do not belong) reveal the map of the imperial world to be, at every point, contested.

The Pirate's Prophecy

Chapter 1, 'It is Not Amiss to Speak of His Beard', focuses on the period just after the demise of Atlantic piracy. In the first decade of the eighteenth century, there were as many as 2,000 pirates on the Atlantic in any given year. By 1724, when Captain Johnson penned his famous *A General History of the Pirates*, very few remained; pirates had been eradicated by a massively successful campaign on the part of European nations (and of Britain in particular). I focus on *A General History* in this chapter because of its complicated status as a post-piracy pirate tale. It is a text that benefits from an historical distance from its subject but simultaneously maintains a sense of immediacy, as the effects of piracy were still very much present. Johnson's introduction makes a point of citing the economic damage inflicted on England by pirates – greater, he says, than what the nation suffered at the hands of the French and Spanish combined. But I argue that, embedded in his account of the violence pirates inflicted, there is a commentary on another serious threat they posed, more ideological than material: pirates rejected the authority of the nation, hierarchies of class and race, and the fundamental principles of ownership and private property. Pirates were physically and ideologically beyond the nation at a time when the nation-state was solidifying; the multiracial and multinational composition of pirate crews reflected this disaffiliation by abandoning race and nationality under the Jolly Roger. The famous pirate cry 'We come from the sea!' was therefore more or less true; having disowned (and been disowned by) their countries of origin, pirates could be said to have come from both nowhere and everywhere. They represented a terrifying other, violent and exotic, and even more menacingly, they represented the danger of cultural mixing. Blackbeard, for example, was a threat not only because of his many violent captures, but because he was suspected to be the son of a mulatto. Captain Johnson spends a disproportionate amount of time describing Blackbeard's appearance, and in particular his fearsome black beard, which, even when it was not adorned with lighted matches, 'frightened America more than any comet'.[27] Johnson's conflation of Blackbeard's explicitly racialised features and the physical and economic danger he posed to England neatly captures the conflation of the material and ideological threat of piracy. In tracing the forces that provoked the war against piracy, this chapter aims to establish the terms of the spirit that underlies the piratical, and thus to set the stage for a discussion of other sites at which an analogous spirit emerges. I argue that, despite the dissolution of actual pirate bands, piracy persisted as a displaced and appropriated force – a spirit of resistance that I will identify in various authors and texts in the chapters that follow.

My second chapter, 'A Pirate or Anything', begins with Lord Byron's surprisingly unpiratical pirate poems. We might expect Byron, who sustained a long interest in pirates (even permitting rumours that he himself spent time as a pirate), to embrace the romanticisation and orientalisation – and the condition of permanent exile and nationlessness – of the pirate. But in Byron's pirate poems *The Corsair* and *The Bride of Abydos*, the pirates are good Christians who have lovers waiting at home; they fight only to protect their religion, their women, and their land. The fictional pirates of these texts, unlike the pirates we know from history, are deeply implicated in the power structures that piracy operates outside of: these pirates are tied to the nation, to the military, to religion, to domesticity, and to a sense of territory more generally. And yet, despite Byron's conspicuous interest in the forces of empire, his pirate poems *The Bride of Abydos* and *The Corsair* strangely elide explicit acknowledgement of the imperial forces that weigh so heavily on their narratives. William Hone, on the other hand, who pirated Byron's *Corsair*, speaks the unspoken political current that courses beneath Byron's own pirate tales. Hone's *Lord Byron's The Corsair* was rewritten in prose and sold at a fraction of the cost of Byron's poem, thus pirating both textually and economically, and it makes explicit the national alliances that are only implicit in its source. As opposed to the vague nationality of Byron's pirates, Hone's corsair is the leader of a 'powerful band of Italian pirates' who settled on one of the Greek Isles in the seventeenth century and is fighting to defend it from an attack authorised by the Ottoman Porte. In both Hone's and Byron's versions, the pirates are defeated and the hero disappears. But in Byron's *Corsair*, the pirates are defeated because of their sentimentality for home, as if the mere fact of their landedness is finally their destruction. With Hone's insertion of an explicitly political element, it becomes national as well as territorial loyalty that dooms the pirates. I conclude this chapter by turning to Byron's final treatment of piracy, the brief appearance of the pirate Lambro in *Don Juan*. *Don Juan*, an international epic, was written after Byron was exiled from England (having, in a literal sense, 'changed his lakes for ocean'). Like Hone's *Corsair*, it is explicit about its pirate's national ties: Lambro is Greek, a symbol of his nation and of his noble inheritance. Reading *The Corsair* and *The Bride of Abydos* through the perspective opened by Hone and by *Don Juan*, I argue that depictions of this particular kind of piratical failure function as a critique of dangerous impositions of nation on territory. In so doing, they offer an alternative model which divorces the ideal of the nation from territory and territory from practiced space.

Nowhere are the contradictory possibilities of supernational, mobile space more evident than in the city of Jerusalem, a city always at once national and extra-national. In the nineteenth century, Palestine was the site of a struggle between the British and Ottoman empires, but it was also the land of God, always necessarily beyond the confines of any nation. Nineteenth-century prophets who imagined rebuilding the city were therefore forced to reconcile a redemptive project with a colonial one – perhaps a familiar prospect to those who already equated empire with a civilising mission, but amped up by the fact that the land to be civilised was the Holy Land itself. My third chapter, 'Coming Up From the Midst of the Sea', focuses on the Jerusalems imagined by prophets Joanna Southcott and Richard Brothers. Despite their interest in the world to come, Southcott and Brothers were also very much invested in the world that was, and they were attuned to the means by which revolutionary prophetic language could be used as a commentary on political revolution. The sheer number of prophets who emerged in the period suggests that the fact of prophecy at this moment was tied to actual revolutions: surely, some figured, the Seven Years' War and the subsequent revolutions in France, America, and Haiti were signs of the apocalypse prophesied in the Book of Revelation. During the years when Southcott and Brothers squabbled over their respective claims to God's word, England was embroiled in the French Revolutionary wars, and slaves in St Domingo were fighting for their independence. These are details registered in their prophecies: Southcott compares Napoleon to Satan and concludes that his defeat is evidence of God's triumph, while Brothers insists that London, with its trade in exotic goods and slaves, is the spiritual Babylon and will be destroyed. Both insist on transforming these historical, material spaces to create the imagined city, and yet their respective Jerusalems are, in at least one crucial respect, polar opposites. For Southcott, Jerusalem is to be built here – that is, in England – and the fact that Jerusalem happens already to be 'there' is of little importance. In contrast to Southcott's Jerusalem-in-Britain, Richard Brothers' Jerusalem is in Jerusalem: but the city that *is* bears no resemblance to the city that should and will be. The present Jerusalem needs to be resettled and then rebuilt, not, as in a British imperial model, by replacing what is there with British customs and goods, but by dismantling empire and distributing its pieces. The stones from the pyramids will be used to rebuild the Temple; the New Jerusalem will be built, quite literally, from the spoils of empire. If Southcott's Jerusalem is uncomfortably British, Brother's is radically anti-national: taken together, they argue for the complicated inscription of prophecy in colonialism even as they gesture towards its extra-national potential.

Chapter 4, 'Jerusalem is Scattered Abroad', expands on the complicated relationship between the actual city of Jerusalem and its literary representation. It begins with travel narratives about the real Jerusalem and concludes with Blake's poem about an imagined Jerusalem, but the argument of the chapter is that Jerusalem is in fact always both real and imagined, simultaneously a material city and the site of an imminent heaven on earth. Chateaubriand writes of his 'surprise' at his first sight of the city in 1806, as he stood at Jerusalem's gates 'seeking in vain the Temple' (that had been gone for two thousand years).[28] Such surprise is a common trope in eighteenth- and nineteenth-century Palestine travel narratives; travellers arrived in Jerusalem, one after another, expecting to find the Jerusalem of the Bible. Instead, they found Muslims. Jerusalem was thus the epitome of British imperial sensibilities: a land to be conquered, developed and saved. My analysis of these Jerusalem travel narratives sets the historical stage for William Blake's visionary poem. Like Southcott and Brothers, Blake was keenly aware of the contemporary political conditions that framed Britain's relation to the East, and in particular to the Ottoman Empire (then in control of Jerusalem); he understood that Britain's investment in Jerusalem, economic as well as religious, was in a Jerusalem that was explicitly Western. But Blake's own Jerusalem is far more complicated, a palimpsest of Britain on Egypt on

Jerusalem on the globe on the body. I argue that in imagining such a Jerusalem, Blake's poem demands a radical remapping, critiquing the version of interconnectedness that is empire and calling instead for a global network of revolution and resistance.

Chapter 5, 'From Here to Timbuktu', treats a very different kind of imagined space: not prophesied so much as invented outright, in the form of two fictional narratives about the West African city of Timbuktu. They are both, I argue, examples of how the nation can be reconceived by those who are outside of it; rather than documenting a rejection of the nation from within, moving out, they depict a reconceptualisation of the nation from the outside, moving in. The first is *The Narrative of Robert Adams*, the story of a mixed-race sailor who was found starving on the docks of London, and who claimed to have gone to Timbuktu. No Westerner had been to Timbuktu since the sixteenth century, and Europeans were anxious for information about the fabled city; Adams was anxious for food, clothing, and passage back to America. The African Company of London recorded and published Adams' narrative, insisting on its legitimacy, and making themselves look rather foolish in the event: Adams, it turned out, had never been to Timbuktu. Five years later, James Grey Jackson published another false Timbuktu narrative by Asseed El Hage Abd Salam Shabeeny, a Muslim merchant who also claimed to have visited the city. Both Adams and Shabeeny stress the primitiveness of Timbuktu, an unlearned, heathen city, and this was precisely what the African Company and the British public wanted to hear. If Timbuktu was an uncultivated land, it had the potential (a potential that, of course, only the West could recognise) to be once again the city of gold: Timbuktu was a Jerusalem-style imperial dream. This chapter argues that Adams and Shabeeny take advantage of British self-conception to manipulate systems of control, rather than merely responding to them. Like pirates – who raise a black flag in parody of the nation, who use their status as outlaws to operate literally outside the law, who deploy the skills they learned on merchant or navy ships to attack the merchants and navies they once worked for – Shabeeny and Adams recognise how to work the colonial system to their own ends. And like prophets, they offer imaginary spaces as antidotes to the violence of state-imposed territory and imperial incorporation, negotiating the fine line between complicity and rebellion. Here is where prophets, pirates, slaves and travellers come together, and here we can grasp the force of their imaginative potential. Their insistent depictions of transformative spaces expose the inadequacy of national models, revealing the fault lines along which imperialism breaks apart. This book is an assemblage of these otherwise only tangentially related moments and texts. It seeks to forge relations from the fragments of an expunged tradition of resistance.

Notes

1. Jean Baptiste Bourguignon d'Anville's 1749 map of Africa marked a shift in cartographic practice. Where his predecessors had filled the centre of the continent with rumoured geographical features, d'Anville recorded only those sites that had been confirmed by European travellers. Depending on your reading, this was either an acknowledgement of the limits of European knowledge or an invitation to colonise those blank spaces. Many critics suggest that it functioned as the latter; see this book's conclusion, as well as Siobhan Carroll, *An Empire of Air and Water: Uncolonizable Space in the British Imagination, 1750–1850* (Philadelphia: University of Pennsylvania Press, 2015), 1.
2. Baudrillard refers here to Borges' 'On Exactitude in Science': 'In that Empire, the Art of Cartography attained such Perfection that the map of a single Province occupied the entirety of a City, and the map of the Empire, the entirety of a Province. In time, those Unconscionable Maps no longer satisfied, and the Cartographers Guilds struck a Map of the Empire whose size was that of the Empire, and which coincided point for point with it. The following Generations, who were not so fond of the Study of Cartography as their Forebears had been, saw that that vast Map was Useless, and not without some Pitilessness was it, that they delivered it up to the Inclemencies of Sun and Winters. In the Deserts of the West, still today, there are Tattered Ruins of that Map, inhabited by Animals and Beggars; in all the Land there is no other Relic of the Disciplines of Geography.' Borges is himself expanding on an idea from Lewis Carroll's *Sylvie and Bruno Concluded*, in which a map is made with a 'scale of a mile to the mile'. [Jean Baudrillard, *Simulations*, trans. Phil Beitchman, Paul Foss, and Paul Patton (Semiotext(e), 1983), 3; Jorges Luis Borges, *Collected Fictions*, trans. Andrew Hurley (New York: Penguin, 1998), 325; Lewis Caroll, *Sylvie and Bruno Concluded* (New York: Macmillan, 1894), 169.]

3. David Ross Stoddart, *On Geography and Its History* (Oxford: Basil Blackwell, 1986), 33; Michael Heffernan, '"A Dream as Frail as Those of Ancient Time": The In-Credible Geographies of Timbuctoo', *Environment and Planning D: Society and Space* 19, no. 2 (2001): 203–25.
4. J. B. Harley, *The New Nature of Maps: Essays in the History of Cartography* (Baltimore: Johns Hopkins University Press, 2001).
5. Catherine Delano-Smith, *English Maps: A History* (Toronto: University of Toronto Press, 1999), 103.
6. Harley, *The New Nature of Maps*, 57.
7. The lines to which Napoleon alludes are from 4.1: 151–3 of *The Tempest*: '. . . the great globe itself,/ Yea, all which it inherit, shall dissolve.' [Christopher Lee, *Nelson and Napoleon: The Long Haul to Trafalgar* (London: Headline, 2005), 161; William Shakespeare, *The Tempest*, ed. John Dover Wilson (New York: Cambridge, 2009).]
8. Edward W. Said, *Orientalism*, Vintage Books ed. (New York: Vintage Books, 1994), 55.
9. David Harvey, *Spaces of Capital: Towards a Critical Geography* (New York: Routledge, 2001), 220, 112.
10. More locally, maps also justified class distinctions. In 1586, the English government confiscated Irish land for the Munster Settlement, using maps to organise rural 'settlements'. Cadastral maps, which show the boundaries and values of parcels of land, were used for colonisation as early as the seventeenth century. They became increasingly common in the eighteenth century, asserting the primacy of ownership as organising criteria. [Norman Joseph William Thrower, *Maps & Civilization: Cartography in Culture and Society* (Chicago: University of Chicago Press, 1996), 93.]
11. Harvey, *Spaces of Capital*, 226.
12. John Agnew, 'The Territorial Trap: The Geographical Assumptions of International Relations Theory', *Review of International Political Economy* 1, no. 1 (1994): 59.
13. For an account of how such solidifications within Britain shaped the national literature, see Penny Fielding, *Scotland and the Fictions of Geography* (Cambridge: Cambridge University Press, 2008).
14. Lauren A. Benton, *A Search for Sovereignty: Law and Geography in European Empires, 1400–1900* (New York: Cambridge University Press, 2010), 11.
15. Not coincidentally, Lefebvre identifies the moment that abstract space came into being with the moment that abstract labour came into being: the moment that labour became distinct from 'the process of reproduction which perpetuated social life.' [Henri Lefebvre, *The Production of Space* (Cambridge: Blackwell, 1991), 289–90, 49.]

16. Benton, *A Search for Sovereignty*, 9.
17. Siobhan Carroll, 6.
18. Having studied with the geographer Allan Pred, I come to this material with what one recent collection calls a *'Predian' perspective*: 'an idiosyncratic form of cultural Marxism', that is 'rooted deeply in geography yet highly transdisciplinary in its scope'. See Heather Merrill and Lisa M. Hoffman's 'Introduction: Making Sense of Our Contemporary Moment of Danger' and Katharyne Mitchell's 'It's TIME: The Cultural Politics of Memory in the Current Moment of Danger' in *Spaces of Danger: Culture and Power in the Everyday*, ed. Heather Merrill and Lisa M. Hoffman (Athens: University of Georgia Press, 2015), 8, 23.
19. Gunnar Olsson, *Abysmal: A Critique of Cartographic Reason* (Chicago: University of Chicago Press, 2007), 410.
20. Bachelard distinguishes between 'inhabited space' and 'geometrical space'. The former always trumps the latter; Bachelard describes the attitude of the one who moves through space: 'I will be an inhabitant of the world, despite the world.' Edward Soja identifies three kinds of space: spatiality (socially produced space), physical space (the space of material culture), and mental space (the space of cognition and representation). The latter two, he says, are incorporated into, and transformed by, the social construction of spatiality. Gaston Bachelard, *The Poetics of Space* (Boston: Beacon Press, 1969), 47; Edward W Soja, *Postmodern Geographies: The Reassertion of Space in Critical Social Theory* (New York: Verso, 1989).
21. Lefebvre, *The Production of Space*, 86.
22. Like Blakean prophecy, Lefebvre's account could be understood as an attempt to uncover the world that already *is*; geographer Derek Gregory describes Lefebvre's work as an 'attempt to construct a history of the present'. [Derek Gregory, *Geographical Imaginations* (Cambridge, MA: Blackwell, 1994), 402.]
23. Lefebvre, *The Production of Space*, 85.
24. Agnew identifies three conditions that have led to this trap: 1. that 'state territories have been reified as set or fixed units of sovereign space', 2. that the 'use of domestic/foreign and national/international polarities has served to obscure the interaction between processes operating at different scales', and 3. that 'the territorial state has been viewed as existing prior to and as a container of society'. [Agnew, 'The Territorial Trap: The Geographical Assumptions of International Relations Theory.']
25. Neil Brenner et al., *State/Space: A Reader* (Cambridge: Blackwell, 2003), 11.

26. Paul Youngquist and Frances Botkin, "Black Romanticism: Romantic Circulations", *Circulations: Romanticism and the Black Atlantic*, ed. Youngquist and Botkin, Par. 10, October 2011, Romantic Circles, <http://www.rc.umd.edu/praxis/circulations/HTML/praxis.2011.youngquist.html>
27. Daniel Defoe, *A General History of the Pyrates*, ed. Manuel Schonhorn (Mineola: Dover Publications, 1999), 84.
28. François-René Chateaubriand, *Travels in Greece, Palestine, Egypt, and Barbary, During the Years 1806 and 1807* (Philadelphia: 1813), 563.

Chapter 1

It is Not Amiss to Speak of His Beard

> For a pirate is not included in the list of lawful enemies, but is the common enemy of all; among pirates and other men there ought to be neither mutual faith nor binding oath.
>
> Marcus Tullius Cicero, *De Officiis*

> It was a pertinent and true answer which was made to Alexander the Great by a pirate whom he had seized. When the king asked him what he meant by infesting the sea, the pirate defiantly replied: 'The same as you do when you infest the whole world; but because I do it with a little ship I am called a robber, and because you do it with a great fleet, you are an emperor.'
>
> St Augustine, *City of God*

The figure of the pirate as we know him can be attributed almost entirely to *A General History of the Pyrates*, written by someone calling himself Captain Charles Johnson and published in two volumes in 1724 and 1728 respectively.[1] Late eighteenth-century accounts of the pirate, in newspapers and fiction alike, echo or duplicate outright this widely published text, and it is from *A General History* that we get our mostly factual accounts of Blackbeard, Bartholomew (Black Bart) Roberts, Captains Avery and Kidd, and the famous female pirates Anne Bonny and Mary Read. David Cordingly writes baldly that 'Captain Johnson created the modern conception of pirates'.[2]

This modern conception of pirates is easy to romanticise, and indeed much contemporary criticism celebrates the radicalism of pirate communities, but it is possible to consider the effects of pirates' ostracisation without idealising their intentions. Eighteenth-century pirates were not on a mission to revolutionise spatial conception, to

Fig. 1.1 'Cap'n Teach commonly call'd Black Beard', printed in *A General History of the Pyrates*, 1724

be sure; their mission was to survive in extraordinarily dire circumstances. But their legal status as *hostis humani generis*, the common enemy of mankind, led them to establish new social structures in response to their exclusion from national identities. If pirates can be thought of as citizens at all, theirs is a citizenship that is non-territorial, or else theirs is a territory that is non-national. Either way, the legal status of pirates had radicalising effects, and it is that radicalism, in part, that led not only to Europe's war against Atlantic piracy, but also to the romanticisation of piracy in the decades (and centuries) to come. Johnson's *A General History* occupies a crucial juncture between these effects: the temporal space between the publication of the first and second volumes marked a shift in the role of pirates in the popular imagination. At the time of the publication of volume one in 1724, Europe's war against the pirates was already underway, but pirates still sailed the Atlantic. By the publication of the second volume in 1728, however, Atlantic pirates were almost entirely eradicated. The two volumes of *A General History* straddle the divide between the Golden Age of piracy and a post-piratical era; seemingly a celebration of the Golden Age, the second volume might just as easily be read as an elegy to it. This chapter's ultimate focus is the story of Captain Misson, which opens the second volume of *A General History*. But first it is necessary to spend some time considering what happened between the two publications, and the particular ways in which piracy was a threat to the nations of Europe.

A Common Enemy

Among *A General History*'s pirates is Captain Teach, aka Blackbeard, whom many historians now believe was a light-skinned mulatto. Johnson makes no mention of Blackbeard's race, but seizes instead on his eponymous facial hair in a disproportionately lengthy description:

> It will not be amiss, that we speak of his Beard, since it did not a little contribute towards making his Name so terrible in those Parts . . . That large Quantity of Hair, which, like a frightful Meteor, covered his whole Face, and frightened *America* more than any Comet that has appeared there a long time.

> This Beard was black, which he suffered to grow of an extravagant Length; as to Breadth, it came up to his eyes; he was accustomed to twist it with Ribbons, in small Tails, after the Manner of our Ramillies Wiggs, and turn them about his Ears: In Time of Action . . . [he] struck lighted Matches under his Hat, which appearing on each side of his Face, his Eyes naturally looking fierce and wild, made him altogether such a Figure, that Imagination cannot form an Idea of a Fury, from Hell, to look more frightful.[3]

The detailed account of Blackbeard's appearance is not typical of the rest of *A General History*, and the attention devoted to his face and hair – perhaps even his name itself – is a means of equating his dark, wild appearance to his inherent violence. One is hard-pressed to imagine why Blackbeard's beard terrorises so – more than a comet! – if not for its serving as a racial marker. Johnson will go on to say that 'if he had the Look of Fury, his Humours and Passions were suitable to it'.[4] This is a common trope, of course, though the fact that his dark beard was styled in the 'Manner of our Ramillies Wiggs' might be as terrifying as the meteoric beard itself: the racial other symbolically taking on a proper English style. But it turns out that Blackbeard, originally Captain Teach, came by his style naturally. Before he turned pirate, he was a privateer with a certificate from the governor of North Carolina, which authorised him to pillage foreign ships. His becoming pirate mirrors Barbary captives who converted to Islam, or 'turned Turk'; even a loyal English privateer might, in turning pirate, turn savage. This seemingly tangential description of Blackbeard's beard therefore speaks not only to fear of African violence, but also to a fear of the mulatto: the fear, in other words, of racial or cultural mixing.[5]

Mixing was a threat manifested more broadly in the composition of pirate crews themselves. Crews were, by necessity, not only multinational but multi-ethnic. Kenneth Kinkor estimates that twenty-five to thirty per cent of pirates were black. Most black pirates were escaped slaves, but some were not; the black sailors on Blackbeard's crew were freemen born in the British colonies, and the black pirates sailing under Captain Roberts were French 'creole negroes'.[6] Their turn to piracy is hardly surprising, given their other options. Black pirates were generally afforded the same rights aboard pirate ships as their white counterparts. They received an equal portion of any prize, were permitted to vote, were allowed to carry firearms, and sometimes even served as captains of predominantly white crews; when pirates captured ships carrying slaves, the slaves were generally freed and offered a place in the pirate crew. 'It would seem', Kinkor concludes, 'that the deck of a pirate ship was the most empowering place for blacks within the eighteenth-century white man's world.'[7]

To some extent, pirates' treatment of black sailors was practical; the money a pirate crew would have saved by excluding black crew-members was insignificant compared to the risk of slaves contributing to the crew's capture.[8] But it was also the case that, while race was an important distinguishing factor, it was of less significance than the distinction between pirates and the rest of society; the former were joined together by what Kinkor calls a 'pragmatic spirit of revolt against common oppressors'.[9] Such a union posed a threat to the nations of Europe and to slaveholders especially, as it offered motivation for slaves to escape or, worse, rebel. In 1718, Lieutenant Governor Bennett of Bermuda wrote to the Council of Trade and Plantations that 'the negroe men . . . are grown soe very impudent and insulting of late that we have reason to suspect their rising, soe that we can have no dependence on their assistance but to the contrary on occasion should fear their joining with the pirates'.[10] Africans who turned pirate were proof that Africans were more than capable of attaining such power, but they were also a confirmation of the stereotype of Africans as fundamentally violent: the barbarity of pirates collapsed easily into the image of African violence. During the trial of John Quelch's crew in 1704, for example, the Queen's Advocate argued that 'The Three Prisoners now at the Bar are of a different Complexion, 'tis true, but it is well known that the First and most Famous Pirates that have been in the World, were of their Colour.'[11] As evidenced by the Queen's Advocate's equation of piracy with blackness (and, implicitly, of blackness with violence), the union of blacks and pirates against the European social order – in defiance of markers of nationality, ethnicity and religion – posed a threat to those nations whose economies were deeply dependent on the perceived inferiority of Africans, and whose slaveholders lived in terror of an uprising. It also posed a threat to the primacy of race as the basis for identity, since, on the pirate ship, ex-slaves and other Africans were in effect citizens.

The particular idea of citizen that emerged on a pirate ship was another threat to European notions of identity, because it challenged the essentiality of national identity: the sailors on board pirate ships were literally motley crews, uniting in the name of something other than the nation. The *Whydah Galley*, for example, included sailors who were originally from England, Ireland, Scotland, Wales, the Netherlands, Spain, Sweden, and the British colonies, as well as Native American, African American, and African sailors. 'Not even sharing a common language,' writes Kenneth Kinkor, 'they were united in a common enterprise transcending considerations of nationality and religion.'[12] It was an enterprise directed against other ships for the purpose of material gain, effectively putting wealth in the hands of a poorer class, a challenge to the social order as much as it was a danger to trade. This class restructuring was mirrored in the social organisation of pirate ships.[13] In *The Many-Headed Hydra*, Linebaugh and Rediker describe pirates as 'democratic in an undemocratic age, egalitarian in a hierarchical age, class-conscious and justice-seeking'. The pirate ship, they suggest, was a 'world turned upside-down', a setting of resistance in which sailors, having suffered under the treatment of merchant ship officers, adopted what Linebaugh and Rediker describe as a 'self-organization of sailors from below'. Though pirates granted their captain unquestioned authority in chase and battle, he was otherwise governed by popular consensus; one observer noted, 'They permit him to be Captain, on condition that they may be Captain over him'. Furthermore, the democratic structure of pirate life extended beyond the ship and constituted a broader connection between and across pirate crews. 'At its most utopian,' writes Srinivas Aravamudan, 'piracy is the circumstantial birth of a "coastal fraternity" that displaces laterally what would otherwise turn into a chain of colonial command'.[14] In that 'coastal fraternity', pirates frequently joined forces with one another, performing an alliance that exceeded any discrete pirate community.[15]

The combined force of these alliances was substantial: from 1716 and 1722, there were between 1,000 and 2,000 pirates in the Caribbean, the Atlantic, and the Indian Ocean every year. As Peter T. Leeson points out, the pirate population was, 'in a good year', equal to more than fifteen per cent of the Royal Navy.[16] And pirates did damage, far beyond the risk of capture or violence. Certainly that threat was real (although captured sailors were, more often than not, given the option of joining the pirate crew), but our sensationalising of piracy tends to eclipse the potentially greater economic threat it posed: '[w]e are fascinated by the violence,' writes Rediker, 'but the blood does hide the gold'.[17] Bodily harm was just a possible outcome of a pirate victory; economic harm was inevitable. Captain Charles Johnson writes in the introduction to *A General History of the Pyrates*:

> As the Pyrates in the *West-Indies* have been so formidable and numerous, that they have interrupted the Trade of *Europe* in those Parts; and our *English* Merchants, in Particular, have suffered more by their Depredations, than by the united Force of France And Spain, in the late War: We do not doubt but the World will be curious to know the Origin and Progress of these Desperadoes, who were the Terror of the trading Part of the World.[18]

More specifically, as Johnson hints, pirates were enemies of mankind because they were enemies of trade; their criminality was more financial than it was overtly political. Marcus Rediker recounts:

> The pirate was an opponent of the government because, as one of the King's men in court explained in 1717, '*It is the Interest of the State that Shipping be improved.*' In this logic, attacks on trade 'may justly be accounted Treason,' as Sir Edward Coke had allowed in his seventeenth-century codification of English law. And of course no 'wise or honest Men ... who love their Country' would turn pirate, since maritime commerce had always produced the 'Wealth, Strength, Reputation and Glory of the *English* Nation'.[19]

The definition of the pirate as traitor depends on a definition of the state as an economic entity, rather than a political one. To commit this kind of treason is not to work against the crown or even the church, but against merchant shipping. Any group that threatened maritime trade was charged with piracy, even if it was – by its own account – nationally affiliated.

Economic losses were not limited to the plundering of supplies, money and ships, and therefore not limited to merchants' losses. John L. Anderson writes of 'indirect' costs, which took several forms. The first was the loss of resources – money, ships and armies – which might have been utilised towards more productive ends but were instead employed in the war against piracy. Mercantile targets, too, could certainly have better used assets which were by necessity put towards protection of their goods. Such losses occurred, Anderson explains, 'because piracy does not represent a simple transaction that is economically neutral; rather, the resources of both predator and victim are consumed in contesting the transfer of the assets'.[20] Besides the loss of potential productivity of governments, armies, and merchants, the pirates themselves were lost potential: they could have paid taxes, and their labour and capital could have contributed towards material production. Finally, losses sustained by merchants and manufacturers were a disincentive to increase or even continue production and trade, and also a deterrent to potential merchants and manufacturers.[21]

But piracy was not merely destructive to the discrete parts of the economic system; it was also a disruption of the system itself. 'Piracy is a service industry', writes David Starkey, one concerned with the distribution rather than production of goods. Pirates either consumed the goods they stole or else sold them to those who were not the intended recipients, those who were, rather, 'consumers in alternate markets'.[22] And by stealing rather than competing in primary markets, pirates threatened the fundamental mechanism of capitalism, replacing it with a mode that more closely resembled Robin Hood's version of 'trade' than a European capitalist model. In distributing goods and money to the poor – particularly the lower-class pirate crews themselves – pirates redistributed wealth. To some extent, this redistribution circled back on itself. As Starkey explains, 'Prize goods surplus to requirements therefore gave rise to a market, a black market in which cheap stolen properties were purchased by merchants and dealers who generally supplied the established, respectable communities of the Atlantic world'. Starkey argues that the increasing importance of piracy in maritime economy 'points to clear weaknesses in the structure of "normal", legal markets', particularly the failure of those 'normal' markets to provide affordable supplies to poorer communities.[23] Piracy reoriented the economic system to incorporate those communities traditionally excluded from it, thus absorbing lower classes and poorer cultures into a system that was designed to exploit them. 'The gold hidden beneath the blood', then, in winding up in the wrong hands, infiltrated and thus subverted the very system that produced it.

War Against the Pirates

Given the significant threat to its economic, military, and political security, Great Britain had no choice but to take on piracy. The war was carried out physically by the state military apparatus, but it was also undertaken ideologically by the construction of an image of the pirate that would justify the war against him. This construction was both cultural and legal; newspaper reports, sermons, and fiction worked in tandem with national and maritime statutes that determined what constituted piratical practice, and hence the pirate himself. The conflation of this culturally defined pirate with the legally defined pirate delineated and maintained what Hans Turley calls the 'piratical subject', the 'merging of representations of both economic criminal and cultural deviant'.[24] The cultural and racial othering of the pirate consolidated the threat he posed by distinguishing him from a potentially sympathetic public, aligning piracy with an alien terror. The pirates' disaffiliation from all nations was blatant, enacted most explicitly in the black flags they raised and in their use of national flags in order to safely approach ships they intended to plunder.[25] It was this disaffiliation that justified nations' refusal to try pirates according to the terms of national law; they were neither domestic criminals nor an international threat, either of which would have warranted the fair treatment required by both law and ethics. Here is the always contradictory position of the outlaw: outside the law and therefore beyond its protection, but nevertheless – or consequently – subject to its harshest treatment and correction.

But that distinction between inside and outside the law is fluid, entirely determined by who is making the laws and for whom. During periods of war, privateers were hired to plunder enemy ships; they did so legally, carrying letters of marque from the government specifying the terms under which they were permitted to attack. At the conclusion of wartime, however, such letters of marque expired; ships were put out of commission, and privateers, like demobilised soldiers, found themselves out of work. It is therefore not surprising that surges in Atlantic piracy consistently corresponded with the conclusions of prolonged periods of war. And so privateers became pirates under the law, though their practices did not change. Previously ordered by the government to attack enemy vessels, the sailors became enemies of mankind for continuing to attack those same ships.[26]

Bidding Defiance to the Power of Europe

It is these circumstances with which Johnson opens *A General History*, providing a straightforward – if cautious – enumeration of the causes of piracy. Despite Johnson's claim that his book will be of interest to the public as an account of the economic threat pirates posed, his description of the motivations for piracy borders on the sympathetic. He writes of the 'Inducements Men have to engage themselves headlong in a Life of so much Peril'; the 'inducement' to which he refers is that their lives are miserable and that piracy, while a dangerous option, is better than the alternative. The 'Multitudes of Seamen at this Day unemploy'd,' to be found 'straggling, and begging all over the Kingdom', are not, Johnson insists, lazy or immoral: it is their 'own hard Fate, in being cast off after their Work is done, to starve or steal'. Between starving and piracy, it is no surprise they choose the latter. Even employed sailors, Johnson suggests, are 'but purely paid and purely fed', mistreatment which 'breeds Discontents among them'.[27]

Johnson's analysis echoes the complaints of pirates themselves. The Golden Age saw a rash of collections of pirates' final words (most famously collected by Cotton Mather), and though most of these speeches – at least by Mather's account – were calls for fellow pirates to repent, some were explicit enumerations, not unlike Johnson's introduction, of the conditions which produced piracy.[28] William Fly, for example, took the opportunity of his execution to make an impassioned speech about the 'bad usage' of sailors, arguing that the barbarity of their treatment 'made so many turn Pyrates': 'We poor men can't have Justice done us. There is nothing said to our Commanders, let them never so much abuse us, and use us like dogs', he charged.[29] Pirate captain Edward Taylor spoke similarly of the royal navy, saying 'Damne my Blood God forgive me for swearing here's a Squadron of Men of War sent to look after us but they don't much care for the seeing of us they are more upon the trading account.'[30] Fly's and Taylor's charges point up the government's failure to protect a certain class of people, whose exclusion from this protection is a marker of their exclusion from civil society. Johnson argues that pirate-free states, like the Netherlands, are a 'reproach' to England for its 'want of industry'.[31] His introduction to the first volume of *A General History* is itself a reproach, a frank acknowledgment of the socio-economic conditions that result in piracy.

The second, post-piratical volume of *A General History*, however, has no explicit introduction, but instead opens directly into a chapter about Captain Misson. While all of the stories in *A General History* are fictionalised to some extent, the story of Misson is one of the few that is entirely invented. If the first volume, as Johnson says, relates 'instances . . . of Inducements Men have to engage themselves headlong in a Life of so much Peril', it does work that no longer needed to be done in 1728. The causes of something that no longer exists, and suggestions for how to get rid of it when it has already been gotten rid of, may provide an illuminating context for the (mostly) factual tales of *A General History*, but those accounts no longer carry the ideological force that they did while piracy was still a significant threat. There is therefore significant pressure on this introductory story to set a precedent for what a post-piratical pirate tale would look like. As is the case with most pirate stories, Misson's tale ends with the pirate's downfall. But embedded in the story of the failure of this particular colony is a hint of what a post-piratical piracy might look like. Anne Pérotin-Dumon argues that *A General History* as a whole is an account of pirates who are 'no longer successful', figures who participated in 'commercial ventures that failed because they were itinerant and improvised'.[32] But we might also say that the tale of Misson is a tale of pirates who failed *not* because they were itinerant and improvised, but because they weren't really pirates.

For one thing, this is a story not of socio-economic oppression but of privilege. The Misson of Johnson's story is far from poor; he is born to an 'ancient family' of fortune in Provence and is given an education 'equal to his Birth'. His father intended him to serve with the Musqueteers, but because of his 'roving Temper' and fondness for travel narratives, Misson takes to the sea instead.[33] Though he is treated quite well on his ship, he is nevertheless plagued by a vague sense that the world is limiting his freedoms. His beliefs are confirmed when, on a brief visit to Rome, he meets a 'lewd priest' named Caraccioli. Caraccioli, too, feels oppressed by government and by his religion; 'tired of the farce' of the priesthood, Johnson writes, Caraccioli eagerly throws off his 'masquerading habit' to join Misson on board ship. Both excellent mariners, the two speak often of 'setting up for themselves'.[34] When their ship's captain, second captain, and three lieutenants are killed in combat, Caraccioli convinces Misson that:

he might with the Ship he had under Foot, and the brave Fellows under command, bid Defiance to the Power of Europe, enjoy every thing he wish'd, reign Sovereign of the Southern Seas, and Lawfully make War on all the World, since it would deprive him of that Liberty to which he had a Right by the Laws of Nature.[35]

Caraccioli's invocation of the Law is general as well as particular, an insistence that the laws of the nation are themselves unlawful if they contradict the laws of nature. But this is not merely about tasting the sweet fruits of liberty. Misson is going to enjoy his freedom by 'reign[ing] Sovereign', equivalent to the 'Power of Europe' against whom he wages war. Caraccioli thus urges Misson that 'he might in Time, become as great as Alexander was to the Persians; and by increasing his Forces by his Captures, he would every Day strengthen the Justice of his Cause, for who has Power is always in the Right . . . Mahomet with a few Camel Drivers, founded the Ottoman Empire . . .'[36] The shift from laws of nature that ensure freedom to the insistence that 'who has Power is always in the Right' is hardly subtle in its implication that rights are not about *right*. Caraccioli's argument has turned circular: he and Misson can wage war against all the world because they are in the right, and the power to do so makes one in the right; right makes might makes right. Misson will be great. He will be Alexander and Mohamet – the latter, crucially, valued here not as a prophetic leader but as the founder of an empire; the 'justice of his cause' is the production of power. The motivation for seizing the ship, in other words, makes impossible the liberty they profess to claim and offer: their pirate ship is going to be another empire.

As Caraccioli has promised, Misson and Caraccioli are able to convince most of the crew to stay with them, and they establish what at first appears to be a typically democratic pirate ship. Misson is elected captain, and he seems to establish a true democracy on board. His terms, however, are hardly democratic. What he actually promises is that he will 'never exert his Power, or think himself other than their Comrade, *but when the Necessity of Affairs should oblige him*' (my italics).[37] This is a subtle but crucial tweaking of the prevailing pirate law, which granted the captain unquestioned authority in battle. The latter rule was of necessity; it would be impractical and dangerous to vote on every choice in the midst of a fight. Misson's declaration, on the other hand, does not specify the terms of his authority; he might be 'obliged' in any circumstance to assume control of his crew.

Misson's offer of rights and liberty to Africans is similarly problematic. His policy seems on the surface to follow the majority of pirate crews in granting equal rights to slaves on board captured ships. Upon taking a Dutch ship, Misson frees the slaves and gives them the Dutch mariners' own clothes, telling the crew that he 'had not exempted his Neck from the galling Yoak of Slavery, and asserted his own liberty, to enslave others'.[38] But Misson's claim that he has been 'enslaved' troubles the entire construction of his society. What might pass for egalitarianism on the ship in fact reflects Misson's and Caraccioli's devotion to that liberty which Misson claims to have been denied: a liberty that manifests itself as power, and in particular the power to conquer and accumulate both goods and men. The unspoken belief that underlies Caraccioli's assertion that the world would 'deprive [Misson] of liberty' is that liberty is as much a right to consume property as it is freedom of body or mind. This is a liberty contingent upon a fantasy of the earth's stores being infinite. If every man has, as Caraccioli insists, 'as much Right to what would support him, as to the Air he respired', that is because there was an unlimited supply of goods to 'support' him. Theirs is a faith in an infinitely exploitable physical world that will remain forever open to appropriation, a fundamental belief in a limitless potential to accumulate. Their attempt to opt out of the system is symbolic of the contradictions of a liberal, expansionist England: the belief that to be born free is to have a right to the goods of creation.

It is no wonder then that Caraccioli insists that he and Misson are not pirates – that they are, rather, 'men who were resolved to assert that Liberty which God and Nature gave them'.[39] This is a declaration at odds with the collection's title, but ultimately true: their particular 'liberty' is not the liberty most often found on pirate ships. It is in this that the distinction between Misson's origin story and the causes of real piracy is laid bare: pirates' practices were primarily a response to dire economic conditions and (actual) poor treatment. This difference is manifest in their fundamentally different relationship to property. The moment at which Misson and Caraccioli's conflation of liberty with accumulation becomes most explicit is when they decide to re-establish their society on land. Their territorial experiment, like their on-ship society, is purportedly an attempt to enact the equality of all and to model an alternative to oppressive European governments. Misson calls their settlement 'Libertalia', and names the people 'Liberi', 'desiring in that might be drown'd the distinguish'd Names of *French, English, Dutch, Africans, &c.*'[40] While this 'drowning' of the distinctions between peoples might be read as an equalising move, putting Africans on the same plane as the English, it might just as easily be read as a scaled-down version of imperialism: every other nation, culture, and ethnic identification is to be subsumed by the identity Misson imposes. Misson is going to be Alexander, after all, and the creation of his own nation – one that insists upon the surrender of all other affiliations – is the ultimate realisation of that dream. And indeed, Misson begins imposing order. He claims the need for laws to protect the weakest, then states to enforce the laws, then officials to manage the states; Misson, naturally, is named Lord Conservator, the head of Libertalia, and Caraccioli his second-in-command as Secretary of State. Most importantly, Libertalians formally institute private property, declaring that 'such Lands as any particular Man would enclose, should, for the future, be deem'd his Property, which no other should lay any Claim to, if not alienate by a Sale'.[41] It is the fatal mistake. Rousseau will warn a few decades later:

> The first person who, having fenced off a plot of ground, took it into his head to say *this is mine* and found people simple enough to believe him, was the true founder of civil society. What crimes, wars, murders, what miseries and horrors would the human race have been spared by someone who, uprooting the stakes or filling in the ditch, had shouted to his fellow men: Beware of listening to this impostor; you are lost if you forget that the fruits belong to all and the earth to no one.[42]

Here again that contradiction of freedom is manifested: Misson and Caraccioli's insistence that 'the fruits belong to all' – and, crucially, the assumption that there will always be fruit – justifies their belief that the earth belongs to them. Lincoln Faller argues that the lesson of Misson's tale is that '[h]owever radically men seek to restructure their social relations, they will tend over time to drift back towards established European norms. In challenging European ideology, then, Libertalia would eventually serve to confirm it.'[43] But Libertalia is never meant to do otherwise. Its 'defiance of the power of Europe' is not a rejection of the principles of imperial expansion; on the contrary, it is a rejection of Europe's sole claim to that expansion – an assertion of the natural, limitless right to accumulate goods.

Misson's tale also tells of another pirate colony established on Madagascar, even more explicit in its performance of 'European norms'.[44] While plundering supplies for Libertalia, Misson captures the ship of a Captain Tew, whose bravery impresses him and whom he therefore invites to join him in Libertalia. Tew and many of his crew accept Misson's invitation, but Tew's quartermaster and some of his men set off to establish their own colony. Like Misson and Caraccioli, the quartermaster insists on his society's freedom from the oppressions of government and equality for all. When Tew approaches his former crew and suggests that they (re)join him, the quartermaster responds that they themselves are 'free and independent of all the World', and that it therefore 'would be Madness again to subject themselves to any Government'.[45] His refusal, however, is qualified:

> [I]f you will go to America or Europe, and shew the Advantages which may accrue to the English, by fixing a Colony here, out of that Love we bear our Country, and to wipe away the odious Appellation of Pyrates, with Pleasure we'll submit to any one who shall come with a Commission from a lawful government.[46]

The quartermaster's pirate colony longs to be an English colony, to transplant English ideals in native territory. Like Libertalia, this colony plays out the fantasy of unlimited stores, but unlike Libertalia, it acknowledges itself as an extension of British colonial practice. The quartermaster sends Tew away with a letter to deliver to England, a letter which describes Madagascar as a land ripe for settling: the soil is fruitful, the seas are full of fish, the woods flush with fowl, and there is doubtless gold and silver to be mined in the mountains. The settlement will produce the spoils of the American colonies 'at a far inferior Expence', the quartermaster promises; even slaves are cheaper, and could be better fed and thus work more efficiently. Perhaps most importantly, a colony in Madagascar can, he argues, produce the silk and cotton currently transported from the Indies and provide a convenient stopping-point for East India ships.[47] To rid oneself of the 'odious Appellation of Pyrate' is, it seems, to think like a colonist.

The quartermaster's offer here reveals the contradiction that underwrites Libertalia: the Libertalians' investment in the principles of British expansion is as great as the quartermaster's. His (however ironic) complaint that Libertalia is a government to which one must submit, a government that suppresses freedoms, turns out to be correct; Libertalia will ultimately fail because of its practices of colonisation and accumulation. 'Without the least Provocation,' mourns Misson, 'the Natives came down upon them . . . and made a great Slaughter, but for what Reason he could not imagine.'[48] Misson's surprise is not surprising. His is the arrogance of the European: what natives wouldn't want such neighbours? Who wouldn't appreciate the improvements Misson and his men have brought to the island? Faller expresses surprise that Johnson chooses to have Libertalia destroyed by the natives rather than letting it fail 'of its own accord'; its 'demonic forces and energies' would, Faller figures, have been 'far better contained' had their settlement failed as a result of those ideals.[49] But it might as easily be argued that Libertalia fails because it has no such ideals; if it had, there would have been no colony, no armed settlement on native land. The Libertalians profess to befriend the natives while colonising their land; they claim to establish a free society, when in fact the expression of that freedom duplicates the oppression against which it claims to be founded. The quartermaster's colony, on the other hand, survives, in part because it is openly hostile to the natives and openly loyal to English values. Together, these two colonies demonstrate how national loyalty invades what looks like a counter-movement: all that remains at the end of Johnson's pirate story is an unpiratical pirate colony that is actually British.

We Come From the Sea

The story of Misson is a fitting introduction to a volume of pirate stories written after the Golden Age of piracy had ended. By playing pirate while betraying the pirate ethos, Misson performs an absence – of the pirates themselves, of the collectivist ethos that sustained them, and of the broader revolutionary impulses that guided them.

In performing that betrayal, Misson's tale also alludes to the forces that repressed piracy and the terms upon which the battle against pirates was fought: the weapons were not only ships of war but also the power of pervasive socio-economic and cultural hierarchies. It was the social structure of piracy as much as its attack on merchants' property that made it dangerous, and so by eradicating the one, authorities hoped to eradicate the other. Governments had the power of the press and public ritual behind them – from newspapers and publications like Mather's, to the spectacle of executions – which they used to assert existing social hierarchies and repress the counter-formations spreading across the Atlantic.

Terror, though, is hard to fight. To the extent that pirates could be located and exterminated, Britain succeeded; British property was saved. But like the present-day 'war on terror' – on terror, not on terrorists – the revolutionary impulse did not reside in any one particular practice; the social world of piracy was more difficult to get to than the ships themselves. The level on which England was fighting pirates was not the only level on which pirates were operating; pirates' exile, both self- and nationally- imposed, meant that the war the nations of Europe were waging against them was not the war that the pirates were fighting in return. Europe's was a war over property and territory, concepts rendered nonsensical by the pirate ethos. There could be no reconciling the rationale for national military battles with pirates' rationale for plundering ships: the former was entirely inscribed in the national paradigm, and the latter lay entirely outside of it. Upon being asked their national origin, pirates were known to declare 'We come from the sea!', an assertion as true symbolically as it was literally. To 'come from the sea' is not merely to live on the sea, as they did, but also to possess values and a culture that were themselves bred to the sea, suitable to the communal, democratic, egalitarian lifestyle the pirates lived. In declaring the sea as their origin, pirates were denying not only national affiliation, but also a national basis for their practices. Pirates did not fight a national war. Their war was fought in defence of their lives but also of their social system, a war fought against and outside of the system from which they were excluded and with which their own lives were fundamentally incompatible.

In this sense, the war against the pirates was not a war that could be 'won' in any traditional terms, and neither was the pirates' war waged against the nations. The pirates' war was one of class resistance and a social revolution, neither of which could be won on the battlefield of the high seas. Neither, however, could be lost there. The pirates themselves may have been eradicated. But the social order they built, the bottom-up restructuring of society and an assertion of the power of the lower classes, could – and did – re-emerge elsewhere, marked by different kinds of mobility. In this light, we might understand Johnson's tale as identifying the specific threat piracy posed and tracing its demise, but in so doing, prophesying its inevitable transformation and re-emergence.

Notes

1. The identity of *A General History*'s author is unknown. In 1932, Defoe scholar John Robert Moore argued that Daniel Defoe authored *A General History*, a decision that was widely accepted until a 1994 study by P. N. Furbank and W. R. Owens argued convincingly against it. Many libraries continue to catalogue *A General History* under Defoe's name, and the most recent complete edition, 'updated' and 'lightly corrected' by Dover in 1999, still names Defoe as the author. All references to the text of *A General History* will be from the University of South Carolina Press edition. [Philip Nicholas Furbank and W. R. Owens, *Defoe De-attributions: A Critique of J. R. Moore's Checklist* (London. Hambledon Press, 1994); Daniel Defoe, *A General History of the Pyrates*, ed. Manuel Schonhorn (Columbia, South Carolina, 1972).]
2. David Cordingly, *Under the Black Flag: The Romance and the Reality of Life Among the Pirates*, 1st Harvest edn, A Harvest Book (San Diego: Harcourt Brace, 1997), viii.
3. Defoe, *A General History of the Pyrates*, 84, 85.
4. Ibid., 85.
5. That image of a European subject 'turning Turk' consolidated the material and ideological terror that pirates inflicted on European nations. The threat of plundering and capture by Barbary pirates was, naturally, terrifying in the most visceral, physical way, and it was a terror to which the British public was frequently exposed. The reading public was familiar with Barbary pirates through the popular genre of Barbary captivity narratives, but illiterate Britons would have known the dangers of Barbary captivity from ransom collectors who spoke at local parishes, collecting donations to free Barbary captives. Their pleas were explicitly ideological: they warned the parishioners that unless the ransoms were met, captives would be seduced by the

'cruel infidels who compelled Christians, with torture and savagery, to renounce their much-loved God and monarch'. In turning Turk, they warned, captives would 'be lost to their families and country'. This is a fear of mixture as contamination; exposure to Islam would make Muslims out of good Christians. [Nabil Matar and Daniel J. Vitkus, eds, *Piracy, Slavery, and Redemption: Barbary Captivity Narratives from Early Modern England* (New York: Columbia University Press, 2001); Suraiya Faroqhi, *The Ottoman Empire and the World Around It* (London: I. B. Tauris, 2006).]

6. Kinkor, 'Black Men Under the Black Flag', in *Bandits at Sea: A Pirates Reader*, ed. C. R. Pennell (New York: New York University Press, 2001), 199–200.
7. Ibid., 201.
8. Pirates would jointly own their slaves, just as they jointly owned their ship and their prize money. The economic benefit of a slave to any one pirate, then, would be fairly small. [Peter T. Leeson, *The Invisible Hook: The Hidden Economics of Pirates* (Princeton: Princeton University Press, 2009), 164–71.]
9. Kinkor, 'Black Men Under the Black Flag', 197.
10. 'Lt. Governor of Bermuda to the Council of Trade and Plantations', *Calendar of State Papers, Colonial Series* (1718): 551.
11. Kinkor, 'Black Men Under the Black Flag', 203–4.
12. Ibid., 198.
13. Critics have also argued that pirates presented a challenge to the social order by their rejection of heteronormativity. [Hans Turley, *Rum, Sodomy, and the Lash: Piracy, Sexuality, and Masculine Identity* (New York: New York University Press, 1999); Erin Skye Mackie, 'The Origins and Regulations of Eighteenth-Century British Privateering', in *Bandits at Sea: A Pirates Reader*, ed. C. R. Pennell (New York: New York University Press, 2001).]
14. See Peter Linebaugh and Marcus Rediker, *The Many-Headed Hydra: Sailors, Commoners, and the Hidden History of the Revolutionary Atlantic* (Boston: Beacon Press, 2000), 144, 162, and Srinivas Aravamudan, *Tropicopolitans: Colonialism and Agency, 1688–1804* (Durham: Duke University Press, 1999), 93.
15. Though every crew had its own 'pirate code', the codes were consistent in their establishment of democracy on-board. And when multiple ships joined with one another, they came to a consensus about the specific terms of their relationship. If any party disagreed with the terms, they were free to go their own way, without fear of attack. Leeson cites an example of a case in which a 'Spirit of Discord' developed between three pirate crews sailing together, 'upon which . . . [they] immediately parted, each steering a different Course'. (Leeson, *The Invisible Hook*, 61.)

16. Ibid., 9.
17. Marcus Buford Rediker, *Villains of All Nations: Atlantic Pirates in the Golden Age* (Boston: Beacon Press, 2004), 176.
18. Defoe, *A General History of the Pyrates*, 26.
19. Rediker, *Villains of All Nations*, 128–9.
20. John L. Anderson, 'Piracy and World History: An Economic Perspective on Maritime Predation', in *Bandits at Sea: A Pirates Reader*, ed. C. R. Pennell (New York: New York University Press, 2001), 85.
21. Ibid. See also R. W. Anderson, *The Economics of Crime* (London: Macmillan, 1976).
22. David J. Starkey, 'Pirates and Markets', in *Bandits at Sea: A Pirates Reader*, ed. C. R. Pennell (New York: New York University Press, 2001), 108.
23. Starkey, 'Pirates and Markets', 114–15.
24. Turley, *Rum, Sodomy, and the Lash*, 41–2.
25. When eighteenth-century authorities attempted to trace the territorial origins of 348 pirates, the bases of pirates' answers varied widely, from place of birth to ancestral connection to home port to most recent port; Marcus Rediker suggests that many answers were pure invention, made up on the spot. [Rediker, *Villains of All Nations*, 51].
26. For an elaboration of the intricate relationship between international law and state sponsorship of piracy, see Lauren A. Benton, *A Search for Sovereignty: Law and Geography in European Empires, 1400–1900* (New York: Cambridge University Press, 2010).
27. Defoe, *A General History of the Pyrates*, 3–5.
28. Mather's first was a 1699 volume entitled *Pillars of Salt*, published in the hopes that 'the *Dying Speeches* of such as have been Executed among us, might be of singular Use, to Correct and Reform, The Crimes, wherein too many do *Live*'. Mather's collection is focused primarily on representing the reformed pirate, the one who urges his fellow criminals to repent, to find God, to submit themselves to the judgement of their law-abiding peers. [Cotton Mather, *Pillars of Salt. An History of Some Criminals Executed in This Land, for Capital Crimes: With Some of Their Dying Speeches; Collected and Published, for the Warning of Such as Live in Destructive Courses of Ungodliness.: Whereto Is Added, for the Better Improvement of This History, a Brief Discourse About the Dreadful Justice of God, in Punishing of Sin, with Sin.: [Two Lines from Deuteronomy]* (Boston: 1699); Cotton Mather, *Instructions to the Living, from the Condition of the Dead. A Brief Relation of Remarkables in the Shipwreck of Above One Hundred Pirates ... With Some Account of the Discourse Had with Them on the Way to Their Execution. And a Sermon Preached on Their Occasion* (Boston,

1717); Cotton Mather, *Useful Remarks An Essay Upon Remarkables in the Way of Wicked Men. A Sermon on the Tragical End, Unto Which the Way of Twenty-Six Pirates Brought Them;With an Account of Their Speeches, Letters, & Actions, Before Their Execution* (New-London: T. Green, 1723); Cotton Mather, *The Vial Poured Out Upon the Sea: A Remarkable Relation of Certain Pirates Brought Unto a Tragical and Untimely End, Some Conferences with Them After Their Condemnation, Their Behaviour at Their Execution, and a Sermon Preached on That Occasion* (Boston, 1726).]

29. Fly also complained that the hangman tied the knot badly, 'not understanding his trade' – sardonic, perhaps, but Mather read Fly's anger as sincere. Whether sincere or in jest, Fly's complaint is not inconsequential, as it contrasts the supposedly legitimate work of the respectable members of society with the work of pirates who, at the very least, know what they are doing. [Mather, *The Vial Poured Out Upon the Sea. A Remarkable Relation of Certain Pirates Brought Unto a Tragical and Untimely End. Some Conferences with Them, After Their Condemnation. Their Behaviour at Their Execution. And a Sermon Preached on That Occasion.*]
30. Rediker, *Villains of All Nations*, 29.
31. Defoe, *A General History of the Pyrates*, 5. For a more accurate account of Dutch piracy, see Virginia West Lunsford-Poe, *Piracy and Privateering in the Golden Age Netherlands*, 1st edn (New York: Palgrave Macmillan, 2005).
32. Anne Pérotin-Dumon, 'The Pirate and the Emperor: Power and the Law on the Seas, 1450–1850', in *Bandits at Sea: A Pirates Reader*, ed. C. R. Pennell (New York: New York University Press, 2001), 40.
33. Defoe, *A General History of the Pyrates*, 383.
34. Ibid., 385, 390.
35. Ibid., 391.
36. Ibid.
37. Ibid., 392.
38. Ibid., 404.
39. Ibid., 392.
40. Ibid., 417.
41. Ibid., 432–3.
42. Jean-Jacques Rousseau, *The First and Second Discourses*, trans. Roger D. Masters and Judith R. Masters (New York: St. Martin's Press, 1964), 141–2.
43. Lincoln Faller, 'Captain Misson's Failed Utopia, Crusoe's Failed Colony: Race and Identity in New, Not Quite Imaginable Worlds', *Eighteenth Century: Theory and Interpretation* 43, no. 1 (2002): 1–18.

44. Misson's tale is continued in the second chapter of *A General History*, 'Of Captain Tew and His Crew'.
45. Defoe, *A General History of the Pyrates*, 435.
46. Ibid.
47. Ibid., 435–6. I am grateful to Ian Duncan for directing me to other eighteenth-century satirical treatments of colonists as pirates, especially *Gulliver's Travels*: 'To say the truth, I had conceived a few Scruples with relation to the Distributive Justice of Princes upon these Occasions. For instance, a Crew of Pirates are driven by a Storm they know not whither; at length a Boy discovers Land from the Topmast; they go on Shore to Rob and Plunder; they see an harmless People, are entertained with Kindness, they give the Country a new Name, they take formal Possession of it for their King, they set up a rotten Plank or a Stone for a Memorial, they murder two or three dozen of the Natives, bring away a Couple more by Force for a Sample, return home, and get their Pardon. Here commences a new Dominion acquired with a Title by *Divine Right*. Ships are sent with the first Opportunity, the Natives driven out or destroyed, their Princes tortured to discover their Gold; a free Licence given to all Acts of Inhumanity and Lust, the Earth reeking with the Blood of its Inhabitants: And this execrable Crew of Butchers employed in so pious an Expedition, is a *modern Colony* sent to convert and civilize an idolatrous and barbarous People.' [Jonathan Swift, *Gulliver's Travels* (New York: Penguin Classics, 2001), 249.]
48. Ibid., 437.
49. Faller, 'Captain Misson's Failed Utopia, Crusoe's Failed Colony', 15n.

Chapter 2

A Pirate or Anything

> Roll on, thou deep and dark blue ocean – roll!
> Ten thousand fleets sweep over thee in vain;
> Man marks the earth with ruin – his control
> Stops with the shore . . .
> His steps are not upon thy paths – thy fields
> Are not a spoil for him . . .
>
> Byron, *Childe Harold's Pilgrimage*, IV: 179–180[1]

The ocean kills Lord Byron's *Childe Harold*. Not our hero Harold (who suddenly and simply is no more), but the poem that only barely celebrates him. In its penultimate stanza, after a prolonged apostrophe to the ocean, *Childe Harold*'s narrator simply gives up:

> My task is done – my song hath ceased – my theme
> Has died into an echo; it is fit
> The spell should break of this protracted dream.
> The torch shall be extinguish'd which hath lit
> My midnight lamp – and what is writ, is writ . . . (IV: 1657–61)

In the 'protracted dream' of the apostrophe, the sea is all about endings. It is the place where people die, sinking into the ocean 'like a drop of rain' and 'with a bubbling groan'. And it is, above all, the limit at which man's control ends – a site, the narrator says, whose 'fields are not a spoil for him'. This is an idealised sea which resists colonising, a space in which such boundaries do not hold. And so it is 'fit' that the poem's power is diminished in relation to the ocean: just as colonial control collapses under the weight of the water, the narrator can't go beyond his dream of the sea. Both narrative and political control 'stop with the shore', as the epigraph suggests: the ocean eludes you.

By the time of Byron's pirate poems, the state's control no longer stopped with the shore, if ever it had; nations were legally entitled to mark the sea with ruin. The Golden Age of piracy had long since been ended by Britain's targeted military campaign; the sudden and efficient eradication of pirates made it clear that the arm of the British government reached far into the ocean. And so Byron's pirate poems are not about the ocean, nor are they about the pirates we know from history. They are, instead, about the inadequacy of such romanticised narratives in the face of the territorialisation of the sea and the expansion (or decay) of empires. I begin this chapter with Byron's two pirate poems, *The Bride of Abydos* and *The Corsair*, which are haunted by the phantom of the Ottoman Empire. The pirate heroes of these poems, in stark contrast to historical pirates, are implicated in the imperial power structures that piracy naturally opposes. But what is striking about these two poems is that neither openly acknowledges the imperial forces that weigh so heavily on their narratives. And so I turn next to a surprisingly different narrative, William Hone's (textual) piracy of Byron's *The Corsair* – sold at a fraction of the cost of Byron's. Hone's story makes explicit the Ottoman-European conflict running through its pirate tale, laying bare the post-piratical sensibility of Byron's own poems. In its exposure of the (perhaps feigned) rigidity of Byron's narratives – and, most crucially, in its Robin-Hood style redistribution of (cultural) capital – Hone's *Corsair* performs the revolutionary spirit of the sea pirate by reproducing and thus exposing the failures of piracy in Byron's pirate poems. I conclude the chapter with Byron's final treatment of piracy, the brief appearance of the pirate Lambro in *Don Juan*. Lambro, like Hone's corsair, is clearly nationalised as Greek, and therefore enacts the invisible narrative surrounding Byron's earlier pirates. Taken together, Byron's and Hone's pirate tales capture and then critique a world in which a particular kind of piratical revolutionary spirit is no longer possible.

For Byron, as for many Romantic-era writers, the failure of revolutionary movements was epitomised by the course taken by the French Revolution. But Byron despaired with a difference – not because of the Revolution's collapse into the Reign of Terror, but because of Napoleon's 'slow downfall'.[2] What had begun with the disastrous Russian campaign in 1812 culminated in 1814 with the fall of Paris to Russia and Napoleon's abdication of the French imperial throne. Byron wrote in his journal: 'Out of town six days. On my return, found my poor little pagod, Napoleon, pushed off his pedestal – the thieves are in Paris. It is his own fault. [. . .] Query – will they ever reach him?' And then, the following day, 'Napoleon Buonaparte has abdicated the throne of the world. [. . .] I am utterly bewildered and confounded. [. . .] But I won't give him up even now; though all his admirers have . . .'[3] If the bewildered and confounded Byron did not give up on Napoleon, he had nevertheless already given up on revolution:

> After all, even the highest game of crowns and scepters, what is it? *Vide* Napoleon's last twelvemonth. It has completely upset my sense of fatalism. I thought, if crushed, he would have fallen, when *fractus illabitur orbis*, and not have been pared away to gradual insignificance; that all this was not a mere *jeu* of the gods, but a prelude to greater changes and mightier events. But men never advance beyond a certain point; – and here we are, retrograding to the dull, stupid old system, – balance of Europe – poising straws upon kings' noses instead of wringing them off![4]

For Byron, to end tyranny is to return to tyranny; the capture of Napoleon amounts to one king wringing the straw from the nose of another. Such was the 'balance' of Europe, a balance that ensured only the impossibility of real progress. This is 'revolution' in the most literal terms, a mere return, a spinning back to what already was.

It was during those two years of Napoleon's demise, as Byron watched his own private revolution die in slow motion, that he became obsessed with pirates. He published two pirate poems, *The Bride of Abydos* and *The Corsair*, in 1813 and 1814 respectively, and in these same years wrote frequently of pirates in his journals. He may even have befriended a pirate around the same time; stories place him in Constantinople in 1814, dining with Greek revolutionary and famous semi-retired pirate Lambro Katsonis, who is mentioned in *The Bride* and is the namesake of the pirate in *Don Juan*. There were even rumours that Byron himself was the pirate hero of

The Corsair, rumours which he only partly denied. '[Hobhouse] told me an odd report', he wrote in March 1814,

> that *I* am the actual Conrad, the veritable Corsair, and that part of my travels are supposed to have passed in privacy [piracy?]. Um – people sometimes hit near the truth, but never the whole truth. H. don't know what I was about the year after he left the Levant, nor does any one – nor – nor – nor – however, it is a lie – but, 'I doubt the equivocation of the fiend that lies like truth.'[5]

The editor's correction, a slip from 'privacy' to 'piracy', performs the same equivocation. To lie like truth is to call Byron a pirate, which he himself does by his stuttering denial: to cite the lie is to make it true.

Still, if Byron was 'about' anything piratical during that year in the Levant, it wasn't the piracy of real pirates, but of his fictional pirate, '*the* actual Conrad', his own only marginally 'veritable' corsair. And a poetic pirate is, for Byron, a contraction. As he wrote in an 1814 journal entry,

> If I have a wife, and that wife has a son – by any body – I will bring up mine heir in the most anti-poetical way – make him a lawyer, or a pirate, or anything. But if he writes too, I shall be sure he is none of mine, and cut him off with a bank token.[6]

Byron's striking indifference to the question of paternity, as well as the unavoidable fact that it is he, after all, who is the writer 'too', gives the impression that it is not actually Byron Junior in question here, that it is Byron himself who should give up writing for piracy. And indeed he tried; with the completion of *The Corsair*, Byron swore off poetry forever. He wrote to John Murray, his publisher:

> It doubtless gratifies me much that our *Finale* has pleased – & that the Curtain drops gracefully . . . We shall now part I hope satisfied with each other . . . Besides I have other views & objects – & think that I shall keep *this* resolution – for since I left London – though . . . tempted with all kinds of paper – the dirtiest of ink – and the bluntest of pens – I have not even been haunted by a wish to put them to their combined uses – except in letters of business – my rhyming propensity is quite gone – & I feel much as I did at Patras on recovering from my fever – weak but in health and only afraid of a relapse – I do most fervently hope I never shall . . .[7]

The 'other views and objects' with which Byron replaced poetry included, appropriately, those most anti-poetical pirates themselves: at the same time as he pre-emptively disowned any son (or even any future wife's lover's son) who thought of writing when he could have thought of piracy, Byron was writing longingly of adventure in his journals and dreaming of being sixteenth-century pirates Hayreddin and Barbarossa. In the face of a failed revolution, Byron chose to align himself with a symbol of the non-citizen: the pirate, the common enemy of mankind.

But the fact is, there is nothing piratical, or at least nothing historically realistic or resonant, about Byron's pirates. With figures like Blackbeard still recent in the national memory – pirates who were genuine inheritors of a revolutionary tradition – Byron puts his own pirates firmly on land, not at sea, gives them Muslims instead of booty, makes them husbands and lovers instead of ex-slaves and criminals. In stark contrast to the pirates of eighteenth-century history, Byron's have national and territorial affiliations and are implicated in the imperial power structures outside of which real pirates had long operated. Rather than taking Byron's corsairs as a celebration of a revolutionary tradition, then, this chapter reads them as a diagnosis of the cause of piracy's demise.

No Land Beyond My Saber's Length

> Know ye the land where the cypress and myrtle
> Are emblems of deeds that are done in their clime?
> Where the rage of the vulture, the love of the turtle,
> Now melt into sorrow, now madden to crime! [. . .]
> Tis the clime of the East; 'tis the land of the Sun –
> Can he smile on such deeds as his children have done?
>   Lord Byron, *The Bride of Abydos*, I: 1–4, 13–14

There is no sea in *The Bride of Abydos*, Byron's first pirate poem. The poem's opening question – 'Know ye the land?' – situates a poem about pirates on surprisingly solid ground: specifically the land of the East, where 'all, save the spirit of man, is divine' (I: 15).[8] Byron's description alternates between orientalising and naturalising: if the East is a land of flowers and trees and turtles, it is also one of virgins and crime and wildness. It is a fitting land to produce a pirate, but it is also the land *Bride*'s pirate Selim will never leave.⁹ He spends the poem on land, as lover and son; we don't even learn that Selim is a pirate until the thirty-first stanza. He will be dead by the thirty-ninth.

Byron describes what little we do know of Selim's piracy, moreover, through this same domestic lens. Driven to turn pirate by a father's mistreatment, Selim is raised 'the son of a slave', as his adoptive father Giaffir calls him – and an infidel one at that, 'from unbelieving mother bred' (I: 81–2). Selim eventually learns that Giaffir is actually his uncle, not his father, and that his real father was killed by Giaffir himself. This is knowledge that gives him license to love Giaffir's daughter, Zuleika, but it also deepens the alienation that, by his own account, drove him to the sea. When Selim finally confesses his piracy to Zuleika, he asks, 'What could I be? Proscribed at home,/ And taunted to a wish to roam' (II: 321–2). Though the poem is itself entirely 'proscribed at home', Selim rhapsodises to Zuleika about the ocean we will never see:

> 'Tis vain – my tongue cannot impart
> My almost drunkenness of heart,
> When first this liberated eye
> Survey'd Earth, Ocean, Sun, and Sky . . .
> One word alone can paint to thee
> That more than feeling – I was Free! (II: 343–50)

It takes Selim only a moment to move from declaring his feelings ineffable to just plain declaring his feelings; what is beyond words finds words five lines later. Or, to be fair, finds *one* word: the only word, Selim insists, adequate to capture his 'drunkenness of heart'. But that one word – 'free' – is not adequate at all. It is nothing but the cliché of the sea, insisting that open waters are actually open, celebrating the ocean as escape and infinite opportunity. This freedom is never evidenced in the poem, in which Selim is bound to the shore and entangled in a family tragedy. It is, furthermore, a freedom absent even from Selim's descriptions of his pirate life at sea, most explicit in his description of his pirate band:

> The last of Lambro's patriots there
> Anticipated freedom share;

> And oft around the cavern fire
> On visionary schemes debate,
> To snatch the Rayahs from their fate.
> So let them ease their hearts with prate
> Of equal rights, which man ne'er knew;
> I have a love for freedom too. (II: 380-7)

The Lambro referenced here is Lambro Katsonis, the same Lambro with whom Byron may or may not have dined. Katsonis was a Greek naval officer who, disillusioned with the Orlov revolt (a 1770 Greek uprising against the Ottomans), turned to piracy, eventually forcing the Ottomans from the island of Kastelorizo; Byron's note describes him as one of the 'two most celebrated of the Greek revolutionists'.[10] Whether a literal or figurative description, Selim's association of his pirates with Lambro is an inscription of them in a national conflict; the freedom Lambro seeks is not Selim's abstract freedom of the sea, but freedom from Ottoman rule. While the pirates' talk of 'equal rights' seems reminiscent of the Golden Age egalitarian pirate ship, those rights will manifest themselves in the dream of rescuing Barbary captives, further reasserting, rather than collapsing, ethnic and religious distinctions.

It is no wonder that Selim seems so dismissive of his band's fireside dreams, in which equal rights and liberation are described in terms of capture. But nowhere are those equal rights evidenced on ship, either. Selim describes his crew:

> 'Tis true, they are a lawless brood,
> But rough in form, nor mild in mood;
> And every creed, and every race,
> With them hath found – may find a place.
> [...]
> But open speech, and ready hand,
> Obedience to their chief's command
> [...]
> Have made them fitting instruments
> For more than ev'n my own intents (II: 337-74)

Like the pirates we know from history, Selim's band is a motley crew, a melting pot of races and religions, united only by their being situated outside the constraints of society and law. But to Selim, the pirates' value lies not in their rebellion, but in their obedience. Whatever Selim's intentions are (and they are not, for all their desperation, exceptionally clear – money? power? to escape his life on land? to avenge his father's death?), his own pirates are truly *his*. By dismissing his band's campfire dreams and celebrating their submissiveness, Selim mocks the egalitarian and democratic ideals of piracy that historians have documented.[11] In this and in his description of 'Lambro's pirates', Selim speaks the unspoken of the poem: this piracy is not about winning freedom, but about gaining power and territory.

Territory will, in fact, be the metaphor that persists throughout the poem; even the sea's freedom is described in terms of the land. Selim rhapsodises: 'My tent on shore, my galley on the sea/ Are more than cities and Serais to me' (II: 390–1). Selim claims to take pride in his semi-homelessness, insisting to Zuleika that he 'ask[s] no land beyond [his] sabre's length', but that formulation nevertheless imagines violent control over the sea (II: 443). Moreover, Selim's notion of space is *domestic* in both senses of the word: it is based on a notion of almost-national territory and has its origins in domestic, familial life. At no point in the action of the poem does Selim leave home, and even the descriptions of his travel are literally grounded by domestic love. He calls Zuleika the 'star that guides the wanderer', asking her to be the 'dove of peace and promise to [his] ark', the 'rainbow to the storms of life', the 'evening beam that smiles the clouds away' (II: 395–400). Selim's descent into the similes of bad poetry reminds us that we are on familiar ground: not the exotic waters of Captain Johnsonesque pirate tales, but the backyard garden of a love story.

When Giaffir discovers that Selim has learned of his father's murder, he fears Selim's betrayal and arranges to have the lovers killed. Selim and Zuleika exchange a final kiss in the grotto as Giaffir's men approach through the thicket; Selim's own pirate band, meanwhile, has made it to shore to join the fight, and Selim could still escape unharmed. But just before he reaches safety, he pauses and turns for one last look at Zuleika, and in that moment he is killed by Zuleika's father: 'That pause, that fatal gaze he took,/ Hath doom'd his death' (II: 565). In that pause, too, is the gap between Selim's piratical ambitions and his domestic life. Selim dies as he lives: as a lover, not a pirate.

Once Thine Own Domain

In contrast to the hermetically-sealed description of the land that opens *The Bride of Abydos*, Byron's *The Corsair* begins with a sea shanty. For forty-two lines, the poem celebrates the sea's boundlessness and its tumult, the thrill of the wanderer, the sailor's soaring spirits. This is what Selim wanted and could not have. But it turns out that the sea song is coming from land, where the pirates are sitting around a watch-fire, repairing boats and wandering on the shore. The first event of the poem is the approach of a 'home-returning bark', further situating the experience of the pirates within the context of the home to which they return:

> 'A sail! – a sail!' – a promised prize to Hope!
> Her nation – flag – how speaks the telescope?
> The blood-red signal glitters in the gale.
> Yes – she is ours . . . (I: 83–6)

Rather than the disaffiliation that a black flag symbolises, this red flag marks the ship as one that returns to the land of a unified people. It is wholly an account of homecoming; as the pirates return to the 'welcome shout' and 'friendly speech' of those who remained behind, 'woman's gentler anxious tone is heard—/ Friends', husbands', lovers' names in each dear word:/"Oh! Are they safe?"' (I.103–11). The poem's first perspective, in other words, is of pirates who aren't pirating and women whose concern is for their safety rather than their exploits; the poem is framed, much like *The Bride of Abydos*, as a domestic story. *The Corsair's* pirate-hero Conrad, more lover than pirate, has never strayed from his love Medora, 'though fairest captives daily met his eye'. For her part, she waits for him at home, alone in her tower singing sadly, Conrad's 'dim and melancholy star,/ Whose ray of beauty reach'd him from afar' (I: 289, 511–12). 'If there be love in mortals,' insists the narrator, 'this was love!' (I: 304). Just as *The Bride*'s Zuleika is the 'star that guides [Selim's] wandering', Medora circumscribes Conrad's travels within the radius of home: his wandering is grounded by the one who waits there.

Immediately upon his return home, however, Conrad learns that Seyd Pasha of a neighbouring island is planning an attack against the Pirates' Isle, and he decides to leave within the hour in order to launch a pre-emptive attack against Seyd. "'Tis rash to meet, but surer death to wait/ Till here they hunt us to undoubted fate', Conrad reasons; beyond this, neither his nor Seyd's motives are clear (I: 315–16). But no one argues; Conrad's rule is absolute:

> [They] marvel where they next shall seize a spoil:
> No matter where – their chief's allotment this;
> Theirs, to believe no prey nor plan amiss. [. . .]
> With these he mingles not but to command [. . .]
> 'Steer to that shore!' – they sail. 'Do this!' – 'tis done:
> 'Now form and follow me!' – the spoil is won.
> Thus prompt his accents and his actions still,
> And all obey and few inquire his will. (I: 58–80)

As soon as his men prepare their ship for the battle, Conrad – mourning, with one last look on Medora's tower – leaves with the crew for Seyd's palace in Coron's Bay, a territory that, at the time *The Corsair* was composed, was still under Ottoman rule. The 'turban'd brave[s]' who patrol it 'seek to flesh their glowing valour on the Greek', a description that clearly aligns them with the Ottoman Empire which controlled what Byron considered to be occupied territory (II: 17–18). But this political context is, like so much in the poem, unspoken; the breadth of the Ottoman–Greek crisis is reduced to primarily superficial differences between the Christian pirates and the Muslims of Coron's Bay. Seyd's men are identified not by their political loyalties but by their dress and manner; the first image of Seyd is a stereotype of the decadent Muslim, reclining in his turban, surrounded by bearded chiefs.

These trappings of Islam are Conrad's way in. Rather than attacking the palace outright, he gains access to Seyd's chamber by dressing as a Muslim, claiming to be a dervise who has escaped from Conrad's pirates. As his men set fire to the palace, Conrad throws off his robes, revealing armour and a sabre. Instead of fighting alongside his men, Seyd 'tore his beard, and foaming fled the fight' (II: 181), a picture of rabid cowardice set in relief against Conrad's nobility and bravery. Conrad orders his men not to attack the harem – '*we* have wives', he says – and as the harem's quarters go up in flames, Conrad's men risk their lives to save the women; Conrad himself rescues the harem queen, Gulnare. Even in battle, the pirates are guided by their domestic loyalties; the safety of anyone's wives, even the enemies', takes precedence. The crew's values drive the poem's plot: Conrad's men spend so much time rescuing the harem that they lose the battle, and Conrad is captured, imprisoned and condemned to death. But Gulnare, 'marvel[ing] o'er the courtesy' Conrad shows, takes pity on him (II: 261). Seduced by his belief that 'his homage were a woman's right', she gains access to Conrad's cell in the night and frees him (II: 268). Before they flee the castle, she urges him to murder Seyd, but Conrad, ever the gentleman, refuses to kill a sleeping man; Gulnare does it for him. At this moment, as soon as she steps beyond the bounds of wife and gentle woman, Conrad ceases to care for her, horrified by the (literal) spot of blood on her face:

> ... [N]e'er from strife, captivity, remorse –
> From all his feelings in their inmost force –
> So thrill'd, so shudder'd every creeping vein,
> As now they froze before that purple stain.
> That spot of blood, that light but guilty streak,
> Had banish'd all the beauty from her cheek!
> Blood he had view'd, could view unmoved – but then
> It flow'd in combat, or was shed by men! (III: 422–9)

Despite the obvious defensive nature of her act – itself a mere continuation of Conrad's attack on Seyd's palace, and the only means by which Conrad can himself escape execution – Conrad considers her actions to fall outside the sphere of battle. She is, therefore, neither proper warrior nor proper woman: truly foreign.

The subplot of Conrad and Gulnare, and all attendant issues of the proper way to treat (or be) a woman, only serve to mask what is really at the centre of the fight between Seyd and Conrad: the Ottoman Empire goes unnamed. But the third and final canto opens with a sixty-five-line tribute to 'fair Athens', which, it becomes clear, is not the Athens of the present day. *The Corsair*'s Athens is populated by Phœbus, Cithæron, Cephisus, and Theseus, a city out of literature and mythology: not an Ottoman territory but the city of gods.[12] This entire section feels wildly out of place, interrupting the action of the poem for an apostrophe to a city that bears no obvious relation to the plot. Byron, in fact, apologises for these stanzas in a footnote, insisting that they 'have, perhaps, little business here ... but they were written on the spot, in the Spring of 1814, and – I scarce know why – the reader must excuse their appearance here – if he can.'[13] But Byron often most vehemently denies control when he is exercising it most strongly, and given his tribute to Greece in *The Giaour* and his own later, fatal interest in Greek independence, it hardly seems likely that he would pay tribute to Athens lightly.[14] The true weight of these stanzas can be found in their single oblique reference to the present political state of Greece, buried amidst the romanticising of mythological Greece. Addressing Athens, Byron mourns: 'His Corsair's isle was once thine own domain – / Would that with freedom it were thine again' (III: 64–5). In the historical context of the poem, this freedom-from is the freedom from Ottoman rule. Ottoman control of Greece *does* matter to the poem, whether or not Byron will admit it; these lines 'have business here' because the battle between Conrad and Seyd is in fact a battle between the West and the East, Greece and the Ottoman Empire. The West prevails for a moment: Seyd is dead and Gulnare is free from the harem. Even Conrad's rejection of Gulnare is evidence of the temporary triumph of Western ideals of propriety (the horror at her crime) and monogamy (his loyalty to Medora). But the triumph is temporary. The poem cannot end happily while the Pirates' Isle and Coron's Bay still belong to the Ottoman Empire: Medora winds up dead, Conrad missing.

The staging of this conflict, and the loss of the poem's pirate hero despite his escape from Seyd, is what structures the implicit argument of the poem, which is a poem about piracy after piracy; it models the inevitable collapse of the piratical into the imperial. The move from *The Bride of Abydos* to *The Corsair* is a progression that allows *The Corsair* to make – but not admit – an argument about the inscription of piracy within an imperial system. The piracy it portrays is no more revolutionary than the vicious circle of Napoleon's tyranny and the tyranny of Napoleon's defeat.

Napoleon Junior

The final footnote to *The Corsair* is a lengthy account of nineteenth-century pirate Jean Lafitte, reproducing an unnamed American newspaper article about Lafitte which marvels that he had, 'mixed with his many vices, some virtues'. Byron claims to add the note out of concern that his audience would find the account of Conrad's 'one virtue' – his love – to have 'been carried beyond the bounds of probability'.[15] The article further reports that when the Louisiana governor ordered the island cleared of its 'banditti', Lafitte spared the life of a captain who had come to execute him; the tale of such generosity from Conrad's 'brother buccaneer' is meant to substantiate his own 'single virtue'.

But Jean Lafitte was mostly likely interesting to Byron because of his association with Napoleon. Lafitte was the head of a pirate colony on the island of Barataria, near New Orleans, and was reportedly a former fencing master, 'which art he learnt in Buonaparte's army, where he was captain.'[16] The rumour that Lafitte was an exiled general from Napoleon's armies was false but prevalent, and one that Lafitte seems to have encouraged.[17] After the arrest and imprisonment of his brother Pierre, Jean Lafitte wrote a letter to *The Louisiana Gazette and New Orleans Advertiser*, defending his brother and Barataria more broadly, arguing that it was in the economic interests of New Orleans residents to protect the pirates' trade. Lafitte identified his men with Napoleon's followers, calling them 'my uncle's faithful band of loyal subjects', and signed his letter 'Napoleon, Junior'.[18] The *Delaware Gazette* would pick up the joke the following year, publishing a parody of Napoleon's protest against his transportation to St Helena from the perspective of Jean Lafitte:

> I, Lafitte, ringleader of the Pirates of Barataria, solemnly protest, before God and men, against the violation of my sacred rights, which is committed, in depriving me of the power of committing piracy, on all nations, more particularly on the U.S. I am not a prisoner, I am an inhabitant of the most enlightened nation of the globe.[19]

At the time Byron wrote his footnote, Lafitte was still an unfallen version of Napoleon, maintaining all the revolutionary potential that Napoleon had lost: Lafitte was, after all, an officer gone rogue. But Jean Lafitte's *future* reveals as much about the systems which alternately produce and prosecute piracy as it does about our hero Conrad. Whether or not Lafitte actually trained in Napoleon's army, his piratical skills were exceptionally compatible with national ambitions, put finally to the task of defending a nation-to-be: by November 1815, Lafitte was famous as a pirate-turned-*hero* of the

War of 1812, having sold his services to Andrew Jackson.[20] The complex end to Jean Lafitte's story – where he is simultaneously enemy of mankind and hero of the state – throws into sharp relief the character of his 'brother buccaneer' Conrad, a pseudo-pirate whose state affiliations remain otherwise buried in Byron's poem.

Pirating Pirates

William Hone, a radical satirist, pamphleteer, publisher and bookseller, was a homebound pirate of sorts, but one who trafficked in textual booty: revising Byron's poems and sometimes inventing them outright.[21] Though his most famous Byron piracy is his spurious third canto of *Don Juan*, his most literally 'anti-poetical' piracy is his rewriting of *The Corsair* – in prose. While Byron permitted rumours that he was the 'actual Conrad, the veritable corsair', it was Hone who went on veritably pirating, selling his own *Hone's Lord Byron's Corsair Conrad, The Corsair: or, The Pirate's Isle* for fourpence – less than a sixteenth of the cost of Byron's *Corsair* – thus bringing Byron to a working-class public. The double possession of Hone's title, 'Hone's Lord Byron's Corsair', insists that Hone's version of Byron is the man himself, even as it recasts Byron as a product of Hone's Whig publishing house.[22] Hone's Conrad is more explicitly tied to state policy and practice, sharing much more with Lafitte than does Byron's Conrad. In a sense, then, Hone's Conrad picks up the prophetic irony of Byron's footnote.

In many respects, Hone's *Corsair* is a faithful prose version of Byron's poem. The plot, though fleshed out, is basically the same, and Byron's rhymes are, in Peter Manning's terms, still 'disconcertingly audible beneath the prose'.[23] Where Hone adds substantial plot, it is only to fill out the characterological background of the (otherwise mysteriously morose) Byronic hero, for whose typically Byronic despair he offers an explanation. Hone's young Conrad had fallen in love with Medora, the daughter of a 'magnifico of Venice', who had 'encouraged his addresses until the result of his imprudence became apparent':

> ... and when the unforeseen mandate was issued for their eternal separation, in an evil hour [Conrad] persuaded the innocent maiden, whose

heart had long been his own, to elope with him beyond the bounds of Venetian authority. Unfortunately for them, they were intercepted in their flight; and the result was the everlasting banishment of Conrad from the dominions of the republic, and the restoration of Medora to the custody of an incensed parent. From this moment, the character of Conrad was determined; and he solemnly dedicated himself to a life of rapine and revenge.[24]

Medora was 'condemned by her relentless parent to a life of celibacy, in a convent on the shores of the Adriatic', and Conrad's pirate band rescued her in a scheme involving Turkish costumes, strikingly similar to the siege they will later make on Seyd's island (5).

The opening of Hone's *Corsair* is notable for Manning because, in contrast to Byron's poem, it situates the tale in time, and specifically in a time that is of the 'comfortably distant past'.[25] But the substantial revision for my purposes is Hone's situating of the tale in *space*, explicitly acknowledging the relationship between the poem's location and its political loyalties:

> In the beginning of the seventeenth century, a powerful band of Italian pirates seized upon one of the small rocky but beautiful islands of the Grecian Archipelago, and made it their head-quarters and home. Regularly fortified . . . this retreat, known to both Mahometan and Christian by the name of the *Pirates' Isle*, was deemed impregnable to any thing less than a national attack, formidably equipped and ably commanded. (3)

To say that the Pirates' Isle is invulnerable 'to any thing less than a national attack' is to afford it the military status of a nation – a nation that, we will learn, is at odds with the Ottoman Empire. Seyd Pasha, a Turk whose authority 'extended over Greece and its islands', was 'stung at the extent of the corsairs' depredations, [and] had represented their insolence to the Ottoman Porte, which had issued its firman, directing him to assemble a force, and root them out' (9). Hone's account of this chain of command provides a stark contrast to Byron's own oblique treatment of Greece. Byron may claim to 'scarce know why' the Ottoman control of Greece is relevant to *The Corsair*, but Hone holds no such pretence; in contrast to the murky account of the conflict between Byron's pirates and Seyd, Hone's Seyd's motives are explicitly political.[26] The Ottoman

Porte, the central government of the empire, has condoned Seyd's attack, and it is as the empire's representative that Seyd plans to conquer the Pirates' Isle and secure Ottoman rule over the islands. Hone's corsairs are uniformly Italians; they therefore pose a threat that is more national than renegade. In contrast to real pirates, the pirates who live on this island are of one original nationality, and their reformation here as exiles is less a rejection of European national authority than an extension of it. Even Conrad's attraction to piracy is a national inheritance: in Hone's account, Conrad acquired his love for naval warfare as a volunteer in the marine force of Venice (5).[27] This is the Conrad behind Byron's Conrad: the post-piratical pirate haunted by Napoleon's downfall, trapped in a national identity and bound to reproduce that 'dull, stupid old system' that Byron warns against in his journals. By making explicit the nationalist strain that runs through Byron's pirate poems, Hone reveals the problem at the heart of this piratical failure: an overinvestment in territory. It is Byron's *Don Juan*, I will argue, that proposes a solution.

Lakes for Ocean

Byron will revisit the figure of the pirate one final time in cantos II–IV of *Don Juan*, five years after the completion of *The Corsair* (and five years after he had sworn to give up poetry forever). Juan, shipwrecked on an island, falls in love with Haidée, daughter of the pirate Lambro. Of Lambro, we learn:

> A fisher, therefore, was he – though of men,
> Like Peter the Apostle, – and he fish'd
> For wandering merchant vessels, now and then,
> And sometimes caught as many as he wish'd;
> Let not his mode of raising cash seem strange,
> Although he fleeced the flags of every nation,
> For into a prime minister but change
> His title, and 'tis nothing but taxation;
> But he, more modest, took a humbler range
> Of life, and in an honester vocation
> Pursued o'er the high seas his watery journey,
> And merely practised as a sea-attorney. (III: 101–12)

Lambro as 'sea-attorney' is the culmination of Byron's pairing of lawyer and pirate in his earlier journal entry, where 'a lawyer, or a pirate, or any thing' places these careers on the same spectrum: lawyers, pirates, prime ministers, apostles – all just jobs. We can find a class argument embedded here as well; a person who is not in the position to be a prime minister or a lawyer will simply do better for himself as a pirate. Echoing St Augustine's pirate, who insists that his practices differ from the emperor only in scale, *Don Juan*'s narrator compares the economic responsibilities of a prime minister with the economic exploits of the pirate and finds the latter the more modest, 'honester vocation'. This is also a reminder, as in St Augustine's account, that the category of pirate is constructed by a legal discourse that is subject to the whims of governmental power. In this respect, *Don Juan* catches up with the fate of Jean Lafitte and the lesson of Hone's Conrad in admitting that piracy is produced by national policy.

Like Selim and Conrad before him, Lambro is not the ruffian of piratical lore. If you assume that Lambro 'show[s] the royal *penchants* of a pirate', *Don Juan*'s narrator warns,

> You're wrong. – He was the mildest manner'd man
> That ever scuttled ship or cut a throat,
> With such true breeding of a gentleman.
> [. . .]
> Pity he loved adventurous life's variety,
> He was so great a loss to good society. (III: 320–3, 328–9)

Despite the narrator's protest, Lambro seems to indeed have 'the penchants of a pirate', at least insofar as he scuttles ships and cuts throats. And yet his demeanour remains genteel; though he likes 'wild seas, and wild men', admits the narrator,

> something of the spirit of old Greece
> Flash'd o'er his soul a few heroic rays
> Such as lit onward to the Golden Fleece
> His predecessors in the Colchian days. (III: 430, 433–6)

Lambro, in other words, is saved from degradation by his noble ancestry. As in *The Corsair*'s song to Athens, the Greece which gave birth to Lambro is the Greece of antiquity – buried, argues Saree Makdisi, more and less literally beneath the Greece of the nineteenth-century Levant. Writing of Childe Harold's travels in the East, Makdisi suggests that the classical history of Greece is 'alien to the people currently inhabiting it', that 'the ruins of paradise are neither "here" nor "there"; separated from modern Europe by a gulf, they are also opposed to the contemporary Greeks and Turks, whose spatial structures and assemblages are superimposed on them'.[28] The fear of European subjects 'turning Turk' thus becomes more complicated in relation to Greece. To 'turn Turk' here would be to inherit the *wrong* Greece: the oriental, rather than the classical. Ancient Greece and the modern Orient are, Makdisi argues, mutually exclusive – the Levant as the 'cultural and historical ancestor of Europe' and the Levant as the 'space and territory of the Oriental other' do not even occupy the same physical place. Though Lambro is born of the former, he shares the political distresses of the latter:

> 'Tis true he had no ardent love for peace –
> Alas his country sho'd no path to praise:
> Hate to the world and war with every nation
> He waged, in vengeance of her degradation. (III: 433–40)

Put another way, Lambro is a Greek in both socio-temporal senses: born with the grace of ancient Greek culture, his nobility drives him to defend contemporary Greece from her Ottoman enemies.

The pervasiveness of this dichotomy – the grandeur of ancient Greece against the degradation of the Ottoman territories – is evidenced by contemporary reviews of the poem. Francis Jeffrey, for example, wrote that:

> [Byron's] lot has fallen among the Turks and Arabs of the Mediterranean; – ruffians and desperadoes ... but capable of great redemption in the hands of a poet of genius, by being placed within the enchanted circle of ancient Greece ... [Our modern poets] have combined the reckless valour of a Buccaneer or Corsair of any age with the refined gallantry and sentimental generosity of an English gentleman of the present day.[29]

Byron's 'genius' is his good taste in finally preferring Western culture to Eastern decadence; his 'ruffians and desperadoes' are redeemed by their Hellenised surroundings. Jeffrey's review suggests that the Eastern elements of Byron's *Tales* are made palatable by their Westernisation; contemporary readers were gradually acclimated to the idea of heroic 'ruffians and desperadoes' by their association with the territorial roots of Western culture. The two spatio-temporal registers of Greece that Makdisi identifies as incompatible in Byron's thinking – 'the Levant as the cultural and historical ancestor of Europe' and 'the Levant as the space and territory of the Oriental other' – are only problematic *because* they happen to share the same physical location.[30] The difficulty is that the cultural history of the West can be traced territorially to the East; the arbitrary determination of national boundaries – now the Ottoman Empire's, then Greece's – means that the Greece that Lambro defends is a palimpsest. Lambro fights for both versions of Greece, and so he chooses his victims indiscriminately; as a pirate, rather than a soldier, he attacks *all* nations and subjects out of revenge for Greece's 'degradation'. In this account, piracy is not merely produced by state policy but is itself figured as a form of national loyalty: Lambro defends the honour of Greece, in theory, by waging war against the world.

It turns out, however, that *Don Juan*'s Lambro, though wise and worldly on the point of his national debts, is no more able than Selim and Conrad to avoid the dangers of home and territory.[31] Lambro's tale ends unhappily – with the death of his daughter Haidée and her unborn child – because his protection of Greece's honour translates into a protection of his daughter's honour. Like Byron's other pirate tales, the story of Lambro is a diagnosis of the problem of failed revolution: Byron's 'utter detestation of all existing governments' is a choosing not to choose when all choices seem equally damned. Mohammed Sharafuddin summarises Byron's national predicament:

> The forces of reaction are corrupt, but the counter-forces of revolution are exhausted. This seems true of England, as it was true, more spectacularly, of Greece. The question then arises as to what role is left for such as Byron, who, like Childe Harold sitting among the ruins of the Parthenon, can *see*, but cannot *do* . . .[32]

Sharafuddin's image of Harold/ Byron sitting among Greece's ruins is especially evocative because it highlights the spatial aspect of Byron's distress. In an 1813 journal entry, Byron exclaims: 'umph! – In this island, where one can't ride out without overtaking the sea, it don't much matter where one goes.'[33] Most obviously, it don't much matter where one goes because to go anywhere, as Byron says, is to run into the ocean. But Byron's island problem may be figured more broadly as a problem of empire: it 'don't much matter where one goes' because to go anywhere is merely to visit the furthest reaches of the British empire – or to risk bringing the British empire to the furthest reaches of the world.

Certainly to be a British poet – to write, God forbid, a *national* epic – is to reproduce precisely these impositions; this is the trap which *Don Juan* must avoid.[34] Writing such naively nationalist poetry is the thing for which – even more than their poetical sins – *Don Juan*'s introduction censures Southey, Wordsworth, and Coleridge:

> You, Gentleman! by dint of long seclusion,
> From better company have kept your own
> At Keswick, and through still continued fusion
> Of one another's minds at last have grown
> To deem as a most logical conclusion
> That Poesy has wreaths for you alone;
> There is a narrowness in such a notion
> Which makes me wish you'd change your lakes for ocean. (I: 33–40)

The danger of living on an island (here the literal island of England and the metaphorical island of Keswick) is that it produces island thinking: the belief that 'poesy has wreaths for you alone'. The mistake that Southey and company make is provincial; they would know better, and they would write better poetry, if only they got out more.

Insularity was not a luxury Byron had. By the time of *Don Juan*, he was firmly in exile; having changed his lakes for ocean, he had become the 'poet of the sea', as he was termed by his Russian contemporaries.[35] Juan, however, can go where Byron could not, and *he* visits England. At the 'first sight of Albion's chalky belt', Juan feels pride that he should be among the English, '[t]hose haughty shop-keepers, who sternly dealt/ Their goods and edicts out from pole to pole, / And made the very billows pay them toll' (X: 516–20). The transformation is complete: when Juan imagines the English subject, he imagines a merchant performing the ownership of territorial waters, insisting that the waves themselves are trespassing on British property. The 'haughty shop-keeper' is the anti-pirate, reasserting with every edict the control that Britain has assumed over Atlantic networks.

Though Juan himself seems content to celebrate Britain by celebrating maritime colonisation, *Don Juan*'s narrator knows better. Confessing some 'mixed regret and veneration' for England's current decay and past greatness, he insists: 'I have no great cause to love that spot of earth,/ Which holds what *might have been* the noblest nation' (X.521–2, italics are Byron's). This is a radical move away from the geographical nostalgia of classical epic and towards a post-nationalist epic, an alternative to the failed revolution of Byron's and Hone's pirates. To refuse to love that 'spot of earth' for what it was or might have been – to refuse to locate potential in a 'spot' – is to reject the territorial sensibility that defangs the revolutionary force of Byron's pirates. This is a piratical move for a new age, an age where piracy fails but its sensibility remains.

Notes

1. George Gordon Byron, *Byron: Poetical Works*, ed. Frederick Page (New York: Oxford University Press, 1970). All subsequent references to Byron's poetry will be cited in-text.
2. George Gordon Byron, *Byron's Letters and Journals: The Complete and Unexpurgated Text of All the Letters Available in Manuscript and the Full Printed Version of All Others* (London: J. Murray, 1973), 3: 218.
3. Ibid., 3: 256.
4. Ibid., 3: 218.
5. Ibid., 3: 250. Byron's quotation is from *Macbeth* Act 5, Scene 5, 42–3. Brackets are editor's correction.
6. Ibid., 3: 252.
7. Ibid., 4: 44.
8. This is an echo of Mignon's 'Kennst du das Land?' in Goethe's *Wilhelm Meister's Apprenticeship*; Pushkin will echo this line yet again in 1828. For a study of these three texts together, see Carlo Testa, *Masters of Two Arts: Re-creation of European Literatures in Italian Cinema* (Toronto: University of Toronto Press, 2002), 126–7.
9. Jerome Christensen describes *The Bride of Abydos* as an 'elemental family romance'. [Jerome Christensen, *Lord Byron's Strength: Romantic Writing and Commercial Society* (Baltimore: Johns Hopkins University Press, 1993), 116.]

10. Byron, *Byron*, 897.
11. Nigel Leask, *British Romantic Writers and the East: Anxieties of Empire*, Cambridge Studies in Romanticism (New York: Cambridge University Press, 1992).
12. M. Byron Raizis writes of a 'Byronic Philhellenism', which 'lacked the stale odour of the museum and the uncertainty and speculative aura of archeology', and instead 'related a glorious past in a direct way to an inglorious and pathetic present'. The outbreak of the revolution in Greece, argues Raizis, 'focused the minds of European intellectuals on the very map that Byron ha[d] shaped'. [M. Byron Raizis, 'Byron's Greece: Ancient and Contemporary', in *Lord Byron the European: Essays from the International Byron Society*, ed. Richard Andrew Cardwell (Lewiston: E. Mellen Press, 1997), 41.]
13. Byron, *Byron*, 899.
14. Perhaps it is especially fitting that this tribute to Greece is a fragment. Padma Rangarajan argues that Byron uses the fragment elsewhere as a 'formal representation of stasis and ruin in those regions that have stalled in the cultural evolutionary process'. In *The Giaour*, she argues, 'it is a fitting tribute to the tyranny of the Ottoman Empire: European colonialism produces the historical novel, oriental despotism necessitates the fragment'. [Padma Rangarajan, *Imperial Babel: Translation, Exoticism, and the Long Nineteenth Century* (New York: Fordham University Press, 2014), 51.]
15. It is not surprising that the two-page preface to Davis's *The Pirates Lafitte* is almost exclusively occupied with a discussion of Byron's *Corsair*, and that each chapter begins with an epigraph from the poem. Slightly more surprising is Davis's insistence that the frequent comparison between Conrad and Jean Lafitte is the result of a *mistaken* association, that Byron had surely never heard of Jean Lafitte. Most surprising of all is Davis's reason for the 'impossibility' of the comparison, even if Byron had known of Lafitte: that Conrad had a single virtue, and Jean Lafitte, at the time of *The Corsair*'s composition, seemed to have none. He writes: 'It is poetically typical of the lives of the brothers Pierre and Jean Lafitte, smugglers, merchants of contraband, revolutionaries, spies, privateers, and pirates as well, that so little in their memory fits their lives, and nothing less so than their persistent association with Byron's poetic epic. When he wrote it, the Lafittes were nothing more than minor figures on the crowded criminal landscape of early Louisiana. The poet likely never heard of either, and certainly his corsair was not patterned after Jean Lafitte. Conrad's single virtue was a romantic device ... And yet, romance and legend will not yield to break the bond between poet and pirate.' (Davis, *The Pirates Laffite*, xi–xii.) It

was, on the contrary, precisely Lafitte's virtue that led Byron to make his comparison.
16. Ibid., 839.
17. When Pierre Lafitte was arrested, one city paper ran the headline 'Another Emperor Fallen', comparing Pierre to Napoleon, exiled in Elba. Pierre was called 'Emperor of Baratraria [sic], King of the smugglers.' For a thorough account of Lafitte's past and the rumour about Napoleon's army, see William C. Davis, *The Pirates Laffite: The Treacherous World of the Corsairs of the Gulf*, 1st edn (Orlando: Harcourt, 2005), 129, 158.
18. Ibid., 163–4.
19. 'Protest [from *The Delaware Gazette*]', *The Western Monitor*, 3 November 1815.
20. Of course, to the extent that the United States was itself a rogue nation, Jean Lafitte (like the Barbary corsairs) was a still a pirate, even as he turned his men against the British in defence of Louisiana's ports; Florida governor Gonzalez Manrique suggested to Andrew Jackson that the 'scandalous notoriety' of America in tolerating Lafitte and his band was sufficient reason to aid the British against them. [Ibid., 181]
21. Byron was frustrated by these piracies, writing to Murray, 'You should not let those fellows publish false "Don Juans"' (*BLJ* 6: 236). Arnold Schmidt suggests that, for Byron, 'the destabilization seen in literary piracy mirrors that of political piracy, evidenced by *The Island*'s associations of Christian with Napoleon, another failed usurper'. [Arnold A. Schmidt, 'Bligh, Christian, Murray, and Napoleon: Byronic Mutiny from London to the South Seas', *The Byron Journal* 32, no. 1 (2004): 22.]
22. Kyle Grimes cautions, however, against over-romanticising Hone's interests: 'More likely . . . Hone had more humble motivations. Early in 1817, the perpetually impecunious Hone was living with his wife and eight children in very cramped quarters behind his tiny shop in Fleet Street . . . If he could also use Byron's work in the service of popular politics, so much the better. But the primary impetus was nonetheless financial.' [Kyle Grimes, 'William Hone, John Murray, and the Uses of Byron', in *Romanticism, Radicalism, and the Press*, ed. Stephen Behrendt (Detroit: Wayne State University Press, 1997), 195–6.]
23. Peter J. Manning, 'The Hone-Ing of Byron's *Corsair*', in *Texts and Contexts*, ed. Peter J. Manning (New York: Oxford University Press, 1990), 227.
24. William Hone, *Hone's Lord Byron's Corsair: Conrad, the Corsair, or, the Pirates' Isle, A Tale* (London, 1817), 5. Subsequent references will be cited in text parenthetically.

25. Manning, 'The Hone-Ing of Byron's *Corsair*', 224.
26. Seyd's palace, in Hone's version as well as Byron's, is in 'Coron's Bay'. John Galt's biography of Byron argues that Byron has made an error, that Coron was never an Ottoman territory: 'There were two islands in the Archipelago, when Lord Byron was in Greece, considered as the chief haunts of the pirates, Stampalia, and a long narrow island between Cape Colonna and Zea. Jura also was a little tainted in its reputation. I think, however, from the description, that the pirate's isle of The Corsair is the island off Cape Colonna. It is a rude, rocky mass. I know not to what particular Coron, if there be more than one, the poet alludes; for the Coron of the Morea is neighbour to, if not in, the Mainote territory, a tract of country which never submitted to the Turks, and was exempted from the jurisdiction of Mussulman officers by the payment of an annual tribute. The Mainotes themselves are all pirates and robbers. If it be in that Coron that Byron has placed Seyd the pasha, it must be attributed to inadvertency. His Lordship was never there, nor in any part of Maina; nor does he describe the place, a circumstance which of itself goes far to prove the inadvertency. It is, however, only in making it the seat of a Turkish pasha that any error has been committed.' [John Galt, *The Life of Lord Byron* (Norwood: Norwood Editions, 1977), 197–8.]
27. I am using 'national' too loosely, here, for lack of a better word. The seventeenth-century Venice from which Conrad hailed was a republic at odds with the Ottoman Empire, but by the time of Hone's writing, Napoleon had ceded the former republic (now a province) to the Habsburg monarchy.
28. Saree Makdisi, *Romantic Imperialism: Universal Empire and the Culture of Modernity* (Cambridge University Press, 1998), 125, 127.
29. Andrew Rutherford, *Byron: The Critical Heritage*, The Critical Heritage Series (New York: Barnes & Noble, 1970), 57, 59.
30. Makdisi, *Romantic Imperialism*, 127.
31. Lambro is literally worldlier; the goods in which he trades seem to originate from all over Europe, Asia, and Africa. See *Don Juan* Canto III. Leask comments on Selim's comparative naiveté regarding the economic conditions in which he labours: 'Although Selim contains elements of his creator, he can't see beyond the horizon of his own class ideology to grasp the socio-economic realities which mould his existence; he is innocent of a knowledge of the cash nexus which Byron scrutinizes in the twelfth canto of *Don Juan*.' (Leask, *British Romantic Writers and the East*, 39.)

32. Mohammed Sharafuddin, *Islam and Romantic Orientalism: Literary Encounters with the Orient* (London; New York: Tauris, 1994), 260.
33. Byron, *Byron's Letters and Journals*, 3: 213.
34. Richard Cronin argues that Lord Elgin's plundering had demonstrated the overlap of the fate of nations and the fate of art: 'in Greece Elgin did no more than imitate what Napoleon had done in Italy ... Lord Elgin's activities, the fact itself that the marbles were transported to Britain by warships, afforded an ample proof that art could no longer claim to transcend politics in a world in which the work of art had become the most prized trophy of success in war.' Furthermore, the poet-pilgrim (Byron, as well as Harold) is, as Cronin demonstrates, dependent on wars for his freedom of movement: 'Byron visited Seville and Cadiz, but had he arrived in Spain just six months later he would have visited neither, for by then Seville had fallen to the French and Cadiz was under siege. He could dally with Mrs Spence Smith at Malta because Malta was a naval base so important that the British had chosen to risk the breakdown of the Peace of Amiens rather than to withdraw and risk losing the island to the French. From Malta he had planned to sail to Friuli, "but, lo, the Peace spoilt everything by putting this in the possession of the French." Byron was flattered by his reception by Ali Pasha in Albania, but the warmth of the hospitality must surely have owed something to the news that only days earlier four of the Ionian Islands had fallen to the British. Byron travelled freely to Constantinople, but there years previously the city had been under blockade by Admiral Duckworth, for Turkey was at war with Russia and Russia was an ally against Napoleon.' Harold, too, relies on the trappings of warfare for his travels, even as he affects superiority to it: 'Harold's contemptuous indifference to "the bravo's trade" is a vulnerable attitude in a man sailing in an armed frigate through waters that have been secured for the British by Nelson in the battle that Harold despises.' [Richard Cronin, 'Mapping *Childe Harold I and II*', *The Byron Journal* 22 (1994): 23, 13, 15.]
35. Alexander Pushkin writes of Byron, 'O sea, he was your poet' in his 1824 'To the Sea'. Though Byron felt trapped by the island of England, Catherine O'Neil points out that his proximity to the ocean afforded him his freedoms: 'Pushkin and Lermontov were not able, like Byron, to travel outside Russia, and the sea for them ... is the realm that keeps them in; the shore becomes the border.' Similarly, Richard Cronin calls Canto 2 of *Childe Harold's Pilgrimage* a 'sea canto': 'In Canto 1 the poem is confined to the peripheries of a Europe over which Napoleon's

armies held sway, but in Canto 2 Byron records how he travelled freely through the Mediterranean, for Nelson's victory at Trafalgar had made the Mediterranean a British sea, and confirmed Britain's status as the "ocean queen"'. [Catherine O'Neil, 'Byron's Sea in Pushkin in Lermontov', *The Byron Journal* 32, no. 2 (2004): 101; Cronin, 'Mapping *Childe Harold I and II*', 21.]

Chapter 3

Coming Up From the Midst of the Sea

> Symbolic reading is probably the worst way to read a literary text. Each time we are bothered by language that is too strong, we say: it is a symbol. [. . .] Yet, if prophetic words reach us, what they make us feel is that they possess neither allegory nor symbol. [. . .] It is a speech that takes up all of space and that is still essentially not fixed.
> Maurice Blanchot, *The Book to Come*[1]

Prophecy just might be the piracy for a new age, a practice that 'takes up all of space and that is still essentially not fixed', in Blanchot's words. Like the space of the sea, the space of God defies borders, but like the sea it is vulnerable to the imposition of territory: the land of God is always about to collapse into empire. Colonists spread Britain, and prophets spread Christianity; if the prophet's word takes up all of space, it might also take *over* all of space. What is the difference between building colonial outposts in Africa and re-building the city in Palestine? Where is the overlap between the Empire and the empire? These are the questions with which Romantic-era prophets had to grapple; their prophetic project was redefining the kind of space that prophecy might take over. The space in question: Jerusalem.

In the late eighteenth and early nineteenth centuries, Jerusalem was part of the Ottoman Empire and therefore complicated by the imperial struggles we've seen in previous chapters – complicated, in short, by its Easternness. Joanna Southcott's and Richard Brothers' prophecies raise geographical questions both concrete and abstract: is the East necessarily in the east? East of what, exactly? Said argues that the East 'alternated in the mind's geography between being an Old World to which one returned, as to Eden or Paradise, there to set up a new version of the old, and being a wholly new place to which one came as Columbus came to America, in order to set up a New World . . .'[2] Said's pairing of Eden with the colonisation of America is telling; the newness of Eden was itself the fantasy imposed on colonial projects, America and Jerusalem alike. The prophecy of the Romantic period was therefore steeped in contemporaneous problems of empire and territory, and prophets were put in the position of reconciling the space of God with the space of the nation. This chapter takes as its subject the prophecies of Joanna Southcott and Richard Brothers, not to argue that these two prophets are somehow representative of their time, but rather to show how wildly solutions to this problem may differ. Southcott conflates divine and national revolution, arriving finally at a Jerusalem that is aggressively British. Richard Brothers, on the other hand, reimagines Britishness to the point of exploding the very idea of nation. Southcott still has followers today; Brothers became an enemy of the state, arrested for sedition and forgotten in an asylum. Theirs is the story of this chapter, Southcott's an illumination of prophecy's inscription in colonialism, and Brothers' a testament to prophecy's radical, extra-national potential.

Where the Visitation Was Made Known

On 11 December 1804, while Joanna Southcott stood in a field in Exeter and announced to a large audience that Christ's return was imminent, disbelievers shouted at her from the opposite side of a canal. The Exeter Canal had been widened 100 years earlier to allow oceangoing ships; Southcott was literally distanced from her disbelievers by Exeter's direct connection to the ocean. But her own connection to the ocean was more circuitous and more subtle, winding through England by way of the Promised Land. As Southcott imagines the building of Christ's kingdom, she collapses Devon with Palestine, the French Revolution with the battle of the end-times; her land-locked prophecies are enabled by her layering of space across ocean and desert. Despite her prophecies' engagement with the divine, they are nevertheless invested in the space of the nation.

Southcott never physically left England. She grew up the daughter of a devout Methodist farmer in East Devon and managed her father's farm when he was ill; she later went to work as a domestic servant in Exeter. It was during her employment there that, in 1792, she received her first communication from God: a communication which revealed her to be the 'woman clothed with the sun' prophesied in the book of Revelation. In 1801, Southcott published her account of this experience, entitled *The Strange Effects of Faith*; she went on to publish sixty-five books and pamphlets between 1801 and 1814, hoping to convince as many people as possible to be 'sealed'. The process required followers to sign a petition that called for the overthrow of Satan and the establishment of Christ's kingdom on earth; having committed themselves, their sealing was made material with a certificate inscribed 'The Sealed of the Lord, the Elect precious. Man's Redemption to inherit the Tree of Life. To be made Heirs of God and Joint-Heirs with Jesus Christ.' Southcott's repeated injunction: 'Sign for Satan's destruction'.[3]

Southcott is estimated to have had as many as 100,000 followers, and the mass appeal of her work must have been due in part to its having been written for the people. James Hopkins notes in *A Woman to Deliver Her People* that her New Jerusalem is described in terms 'easily understood by Joanna's audience'; Eitan Bar-Yosef describes them as terms 'with which Joanna herself was most familiar: a roof, good crops, rest, land . . .'[4] Southcott's prophesying, in other words, is an act of translation: she makes the word of God into the word of the God of regular people, translating the divine into the common. 'Joanna was no Joan of Arc,' writes E. P. Thompson, 'but she shared one of Joan's appeals to the poor: the sense that revelation might fall upon a peasant's daughter as easily as upon a king.'[5] But even more important than the possibility that the poor might be chosen is Southcott's suggestion that the New Jerusalem will come about by what the poor best know how to do: labour. God describes to Southcott a Jerusalem that will be built with the tools of the farmer, as she records in *Sound an Alarm*:

> Now I shall come to some particulars concerning the people. It is not a trifling matter for people to put their hand to the plough and draw back; it is better for them never to sign at all, than, after they have signed, to destroy their seals; because they first sign for Satan's destruction, and afterwards destroy the seal of Christ's protection . . . [N]ow I tell all men, he that putteth his hand to the plough and draweth back, cannot

enter the kingdom of heaven; for this is the plough that must break the ground for my Kingdom to be established upon earth, and Satan's kingdom to be destroyed. So let the Sealed stand steadfast, and they shall reap if they faint not.[6]

It is better not to begin at all than to leave the work unfinished, better not to sign at all than to break Christ's seal: dabblers are dangerous in the Kingdom of God. Workers are therefore the most chosen of the chosen people; they know what to do with a plough, and they know how to follow through. Southcott's seals are the plough that will prepare the land for the Kingdom of God, and the poor are particularly well-suited to the labour of belief. But the 'Kingdom to be established upon earth' differs from the land of Britain in one crucial respect: the land that the poor plough might, in the world to come, actually belong to them. 'This', argues Bar-Yosef, 'is precisely what Southcott promises her followers, as she transforms the image of the Promised Land to, simply, the promise of land.'[7] The labour of Adam and Eve taming the Garden is rewritten as the poor labouring at the plough; the divine inheritance of Eden becomes the gift of a plot of land.

If belief is labour, as Southcott suggests, there is a terrible pun to be made here, because in 1813, the Spirit informed Southcott that 'a second Son must be born, like the first; that is, of God, and not of man', – and that she, a sixty-four-year-old virgin, was to bear this Son of God.[8] In her willingness to bear the Son of God, to *labour* in his birth, Southcott was the most devout of believers. Shiloh was to be born in the autumn of 1814, and that summer Southcott began readying for the birth. She was examined by at least twenty-one doctors (including Richard Reece, a distinguished London surgeon), and seventeen of them confirmed her pregnancy. She married her friend John Smith to legitimate her future son, and believers sent gifts for the baby. Though the birth was expected sometime in autumn, Southcott grew ill and died on 27 December 1814, without delivering the child. An autopsy determined neither the cause of death nor evidence of a pregnancy.

After her death, some followers maintained faith, arguing that the birth was a 'spiritual' one, or that Shiloh had in some other way disappeared. In 1814, partly in response to the continued enthusiasm for Southcott's teachings, Dr Reece (who had, after Southcott's autopsy, retracted his confirmation of her pregnancy) published *A Statement of the Circumstances that attended the Last Illness and Death of Mrs. Southcott, with an account of the Appearances exhibited on Dissection* as a warning 'to the weak, ignorant, and deluded' of the 'lengths to which fanaticism will go'.[9] Despite this purported mission, Reece's *Statement* is primarily a medical account; it does not concern itself with Southcott's experience or the content of her prophecies. 'I lay aside entirely the idea of her prophetic functions. These must rest with those who are able to judge of their truth or otherwise', writes Reece.[10] Of society's *need* for the prophetic, on the other hand – and of Southcott's therefore well-timed arrival – Reece explains that recent events, 'unparalleled in former times', make it only natural for people to look for an explanation 'in that record which is given us as our rule of life and conduct'.[11] Reece moves here from biology to politics, from the medical fact of Southcott's body to the political context in which it functioned symbolically. By Reece's account, it was the current political climate that lead Southcott to make the mistake she made, but it was also the current political climate that readied the world to hear her message. Revolution, in other words, is both produced by and productive of prophecy, and Southcott's prophecies directed what Reece calls 'fanaticism' towards a political end.

But that end was British. Southcott's God, it turns out, is a British God, speaking through her always, and exclusively, to the British people. As Southcott records in *The Third Book of Wonders*:

> ... I now tell thee, if it were not for the laws of your land, the persecution would now be as great as it was by the Jews, when they put their prophets to death, and when they clamoured for my blood: and this, thou knowest, has been the desire of many, to see thee put to death, as I was; and therefore, *it is the laws of your land that have made ME defend this nation from the foreign enemy, while mine anger and indignation are kindled, to hear the blasphemy throughout the land* ...[12]

Britain's laws protect it from making the mistakes of ancient Israel; despite the ignorance of the British people, who blaspheme their God and refuse His message, their laws prevent them from repeating the crucifixion. In this account, the law of the nation is conflated with God's law, and to be British is to be chosen. But for Southcott,

Britain's chosenness is circular: Britain is saved because of its law, and it has its law because it is saved:

> ... at the beginning, when man fell from the perfection in which he was first made, he fell under the powers of darkness; and had it not been for prophecies, man would soon have become like the wild ass's colt. The wild Indians, and the complete heathens, who worship stocks and stones, shew you what man was fallen to; and what all men would be, had I not sent my Spirit amongst them, to instruct and direct them; and by prophecies foretold what lay before them.[13]

The narrative of development which positions Christianity at the opposite end of rock-worshiping heathens is in this case attributed not to the essential superiority of any race or nation, but to the word of God itself: prophecy, here, produces progress, which then enables prophecy.

Here lies the most interesting aspect of Southcott's prophecy: if the geographical particularity (west versus east) is not what guarantees Britain's authority, the particular land of the Holy Land need not matter either. And so Southcott's Jerusalem will not necessarily be rebuilt in Jerusalem. Referring to the Book of Revelation 21: 2, in which John sees 'the holy city, new Jerusalem, coming down from God out of heaven', Southcott writes: 'The new Jerusalem, coming down from heaven, meaneth where the visitation is made known: it does not mean Jerusalem where it stood'.[14] The 'place where the visitation is made known' happens, not so incidentally, to be *Britain*; in this way, Southcott aligns herself with an Anglo–Israelist movement that means, often quite literally, to rebuild Jerusalem in England. But where, precisely, is the space 'where the visitation was made known'? Does that mean London? Or Southcott's kitchen? Or is it in the written prophecies? Or is Jerusalem finally to be rebuilt in Southcott's body – where the visitation is most literally made known – housed in the soul or belly of the prophet? In privileging the space of prophecy over the space of the nation, Southcott divorces her rebuilt Jerusalem from the nationalised city; she allows Jerusalem to happen wherever it happens to happen. Elsewhere, however, Southcott *does* seem to mean to build Jerusalem where Jerusalem was; in *The Fourth Book of Wonders*, she writes:

for I shall . . . establish the THRONE OF DAVID for ever in Jerusalem, as I have promised. For, *where I was crucified, I will be exalted; where I died for MAN, my SON shall reign over MAN.*[15]

Bar-Yosef, in reading Southcott's contradictory accounts of where Jerusalem is to be built, argues that 'although a certain ambiguity does exist in her teaching in relation to the situation of Jerusalem, the tension is not so much between England and a present-day reality in the East, but between England and a textual representation that can always be applied, yet again, to the happy land that is England'.[16] But there was also a tension between that ever-portable textual representation and the 'present-day reality in the East': the former could not escape the latter. The clash of Britain's political and military aims with the Jerusalem of the Bible was strong enough to prompt Southcott to a few rare gestures towards the international sphere:

Of France, and Spain, and every distant coast
I'd save a remnant; but one nation lost –
And that should be for the sake of the Jews, that I should destroy the nation that had their possession; for I said I gave it to the heathen, and they that called not upon my name; therefore it is said, in the second Psalm, 'Ask of me, and I shall give thee the heathen for thine inheritance, and the uttermost parts of the earth for thy possession.'[17]

Southcott's God seems here to be referring not only to the heathenism of biblical times, but also to the 450-year Ottoman possession of Palestine. The Muslim 'heathens', in fact, are worse even than the heathen Catholic nations; the Ottoman Muslims had every chance, and they didn't take it. Despite being in the land of God, they failed to accept Christ, while those in exile nevertheless carried on in their faith. It is not, then, as Southcott's relocation of Jerusalem at first seems to suggest, that the geographical land is unimportant. The specificity of the land matters very much, or could have mattered; finally, of all the land in the world, it is only the Holy Land that is not holy enough to be saved.

And so this is the problem Southcott's prophecies are meant to solve: God has been exiled from His land. The work of the prophecies is not only to restore the Jews to 'their land', but to make

England – indeed, all the earth – into God's land. The work of the prophet is therefore to put everything in its proper place:

> The Sealing must first take place before the end can come. Satan must be fixed to bounds; as man was fixed to bounds. For, in me there is no variableness, nor shadow of turning. Then how shall I turn from the manner I first began? All things have their time, and their bounds – winter and summer, seed time and harvest, life and death have their appointed time . . .[18]

To everything there is a season, and a *place* to every purpose under heaven; 'all things have their time' morphs into all things have their 'bounds'. Southcott's sealing is a spatial practice, a redemptive inverse of the original fall; this is how God 'turns' from the punitive geographies of Genesis. When Adam and Eve were cast out of the garden, their bounds were fixed by their exile; now Satan's bounds will be fixed by *his* exile from earth, literally making space for the kingdom of God. There is no going back to Eden.

There may, however, be some negotiating to be done about what constitutes Satan's space. If Reece is correct that Southcott's prophecies were made necessary or relevant by 'recent events' (to read the Bible in the shadow of the French Revolution is to become a prophet), then the space that God was meant to (re)inhabit was nationally and militarily contested. The Holy Land itself was the site of battles between the British and the French. Napoleon was thwarted by the British and Ottomans at the Battle of Acre in 1799, and while historians disagree about whether he intended to take Jerusalem, Palestine was to be his gateway to the rest of the empire: had he been able secure Acre, he declared, he would have made himself 'Emperor of the East'.[19] Southcott was aware of the rivalry. In explanation of her claim in *The First Book of Wonders* that 'the Woman clothed with the Sun shall make all nations shake', she writes:

> It is not the WOMAN that makes the nations shake, that is with child, travailing in birth and pained to be delivered; but it is the CHILD, when he is born; then the nations will begin to shake, and then they will know, if thou art the WOMAN MENTIONED IN THE *Revelation*, to bring the MAN-CHILD into the world; then BONAPARTE is the *Beast* in the *Revelation*, whom they have worshiped.[20]

If this prophecy is true, Southcott suggests, then it has political currency; the end will come about not only through spiritual battle, but also through a political war with national and territorial stakes. The birth of the messiah will alert the world to the sins of Napoleon; the spiritual revelation will result in a political awakening. Furthermore, if the birth of the 'man-child' revealed Napoleon to be the beast of Revelation, the reverse also held true: Napoleon's exile was a sure sign that the birth of the saviour was imminent. Southcott writes in June 1814, two months after Napoleon's exile to Elba:

> And now discern the shadows of this year, that I have told thee the Prince of Peace shall be born; because I have told thee it is by him that I shall establish Peace throughout the Earth: and now discern the Shadow of Peace, which they say the Kings are making with England, while at the same time Buonaparte, as I told thee – 'If England would take care, I'd rid him from this coast:' and let them see how far he is gone from the coast.[21]

The Beast Napoleon, as Southcott's earlier prophecies promised, had been put in his proper place, sealed in an entirely different sense. The measure of 'how far' Napoleon had gone was his removal from the (British) coast and his confinement to an island, the most material representation of bounds Southcott could have hoped for. The Napoleonic Wars collapse entirely into cosmic war: finally, the fulfilment of Southcott's prophecy is territory.

Like No City You Have Ever Seen

Although Richard Brothers also planned to build a New Jerusalem, his prophecies imagine space in a radically different way from Southcott's: not as land but as movement. And no wonder; Brothers was supposed to be a sailor, not a prophet. At thirteen he became a midshipman with the Royal Navy and then served as a lieutenant; after he was discharged in 1783, he travelled in France, Italy and Spain, most likely as a merchant sailor, before rejoining the navy. But God interfered (in what would be the first time of many): Brothers eventually decided he could not serve a King who was the head of the Church of England, and so he left the navy in 1789. It was a year later, when

Brothers was thirty-two, that the Spirit of God 'began first . . . to enlighten [his] understanding', though he had always, he writes, 'had a presentiment of being sometime or other very great'.[22] By Brothers' reasoning, we were due for another prophet born on Christmas day, as he himself had been, and he argued that his surname was proof that he was a descendent of Jesus' brother, making him, as he termed himself, 'the nephew of the Almighty'.[23] Although Brothers was literally born for his job, he did not choose to be Chosen, and in 1792, he decided to abandon his prophesying and leave England forever. He set off walking for Bristol, intending to emigrate, carrying a rod he had cut for himself in emulation of Moses. After sixteen miles, Brothers threw the rod away in anger; after twenty-five miles, 'on a sudden, God by his power stopped the action of every joint and limb, and turned me feelingly around with more ease than a strong man would a young child; commanding me, at the same instant, to return and wait His proper time.'[24] This Brothers did, finding the discarded rod on his way back, and he never again tried to flee from the presence of the Lord.

In 1795, Brothers was arrested on the basis of an Elizabethan statute for 'unlawfully, maliciously, and wickedly writing, printing, and publishing various fantastical prophecies, with intent to create dissensions, and other disturbances within this realm'. Authorities claimed that Brothers had 'for several years alarmed and agitated the minds of the people (crowds of whom have resorted to him daily)'.[25] According to the *European Magazine*, Brothers 'told the two messengers who had come to arrest him that they must "oblige" him to get into the coach, "as then his great prophecy would be fulfilled"'. Once seated in the coach, Brothers 'exclaimed with great energy, "now my prophecy is fulfilled", after which he was silent and submissive'.[26] He was imprisoned for treason, but after orientalist and ardent supporter Nathaniel Brassey Halhed brought Brothers' case before Parliament, he was moved to a private madhouse, where he remained until 1806. These were productive years for Brothers. It was during this time that he laid plans for the rebuilding of Jerusalem, elaborated in the impressive *A Description of Jerusalem, Its Houses and Streets, Squares, Colleges, Markets, and Cathedrals, the Royal and Private Palaces*. It may be that Brothers' confinement was a necessary condition for the production of his Jerusalem, a particular imagination of freedom that is produced by its absence. In the

Description Brothers endeavours, 'notwithstanding my confinement, to make the description of Jerusalem plain, that every woman, as well as man, throughout the land shall clearly understand it'.[27] This, he admits, is an 'extremely inconvenient' task – the kingdom of God is not easily translated into a kingdom on earth – but like the 'man with the measuring line' of the forty-third chapter of Ezekiel, Brothers will plan every Jerusalemitic square down to the last inch. It is time, he says, for 'the city that was shewn in a vision . . . to be openly realised; all its knotty metaphors and parts difficult to be understood are now made plain to every body'.[28]

The new Jerusalem will be a city like no city you have ever seen. 'Look at London and Paris, those two great and wealthy cities', Brothers declares,

> there are no such regular streets in either, or healthy accommodations as in ours. Their streets in general are narrow, and very crooked, their houses in many parts are confusedly crowded together, some high, some low, and very few gardens except those of the most wealthy men. But with us every house throughout the city has its regular portion of ground for a garden, where the poorest families may walk and enjoy themselves – where their children may play in safety, to acquire daily fresh health and strength.[29]

There will still be poverty in Brothers' Jerusalem, but unlike the poor neighbourhoods of London and Paris, Jerusalem will have safe, pleasant gardens for its poorest to relax in. Brothers' *Description* is marked, above all, by attention to these mundane details: his is not a city of gold, but a city to be lived in. He designs the buildings with an eye toward fire prevention (God orders the adoption of this method 'to prevent the expense' of fire damage); the splendour of the city, while it 'astonish[es] one moment', will 'draw the most lively feelings of sensibility from the heart' in the next. Even the 'garden of Eden' at its centre is made for the practical use of its citizens – provided, of course, that they are 'in a cleanly dress'.[30] And Jerusalem's citizens will have every opportunity to make a decent living. There is oil and coal to be mined in the Holy Land, Brothers insists, and he urges the publication of pamphlets to aid Jerusalem's future citizens in making the (financial) best of the land's natural resources. The economy will thrive.

But, as in Southcott's Jerusalem, there is material labour to be done. Relying on the accounts of geographers James Bruce and Robert Wood, Brothers imagines the Holy Land to be quite empty: 'quite desolate and barren', without trees, and sprinkled with 'poor' and 'mean' villages, ruined by the 'robbery and oppression of the enemy'.[31] 'Although we have no desert to travel through,' warns Brothers, 'yet we have a naked country to plant with trees, and over with cattle; we have a barren land to sow with corn, and fill with cities.'[32] Even the geography of the Holy Land is flawed; 'it now solely belongs to God to restore it at least to some part of its original level and beauty', Brothers writes, 'for otherwise, unless the present form was altered to a necessary level by sinking the Mount of Olives, or removing it, and by bringing again a good river of water through that ground, the great and splendid city. . . could never be built by man'.[33] But in the meantime, there are practical, human matters to be tended to. Britain should, for example, 'employ masters of ships to take a good survey of the ground, the depth of water, rocks, or sand-banks, whether they are injurious to obstruct shipping or beneficial to break off the violence of the waves; whether the bottom is level, steep, or gradually shelving'.[34] Brothers' is a practical vision: his vision of what the Holy Land will be must finally yield to what already is.

Brothers' prophecy, in other words, doesn't have the luxury of fantasy: he knows that harbours depend on the shape of the land. He is a sailor first. Brothers admits:

> It will, no doubt, appear astonishing that I should be so perfect on a sudden in architectural deliniation, never having studied it; and when it is considered I have been bred up to the sea, a profession as opposite to that for forming the splendid city of Jerusalem and its elegant houses, as the knowledge of astronomy is to mining in the bowels of the earth.[35]

But the progression from sailor to prophet is not as surprising as we might imagine, argues Brothers; the one who will fulfill God's prophecy *must*, he insists, come from the sea. Brothers references 2 Esdras 8: 25–6: 'Whereas thou sawest a man coming up from the midst of the sea: The same is he whom God the Highest hath kept a great season, which by his own self shall deliver his creature: and he shall order them that are left behind.' This is just what Brothers wants to hear; his time as a sailor was a necessary prerequisite to his service in God's kingdom: 'I am the man alluded to in this chapter; coming from the sea . . . is to signify that I should, *as the person meant*, live on the ocean. I have; having been *in the English navy*: but am now rising from it, to fulfil this prophecy . . .'[36] Like the famous pirate cry 'we come from the sea', Brothers' declaration emphasises the mobility of his experience: place, for Brothers, is never static. Consequently, the Jerusalem he imagines is full of movement; alongside his elaborate plans for how the city is to be built are instructions for how it is to be used. But his aim is always to balance the freedom of movement with the orderliness required (by biblical imperative) in the new City – a delicate position for one who was so often cited for using space incorrectly. Of the college gardens, for example, Brothers writes:

> There must not be any roads made through them for carriages or even people on foot, as they are intended solely for exercise, recreation, and to take the air in. On the six working days they are entirely for the use the students and their officers, but on the Sabbath and public holidays they are to be, without fail, for the free use of all people poor and rich, to walk in them.[37]

The prohibition of roads offers a freedom to those who want to 'take the air in' – sparing them the trouble of watching for carriages, freeing them to focus on their exercise and recreation. And the absence of even pedestrian paths seems likewise a liberating gesture: no one in the gardens of Jerusalem will be told where to walk. But the prohibition of roads suggests more generally that gardens are not made to be travelled through; they are meant to be an end in themselves rather than a means to somewhere else. To 'walk *in*' these gardens, then, is also to have one's movements circumscribed by the garden's boundaries. In the absence of roads leading through – which is to say, in the absence of roads leading in or out – the students who are 'free' to stroll around the gardens are also contained by their perimeters. This is, finally, the city drawn by a man in confinement, whose best notion of freedom can only be articulated in forms of orderly movement.

And so in an effort to distinguish his city from those other great cities which have 'no such regular streets', Brothers' Jerusalem will be laid out on a grid, as orderly as a city can be:

> The 12 great streets of 144 feet each, after passing from the square beyond the palaces, are intersected by the letter streets of 72 feet wide, regularly at the distance from each other of 1528 feet; all these streets cross each other at right angles in the north-east, south-east, south-west, and north-west quarters, forming in them 56 squares, fit for the residence of the most noble and wealthy from all nations, as well as our own... Between the divisions of the streets 72 feet wide, are to be seven regular lesser streets 36 feet wide, each with their houses and gardens running straight in a parallel line with each other.[38]

In this way, Brothers promises, his city will be 'agreeable to the plan laid down when given to Ezekiel 2328 years ago'.[39] But the hyper-organisation of Ezekiel's city is disciplinary; meant at once to control the practices of its residents and to insure the inheritance of the tribes of Israel. The land 'set apart for the Lord', the 'holy portion' for the consecrated priests and Levites, will never change hands. Ezekiel 48: 14 reads: 'They shall not sell or exchange any of it. They shall not alienate this choice portion of the land, for it is holy to the Lord.' Brothers' city, too, with all the precision of Ezekiel's, seems to restrict movement as much as it enables it, limiting how and where roads may be built. 'There must not be any private thoroughfares, alleys, or narrow lanes in the city', he writes: 'The three distinctions of streets already mentioned are the only proper ones for the advantage of cleanliness and intercourse.'[40] Brothers' duty as the Nephew of the Almighty is to personally ensure the 'proper' use of God's city, which means keeping control over the city's appearance in the hands of the government, which is to say himself. The prohibition against smaller, private roads also ensures that the movements of the city's residents will be public and traceable; no one in Jerusalem will travel in secret.

There is, nevertheless, a liberatory aspect to Brothers' rigidity. If the organisation of the city is regulatory, it is also regular, and the meticulousness of Brothers' account makes its regularity comprehensible to all:

> From the regular methodical description I have given, any person that pleases may draw the plan with a pen on paper. Ladies may do it for

amusement, gentleman as an honourable employment to enlarge the sphere of their knowledge, and add new strength to their minds: for they may rely on it as a positive truth, that many of their descendants, sons and daughters, will be respectable inhabitants of the city.[41]

In describing the city in minute detail, Brothers ensures that his readers can do what he has done: they can map the city, and therefore master it. Though Brothers designs a city that seems to control the movements of its residents, he nevertheless gives them the tools they need to own it, by way of a cognitive map that makes the city universally available. The readers and their children and their children's children will live in a city that is their own, and, thanks to the logic of its arrangement, they will have incorporated its organisation into their own minds. Paris, maybe, can never be owned. London can never be owned. These are cities whose streets sprung up by accident, meandering and irregular, built for local needs and therefore private. But the streets of Brothers' Jerusalem will be built for all, to be understood by all; in that sense, they make up a city that, as he declares, is 'our own'. The challenge for Jerusalem's citizens, then, is to enact a kind of freedom within the limits placed upon them. This is not unlike, for Brothers, the problem of the nation: Britain's laws, designed to ensure its citizens' rights, necessarily restrict their freedoms. Arrested for obeying what he believed to be the Lord's command, Brothers understood this as well as anybody. In planning his city, the nation of God, he was therefore faced with the problem of balancing its order with its liberation.

And yet for a moment, it seems that Brother's Jerusalem, like Southcott's, will be British. Reading the history of the world in the Bible, Brothers' *Correct Account of the Invasion and Conquest . . . by the Saxons* traces a lineage from the ancient Israelites to the Britons. The new Israel might be British, in other words, because the British were themselves (already) the Israelites. In that case, the new nation might as well be modelled on the best of Britain. 'The English have shown a similarity of wisdom to the Hebrews in their choice of their sovereign', Brothers writes; the government of God's city – with Brothers at its head – will look suspiciously like the government of Britain.[42] The Holy Land, Brothers concludes baldly, 'is our own country, and the only one we can live free in'.[43]

The fact that the Holy Land is already 'our own country', coupled with his belief that the land is unpopulated, 'as if never inhabited by our ancestors', frees Brothers from the responsibility of worrying about Palestine's indigenous population. He can therefore criticise Britain's imperial policies without irony:

> A little time longer, and England will be so much entangled as not to be able to go forward without feeling the pains of that *colonial conquest* which is to be the cause of her death; nor to retire, without falling under that foreign blow, which will break the empires in pieces, and throw herself down on the ground; from whence she is never to rise up any more.[44]

If Britain is chosen as the harbinger of the rebuilt Jerusalem, it is also – and necessarily – destined for ruin. 'Colonial conquest', the means of Britain's rise to prominence, will also bring about its downfall. Britain cannot 'go forward' without feeling these 'pains'; any progress, in other words, condemns Britain to its demise. This, too, is foretold in the Bible; London, Brothers argues, is the 'spiritual Babylon' described in Revelation 18: 11–19:

> And the merchants of the earth weep and mourn for her, since no one buys their cargo anymore, cargo of gold, silver, jewels, pearls ... and slaves, that is, human souls. [. . .] The merchants of these wares, who gained wealth from her, will stand far off, in fear of her torment, weeping and mourning aloud. [. . .] And all shipmasters and seafaring men, sailors and all whose trade is on the sea, stood far off and cried out as they saw the smoke of her burning, 'What city was like the great city?' And they threw dust on their heads as they wept and mourned, crying out, 'Alas, alas, for the great city where all who had ships at sea grew rich by her wealth! For in a single hour she has been laid waste.'

The 'great city' of Babylon is easy enough for Brothers to identify: a port city that trades in gold and silver, spices and, most damningly, slaves. London is Babylon, London is to fall in the apocalypse, and London has brought this on itself. In its attempts at 'go[ing] forward', in the mistaken desire for progress, Britain has trafficked in slavery and mistreated its poor. Brothers' first-hand knowledge of the wretched conditions in which London's prisoners live qualifies him especially to identify the cause of London's fall: 'No man, who has any knowledge of God, can justly say, that London is without guilt, and her people without sin; when her streets are full of vice, and her prisons are full of oppression.'[45] And so unlike Southcott's, the 'Britain' that Brothers' Holy Land is meant to replicate is not the actual Britain but an ideal of Britishness – the Britain that was, is, and always will be Israel. Brothers is explicitly critical of colonialism in a way that Southcott is not; he therefore strives to honour the essential Britishness of the Holy Land without allowing his new nation to stoop to that 'colonial conquest' that so plagues his current country.[46]

As if in a gesture of his good faith, Brothers' *Letter to Miss Cott* divides the labour and the sacrifice rebuilding Jerusalem among all the nations of the earth, specifying the provisions every government should donate. Even Turkey and Russia, whose mutual destruction Brothers will prophesy just three years later, are asked to contribute.[47] Included in the catalogue of Russia's required donations are 'four hundred ship loads of timber in balks and boards of such different kinds as may be most suitable, with a proportionate quantity of nails' and 'forty-thousand tents, with a rug and blanket, or two blankets to each tent as is most convenient, with kettles and ovens in proportion'.[48] Of the 'Emperor of Turkey and his people', Brothers asks for 'thirty thousand cows with a proportionate number of bulls, thirty thousand sheep, three thousand draught horses, three thousand camels, and as many buffaloes as can be spared, with proper harness'. He concludes his catalogue to the Emperor with a confident and comprehensive request: 'All other requisites necessary for my people and the building of Jerusalem I'll be much obliged to your highness for'.[49] Unfortunately for Turkey, among the requisite items necessary for the building of Jerusalem is the land itself. The Holy Land, Brothers cannot help but notice, sits squarely in the middle of the Ottoman Empire; to rebuild the city, Brothers is going to need to get his hands on the land. But, in light of his criticisms of Britain's colonial projects, he can hardly justify taking it by force. Instead he offers the following promise to the Emperor:

> Although I am obliged to take off a little from the limits of your empire, as decreed in the scripture, and now commanded by Almighty God, it is not done from enmity, or any intention of future destruction, but on the contrary you may be firmly assured of my favour; for the countries

that I shall take possession of were designedly by God put under your care as guardian until the fulness of time was expired for his people the Hebrews to return and enter on their inheritance. As to the part I take for my own private maintenance, it is the free gift commanded by God, and as such I take it for me and mine forever. Your highness may think the loss of Egypt a great injury to your capital from its fertility and frequent supplies of grain; but God who orders what I do, and separates from your empire what I take, can easily give you another country for it, much more convenient, and at present more fertile.[50]

It is a trade, and the Turks will profit by it. They only need give up the land of God – not exactly *their* god anyway, Brothers seems to suggest – and God will likely give them some land better suited to their purposes. But for once Brothers does not claim to speak for God; he goes on to warn that he in no way intends to 'bind the Almighty to any terms of agreement as a compensation for Egypt and Cyprus or any other country and island he may choose to take hereafter'.[51] Brothers and God will take the land whether or not they can pay for it, and Turkey should sacrifice it happily for the good of the world (to come). Brothers goes on to warn that, though the Turkish are favoured as descendants of Isaac and therefore 'the brethren and nearest relatives that the Israelites may have on earth', they nevertheless risk 'perish[ing] by fire' if they oppose him. 'I fight alone,' Brothers declares, 'not with sword or gun, but with the delegated power of God in fire. You will, I hope, live to see it, and with many other princes bow before it.'[52] God is a weapon, and Brothers is not afraid to use Him.

Brothers' Jerusalem teeters dangerously on the edge of British imperialism here, substituting redemption for progress, God for nation. He insists that 'all houses . . . must be built in the English manner', and that the Hebrews wear hats instead of turbans, being a 'better defense against the sun than turbans, more cool, more supportable to health, and certainly more convenient to put on or take off'.[53] How will Jerusalem not be another Babylon, another Egypt? Brothers' answer: tear down the pyramids, and use their bricks to build the new city. The 'pieces' of Egypt and of all great nations are to be the material stuff of the new Jerusalem. This is not merely symbolic. Brothers has no time for metaphors; he has a city to build. And so he suggests that the stones of the pyramids might actually be used to rebuild the Temple, requesting that 'the greatest care may be taken to preserve the stones entire', and that 'all slabs of polished marble, with every other thing rare and curious, may be carefully laid by for my own use'. Retired ships of war, no longer necessary in the Kingdom of God, could be used to transport people to the Holy Land. And maybe, with luck and the grace of God, the Roman government would be 'so kind' as to send 'home' the pillars Titus removed from the Temple.[54] Unlike British ambitions to expand their own empire to include the Holy Land, Brothers' city depends upon Britain's own destruction, even as it insists on Britain's universality. The Holy Land may be British, with its British houses and British hats, but it can only exist if the empires that exist now and have existed in the past are dismantled to build Jerusalem. London, remember, is Babylon, and so will be 'laid waste' and with the destruction of Turkey and Russia, 'all' – the British too – 'shall be as one people, and of one mind'.[55] Brothers reorganises space in such a way that Egypt is a place of freedom: Egypt, the 'free gift' of God, is simultaneously Egypt and the Holy Land. The stones of Egypt will be the stones of Jerusalem, and the slave labour of the ancient Israelites will be redeemed in the free labour of the new Hebrews. Rebuilding the city does not undo what has been done, and it does not guarantee that what is done will not have to be done all over again. It is not a permanent solution. But then, that is the point: this emancipation is an ongoing practice, one that takes advantage of the instability of space and the productivity of bodies. The city is its being built – not a space to be finished but a process always to be carried out, not a territory but an event.

First Day of the Millennium

An epilogue. In May of 1838, Sir William Percy Honeywood Courtenay (real name: J. N. Thom) led what E. P. Thompson calls 'the last peasants' revolt' in Kent, which resulted in the Battle of Bossenden Wood, with a higher death toll than Pentridge or Peterloo.[56] But this was not just a peasants' revolt. Courtenay was a prophet, believed by his followers to have miraculous powers; in his journal *Lion* he declared himself 'King of Jerusalem, Prince of Arabia, King of the Gypsies, Defender of his King and Country'.[57] Some supporters swore he had stigmata, and Courtenay certainly encouraged such associations, insisting that if he died he would rise again: 'this day', he told his followers, 'I will put the crown on my head'. He declared it to be the 'first day of the Millennium' and promised the poor that they would own land in the days to come.[58] Riding on horseback beneath a blue and white lion flag – wearing Eastern dress, bearing a loaf of bread speared on a pole, and carrying a sword he claimed was Excalibur – he led a crowd of 150, roaming from village to village in protest of the New Poor Law. After killing the constable sent to arrest him, he and his followers took cover in Blean Wood. There he sounded a trumpet and – incredibly – declared that it was heard in Jerusalem, where a troop of 10,000 were waiting to obey his command.[59]

Courtenay is a perfect distillation of all the paradoxes of the British prophets, who must reconcile the undeniable Easternness of the Holy Land with their own claim of entitlement to it, the myth of Western history with a biblical inheritance, the words of the prophet with the inarticulate word of God. Courtenay is the King of Arabia and the Gypsies even as he is 'Defender of his King and Country', and he is dressed in Eastern clothing but carrying Excalibur – at once a traveller from the Orient and inheritor of Britain; the warriors of the millennium, after all, wait in Jerusalem but can hear the trumpet sounded in England's green and pleasant land. In bringing together the East and the West, the biblical and the British, as an attempt to acquire land, Courtenay can believe what the other prophets still hope to accomplish: Jerusalem is already here.

Notes

1. Maurice Blanchot, *The Book to Come*, Meridia (Stanford: Stanford University Press, 2003), 85.
2. Edward Said, *Orientalism* (New York: Vintage, 1979), 58.
3. J. P. Jewett, *Remarkable Women of Different Nations and Ages*, 1858, 67.
4. James K Hopkins, *A Woman to Deliver Her People: Joanna Southcott and English Millenarianism in an Era of Revolution*, The Dan Danciger Publication Series (Austin: University of Texas Press, 1982), 145; Eitan Bar-Yosef, 'Green and Pleasant Lands', in *A New Imperial History: Culture, Identity and Modernity in Britain and the Empire,*

1660–1840, ed. Kathleen Wilson (Cambridge: Cambridge University Press, 2004), 162.
5. E. P. Thompson, *The Making of the English Working Class*, A Vintage Giant, V322 (New York: Vintage Books, 1966), 369.
6. Joanna Southcott, *Life and Works: A Collection of Pamphlets*, 1813, 9.
7. Bar-Yosef, 'Green and Pleasant Lands', 65.
8. Southcott, *Life and Works*, 4. The scriptural basis for the prophecy is Genesis 49: 10, translated in the Geneva Bible as 'The scepter shall not depart from Judah, nor a Lawgiver from between his feet, until Shiloh come, and the people shall be gathered unto him.'
9. Richard Reece, *A Correct Statement of the Circumstances That Attended the Last Illness and Death of Mrs. Southcott: With an Account of the Appearances Exhibited on Dissection: and the Artifices That Were Employed to Deceive Her Medical Attendants* (Printed for the author, 1815), 3.
10. Ibid., 2.
11. Ibid., 1.
12. Southcott, *Life and Works*, 33.
13. Joanna Southcott, *The Strange Effects of Faith: With Remarkable Prophecies (made in 1792, &c.) of Things Which Are to Come: Also Some Account of My Life* (Printed for the Author (formerly) by T. Brice, 1801).
14. Joanna Southcott, *The Scriptures of the Holy Trinity* (Printed and published by Daniel Jones, 1861).
15. Southcott, *Life and Works*, 492.
16. Bar-Yosef, 'Green and Pleasant Lands', 163.
17. Southcott, *Life and Works*, 22.
18. Ibid., 6.
19. J. Christopher Herold, ed., *The Mind of Napoleon: A Selection from His Written and Spoken Words* (New York: Columbia University Press, 1955), 49; Franz Kobler, *Napoleon and the Jews* (Tel Aviv: Massada Press, 1975); Philip Guedalla, *Napoleon and Palestine*, ed. David Lloyd George (London: G. Allen & Unwin, 1925); Antoine-Vincent Arnault, *Memoirs of the Public and Private Life of Napoleon Bonaparte: With Copious Historical Illustrations and Original Anecdotes* (Sherwood, Gilbert, and Piper, 1826).
20. Ibid., vol. 7, 32.
21. Southcott, *The Scriptures of the Holy Trinity*, 96.
22. Richard Brothers, *A Revealed Knowledge, of the Prophecies & Times. Particularly of the Present Time, the Present War, and the Prophecy*

Now Fulfilling . . . and Published by His Sacred Command. . . By the Man That Will Be Revealed to the Hebrews as Their Prince and Prophet (London, 1794), 57. Otherwise, there was nothing about him to suggest his prophetic leanings; 'all agree', reports Clarke Garrett, 'that he was very tall and handsome, well-bred, with nothing of the "enthusiast" in his manner'. Clarke Garrett, *Respectable Folly: Millenarians and the French Revolution in France and England* (Baltimore: Johns Hopkins University Press, 1975), 181. Also see J. F. C Harrison, *The Second Coming: Popular Millenarianism, 1780–1850* (London: Routledge & Kegan Paul, 1979).

23. 'You may inform the King of England,' God tells Brothers, 'that I call you my nephew.' [Brothers, *A Revealed Knowledge, of the Prophecies & Times. Particularly of the Present Time, the Present War, and the Prophecy Now Fulfilling . . . and Published by His Sacred Command. . . By the Man That Will Be Revealed to the Hebrews as Their Prince and Prophet*, vols. 2, 88.]

24. Richard Brothers, *An Exposition of the Trinity with a Further Elucidation of the Twelfth Chapter of Daniel; One Letter to the King, and Two to Mr. Pitt, &c. by Richard Brothers. The Descendant of David, King of Israel, &c* (London: printed for G. Riebau, No. 439, Strand; and sold by J. Wright, Dorset-Street, Manchester-Square; H. Wood, No. 9, Worcester-Street, Ratcliffe-Highway; Parsons and Symonds, in Paternoster-Row, 1795), 34–5.

25. 'Domestic Occurences', *Gentleman's Quarterly* 1, no. 65 (1795): 250. One of Brothers' predictions that London was to be destroyed was taken serious enough that some Londoners considered leaving the city. John Binns, en route to a London Corresponding Society meeting, ducked into an ale-house where he found the customers 'awaiting the consummation of all things'. [Thompson, *The Making of the English Working Class*, 117.]

26. *The New Annual Register or General Repository of History, Politics and Literature for the Year 1795* (London, 1796), 20.

27. Richard Brothers, *A Description of Jerusalem: Its Houses and Streets, Squares, Colleges, Markets, and Cathedrals, the Royal and Private Palaces, with the Garden of Eden in the Centre, as Laid Down in the Last Chapters of Ezekiel* (London, 1805), 12.

28. Ibid., 14.
29. Ibid., 34.
30. Ibid., 40.
31. Ibid., 42–3.
32. Ibid., 46.
33. Ibid., 16.

34. Ibid., 48.
35. Ibid., 49.
36. Brothers, *A Revealed Knowledge, of the Prophecies & Times*, II: 50. Elsewhere, Brothers writes, 'In the second Book of Esdras, particularly in the 13th chapter, I am described as coming up from the sea; which is an inference plain enough that the deliverer of the Jews would professionally belong to that element . . .' See: Richard Brothers, *A Letter to Miss Cott, the Recorded Daughter of King David, and Future Queen of the Hebrews . . .: With an Address to the Members of His Britannic Majesty's Council, and Through Them to All Governments and People on Earth* (G. Riebau, 1798), vi.
37. Brothers, *A Description of Jerusalem*, 33–4.
38. Ibid., 20–1.
39. Ibid., 21.
40. Ibid., 39.
41. Ibid., 27.
42. Richard Brothers, *A Correct Account of the Invasion and Conquest of the Roman Colony of Ailbane, or Britain, by the Saxons,: Never Published Before; and Which Is Very . . . Are Descended from Those Great and Brave Men* (London: R. George, 1822).
43. Brothers, *A Description of Jerusalem: Its Houses and Streets, Squares, Colleges, Markets, and Cathedrals, the Royal and Private Palaces, with the Garden of Eden in the Centre, as Laid Down in the Last Chapters of Ezekiel*, 44.
44. Brothers, *A Revealed Knowledge, of the Prophecies & Times. Particularly of the Present Time, the Present War, and the Prophecy Now Fulfilling . . . and Published by His Sacred Command. . . By the Man That Will Be Revealed to the Hebrews as Their Prince and Prophet*, II: 21.
45. Ibid., II: 54.
46. Richard Brothers, *Brothers's Prophecy of All the Remarkable and Wonderful Events Which Will Come to Pass in the Present Year Foretelling . . . the Downfall of the Pope; a Revolution in Spain, Portugal, and Germany; The Death of Certain Great Persons in This and Other Countries; Also, a Dreadful Famine, Pestilence, and Earthquake, That Will Desolate the Land at the Latter End of the Present Year* (London, 1795), 7.
47. 'Turkey and Russia will be plunged in war, ending in the destruction of the Ottoman Porte, the Mahometan Faith, the Russian Empire, and the Greek Church . . . All shall be as one people, and of one mind . . . The *Christian*, the *Turk*, and the *Pagan* shall no longer be distinguished the one from the other.' [Richard Brothers, *Brothers's Prophecy of All the Remarkable and Wonderful Events*, 7.]

48. Brothers, *A Letter to Miss Cott, the Recorded Daughter of King David, and Future Queen of the Hebrews* . . . 49.
49. Ibid., 57.
50. Brothers, *A Letter to Miss Cott, the Recorded Daughter of King David, and Future Queen of the Hebrews* . . . 57.
51. Ibid.
52. Ibid., 58.
53. Ibid., 57–60.
54. Ibid., 60; Brothers, *A Description of Jerusalem*, 53–4.
55. Brothers, *Brothers's Prophecy of All the Remarkable and Wonderful Events*, 7.
56. Thompson, *The Making of the English Working Class*, 784–5.
57. Canterburiensis, *The Life and Extraordinary Adventures of Sir William Courtenay: Knight of Malta, Alias John Nichols Tom* (James Hunt, 1838), 253.
58. Ibid., 410.
59. Ibid., 465.

Chapter 4

Jerusalem is Scattered Abroad

> They came up to Jerusalem; they walked before Albion
> In the Exchanges of London every Nation walkd
> And London walkd in every Nation mutual in love & harmony
> Albion coverd the whole Earth, England encompassd the Nations . . .
> From bright Japan & China to Hesperia France & England.
> The footsteps of the Lamb of God were there: but now no more . . .
> William Blake, *Jerusalem* (24: 42–51)[1]

Though it is in his preface to *Milton* that Blake famously calls on his readers to build Jerusalem 'In Englands green & pleasant Land', it is *Jerusalem* that synthesises the national and apocalyptic interests of his earlier prophecies.[2] Blake's ambiguously utopic vision of Albion covering the earth treads a very fine line between eternity and empire: 'Bright Japan and China' might just as well be another stop along the Silk Road; the land where the Lamb of God walked is at once the Holy City and London, the Temple and a financial exchange. *Jerusalem*'s collapse of the real and the imaginary does indeed lead many critics to read it as an unapologetically imperialist poem. Julia Wright, for example, calls it 'tyrannical', charging Blake with 'plotting the assimilation of the globe into his own political and religious vision'. She argues that *Jerusalem* 'envisions a kind of imaginative colonisation . . . in which Albion's and Jerusalem's prior universality is reinstated over the national and cultural divisions of the present'.[3] Saree Makdisi offers a very different reading of Blake's seeming Anglocentrism, arguing that his Universal Empire, which conflates all other nations and peoples with England, carries within itself the seed of its own destruction; in the process of binding people together, Makdisi suggests, the Universal Empire creates a unified people capable of overthrowing it.[4] Other critics argue against any social content at all; Mark Ferrara writes that *Jerusalem*'s utopia is 'stripped of its social dimensions and is instead a meditative, internal, and subjective experience . . .'[5]

This dizzying range of interpretations is made possible by Blake's removal from direct political engagement; a text like *Jerusalem*, the subject of which has such a clear referent in the outside world, can be read more or less literally depending on one's understanding of Blake as a political agent.[6] Our sense of Blake as radical is maintained by what Steven Goldsmith calls an 'historicist tendency to radicalize Blake by association' and a willingness to map his 'oppositional aesthetic strategies' onto contemporary radical movements. 'The general result', in Goldsmith's summary, 'has been a Blake with solid political credentials because he lived in a politically saturated world and created his works as if they were momentous public acts determined to transform and liberate a general audience.'[7] This is the sense in which I understand Blake as prophet as well. He lived in a *prophetically* saturated world: a world in which seventeenth-century antinomian tracts were back in circulation, and a world in which Richard Brothers was making plans in earnest for Jerusalem to be rebuilt. The tension between real location and imagined representation is fundamentally characteristic of any conception of Jerusalem during the Romantic period, and that it is a tension Blake uses to deterritorialise his own geographic spaces. While I take my inspiration here from Makdisi, who describes *Jerusalem* as a 'vision of an anti-imperial imperialism', I would like to suggest an alternative: the spaces *Jerusalem* describes are neither imperial nor anti-imperial, but can be better imagined as extra-imperial. They are radical reimaginings of the space of London, of Jerusalem, and of the globe.

The simultaneity of history and vision in *Jerusalem* in fact requires a constant refiguring of Britain: it is at once the origin and end of Jerusalem. Late in the third chapter of *Jerusalem*, we find a roll call of the 'Thirty-two Counties of the Four Provinces of Ireland', the 'Land of Erin'. The counties are a mixture of Irish and biblical inheritance; each Irish county is a direct descendant of one of the sons of Jacob. This gesture to the non-English history of Britain, however, is short-lived, for we soon learn that

> *All these Center in London & in Golgonooza.* from whence
> They are Created continually East & West & north & South
> And from them are Created all the Nations of the Earth

Europe & Asia & Africa & America, in fury Fourfold. (3: 72.28–31, my emphasis)

Golgonooza is Blake's earthly Jerusalem; the centering 'in London & in Golgonooza' not only locates Golgonooza in London but also situates both London and Jerusalem at the centre and origin of all the other 'Nations of the Earth'. Though this call to return to Jerusalem is a call to 'dwell together as of old', the return, just as it is in this chapter's epigraph, is a return to a time when one nation encompassed all: 'O Albion let Jerusalem overspread all Nations/ As in the times of Old' (3: 72.35–6). The particular nations in question are then named in one of *Jerusalem*'s most impressive catalogues:

> France Spain Italy Germany Poland Russia Sweden Turkey
> Arabia Palestine Persia Hindostan China Tartary Siberia
> Egypt Lybia Ethiopia Guinea Caffraria Negroland Morocco
> Congo Zaara Canada Greenland Carolina Mexico
> Peru Patagonia Amazonia Brazil. Thirty-two Nations
> And under these Thirty-two Classes of Islands in the Ocean
> All the Nations Peoples & Tongues throughout all the Earth. (3: 72.38–44)

Notice 'Negroland' in the catalogue, right alongside France and Italy. Strange as the term may sound to our ears, a glance at contemporary maps of Africa will in fact show, more prominently than any actual nation, Negroland taking up the bulk of Northern Africa, south of the Sahara (Figure 4.1). But Blake's inclusion of Negroland is less a nod to its geographical legitimacy than a magnification of the difficulties of Blake's own nation, of national boundaries that are necessarily constructed by a faulty imperial perspective. What *Jerusalem* reveals is the inadequacy of the concept of 'nation', and all the ways human experience and capability exceed and betray such categorisations. In so doing, *Jerusalem* calls the bluff of imperialism, making its aims literal to the point of impossibility: England *is* Israel. The nations here – Negroland and France, England and Israel, 'mutual within each other's bosoms' – are a caricature of global expansion, mocking its ideals and marking the unfeasibility of complete inclusion. This representation of space does double work, mourning an imaginary past when nations were united, even as it critiques an empire made dangerous by its visions of unification.

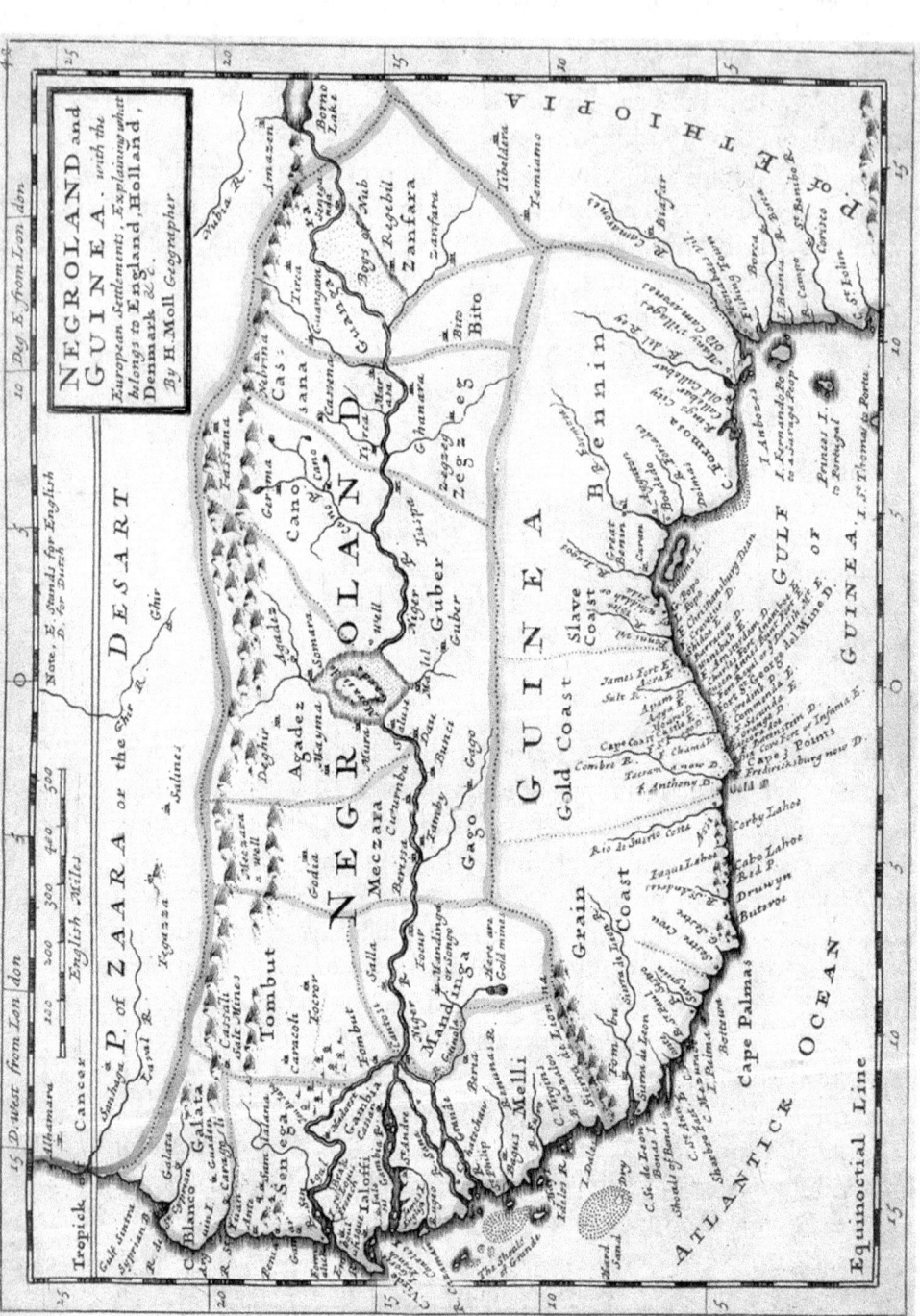

Fig. 4.1 'Negroland and Guinea. With the European settlements Explaining what belongs to England, Holland, Denmark &c.', H. Moll, 1729

You Would Scarcely Recognise Jerusalem

In order to understand the relationship between Blake's idea of empire and his imagination of the city of Jerusalem, it is necessary to backtrack several years, and then fast-forward several more. Europe's colonial interest in Jerusalem, Britain's own limited control of Palestine, and the tenor of other treatments of Jerusalem form the ground on which Blake's own city is imagined. Northern Europe rediscovered the Holy Land only a few years before Blake began composing *Jerusalem*. Napoleon's invasion of Palestine brought the British military, paving the way for religious and cultural exploration by other European Christians, disguised in their finest Muslim attire. In spite of the newfound secular interest in the Holy Land, awakened by the studies of scientists and explorers who followed the military campaigns, travel accounts were nevertheless more often overwritten by scripture. 'Palestine was perceived as a sort of heavenly holy land,' argues Joseph Shadur, 'linked only incidentally to the down-to-earth country through which the Western visitors wound their way.'[8] Some went to Palestine, as John James Moscrop's study of the Palestine Exploration Fund suggests, for economic reasons – to 'rehearse living as an Arab in a Moslem land in order to make journeys into Africa'[9] – but most went in search of the living Bible. What they found, instead, was its ruin.

And yet, the state in which these travellers found Jerusalem only strengthened for them its biblical associations. Most Judeo-Christian holy sites were profaned or inaccessible, the people were poor, and travel was dangerous. In 1806, François-René de Chateaubriand described Jerusalem:

> When you enter the city you find no consolation for the sadness of its exterior. You wander in the tiny unpaved streets which rise and descend over the uneven terrain and you walk amidst clouds of dust and over slippery gravel. The cloths thrown between one house and the other add to the darkness of this labyrinth; vaulted and filthy bazaars succeed in banning the light from the desolate city . . . There is no one on the streets, no one at the gates of the city . . .[10]

William Rae Wilson, in his 1831 *Travels in The Holy Land, Egypt, &c. &c.*, agrees with Chateaubriand that 'on entering [the city] all expectations of magnificence are shattered. Within the walls all is ruins, wretchedness, desolation, narrow streets, miserable bazaars...'[11] The residents of Palestine – when their existence is acknowledged at all – do little more than obstruct the view of the Holy Land, building huts and mosques that interrupt the biblical skyline. Constantin François Volney writes in his 1798 *Journey in Egypt and in Syria*:

> To see its destroyed walls, its debris-filled moat, its city circuit choked with ruins, you would scarcely recognize this famous metropolis which once fought against the most powerful empires in the world; which for a moment even held Rome at bay; and which, by a bizarre twist of fate, gains honor and respect in its disgrace. In short, you would scarcely recognize Jerusalem.[12]

The repeated insistence that 'you would scarcely recognize' Jerusalem, directed towards a 'you' who has never been to Palestine, suggests that the Jerusalem you are meant to vicariously recognise is the Jerusalem of the Bible. Even Chateaubriand, who revels in descriptions of the horrors of Ottoman Palestine, frames his impression of Jerusalem in its biblical terms. He writes of his first sight of the city:

> Then I understood what the historians and travellers reported of the surprise of the Crusaders and pilgrims at their first sight of Jerusalem... I stood there, my eyes fixed on Jerusalem, measuring the height of its walls... and seeking in vain the Temple, on which 'not a stone rests upon a stone'.[13]

What strikes Chateaubriand is not the splendour of Jerusalem but its fall from biblical greatness – not the height of its walls, but the strangely conspicuous absence of the Temple which had, after all, been destroyed 2,000 years earlier. In all of these accounts, the Bible is what lends coherence to the fragmentation and disarray of the city that spreads before the travellers.[14] These writers approach Jerusalem as a layered text, seeing the buildings of ancient Jerusalem in – or in place of – its domes and mosques, replacing its 'filthy bazaars' with the image of the land where Jesus walked.

Though such superimpositions of Jerusalems are Blakean in their multiplicity of visions, these particular substitutions are the privilege of a Christian-European imperial sensibility; they mean, in every case, to chart what they imagine to be an uncharted land. The overlaying of Christian interest and claim is really less an expanse of vision than blindness to the Jerusalem that already is. For British travellers, such oversights are also the work of those whose access to the actual Holy Land was, of all the peoples of the Book, the most limited. The British, as Protestants, were significantly underrepresented in Palestine in the late eighteenth century. Despite Britain's important role in the Battle of Acre, it continued to wield little control over the Holy Land. For Orthodox Christians, Roman Catholics and Jews, 'the Holy Land had never ceased to exist', explains Moscrop:

> They had religious communities there, they visited it on pilgrimages, they knew it, and for them it was a living entity. It was the northern Europeans, and in particular the Protestants, who had lost touch with the land of the Bible, and during the nineteenth century the rediscovery of the Holy Land was largely a Protestant rediscovery.[15]

There was a history to Protestants' absence from the region. Beginning in the seventeenth century, European nations trading at the Porte at Constantinople received capitulations from the Ottoman sultans, which granted them exemption from Ottoman law and custom and the right to reside under the jurisdiction of their own embassies. By 1800, the millet system was in place, which divided non-Moslem Ottoman subjects along religious lines and granted control of these religious groups to local priests, rabbis, or patriarchs.[16] Here the Protestants were left out, 'too new' writes Moscrop, to have a separate millet; they therefore 'did not control any traditional sites of religious significance'.[17] In short, Protestants took little part in the establishment of a significant Christian presence in Palestine before the nineteenth century. This accounts for the Protestant rediscovery of the Holy Land after Napoleon, and it should have relegated the British to the status of mere tourists or pilgrims in Palestine, while the other nations of Europe enjoyed significant control over the region.[18]

But the British didn't *feel* like tourists in the Holy Land – they felt, in fact, that Palestine was somehow essentially British – and they became increasingly anxious to bear this Britishness out in physical terms. The solution? Not to send Protestants, whose lives and livelihoods might be at risk in the wilds of a predominantly Muslim territory, but to send the Jews. According to Michael Ragussis, 'what had been throughout most of the eighteenth century a steady (if somewhat negligible) stream of literature on the conversion of the Jews and their restoration to Palestine became nothing short of a torrent in the 1790s.'[19] The advantages of restoration were fourfold, and not in a Blakean sense: the return of the Jews to Israel would at once cultivate the wilderness, secure trade routes to India, increase British influence in the Levant, and bring about the Second Coming. The London Society for Promoting Christianity Among the Jews (the Jews Society), established in 1809, intended to make the way for Christ's return by converting the Jews to Christianity and returning them to Palestine – 'the exact order of events,' quips Eitan Bar-Yosef, 'was much disputed'.[20] As Bar-Yosef shows, the ostensible religious rationale often disguised the political, and vice versa, as the fact of Britain's empire was taken by Christian Zionists '*a priori* as a sign of divine election' – election that obligated the British to return the Jews and bring about the apocalypse.[21]

Though many Christian Zionists were 'venerable members of society', their beliefs were nevertheless too close to religious enthusiasm for them to gain much cultural traction: 'no one', writes Bar-Yosef, 'was more aware of the marginality of their beliefs than the Christian Zionists themselves'.[22] But there were political as well as eschatological reasons for the urgency to settle Palestine. By the mid-eighteenth century, Barbary captivity narratives were in wide enough circulation to let people know what was going on in those 'uninhabitable downs', as Jonathan Swift would call them – uninhabitable because they were not uninhabited. '[The British] could not know', explains Linda Colley's *Captives*:

> that – in due course but briefly – theirs would be an empire on which the sun never set. Instead, they regarded the Islamic presence in the light of what they *did* know: the sheer scale and continuing grandeur of the Ottoman empire, the well-publicised depredations of Barbary corsairs, and the resilience and toughness of the regimes that backed them.[23]

Well into the nineteenth century, argues Colley – even after Britain's strength as its own empire was firmly established – the British government continued to avoid angering Islamic powers, even in cases of direct threats or offenses. Plans for populating Palestine, then, were overwritten with a fear of the Ottoman Empire. The size and strength of that empire meant that the London Jews Society knew full well what the Holy Land was: a foreign territory, under the control of an empire that still posed a significant threat to Britain's own.[24] 'Writ large in this Mediterranean zone', concludes Colley, 'are persistent reminders of the compromises and collusions that the imperial appetite necessarily imposed on the British, a small people who could therefore be caught and caught out.'[25]

When the British fought Napoleon in the Holy Land in 1799, Britain's interference made visible these previously subterranean British-Ottoman entanglements. The battle at Acre distilled in the British imagination both the clash and the cooperation of Jerusalem and Albion. Sir Sidney Smith wrote to Nelson in May 1799: 'indeed the [Acre] is not, nor ever has been, defensible according to the rules of art; but according to every other rule, it must and shall be defended'.[26] Years later, in a 1925 address to the Jewish Historical Society of England, Philip Guedalla, citing Smith's description of Acre, would refer to Smith as the 'presiding humourist of the scene', who saw the joke he was playing on history, and on Napoleon:

> Across the bay from Haifa some crumbling walls declined to be a ruin, and insisted in face of all the facts that they were a fortress; an odd collection of Turks, bluejackets, and Albanian marksmen, with a French engineer, a mad Englishman, and a Pasha escaped from the *Arabian Nights*, masqueraded as a garrison; and a museum of antique artillery completed the charade.[27]

Smith sees what countless European explorers and pilgrims found as well: the refusal of the Holy Land to 'be a ruin'. Here, for Napoleon, the result is disastrous, and the joke is not only his defeat (against all the 'rules of art') by an indefensible city, but his defeat at the hands of this motley crew – 'an odd collection of Turks, bluejackets, and Albanian marksmen, with a French engineer, a mad Englishman, and a Pasha escaped from the *Arabian Nights*'. Napoleon fights against the cast of a bad Oriental tale, and he loses. Guedalla's retrospective bringing together of the mad Englishman, the Pasha and the French engineer is an allusion to the less visible affiliations already long at work in the Levant, an acting out of European political and religious interest in the region. Representatives of England and France, here masquerading as a garrison, embody the long line of negotiations and treaties between the European nations and the Ottoman Empire. After the Siege of Acre, the intertwined economic, political and religious interests of Europe and the Levant were revealed, marked in the public consciousness.

These inextricably entangled interests in Palestine – travel narratives depicting a biblical and yet strangely empty Jerusalem, British plans for populating the city, and even military ambitions – should suggest that there is no simple distinction between the actual Jerusalem and Jerusalem as it was imagined, feared, appropriated, lived in and dreamed of. Jerusalem is precisely that constellation of material and imagined cities: the site of the ancient Temple and modern bazaars, the culmination of a pilgrimage and a convenient stop along trade routes, simultaneously deserted and overrun with Turks – the lived city. What would it mean to account for such a city? The planetary perspective of Blake's *Jerusalem* is, I will argue, an attempt to do just that.

Jerusalem in Westminster

Of course, Britain had its own planetary ambitions, reliant on an imperialist history which located the origins of culture and of Christianity squarely in England. An extreme version of this narrative was the belief that England was the historical site of Jerusalem, or that the British were the true Israelites.[28] This was the Anglo-Israel movement, whose enthusiasts, in the words of Barbara Tuchman, 'by a tortured interpretation of stray passages from the Bible have convinced themselves that the English are the true descendants of the ten lost tribes of Israel'.[29] Blake overtly engages the Anglo-Israelists is in the subtitle of *Jerusalem*, 'the Emanation of the Giant Albion', and his treatment of that subtitle in his address 'To the Jews':

> Jerusalem the Emanation of the Giant Albion! Can it be? Is it a Truth that the Learned have explored? Was Britain the Primitive Seat of the Patriarchal Religion? If it is true: my title-page is also True, that

> Jerusalem was & is the Emanation of the Giant Albion. It is True, and cannot be controverted. (27)

Faithful to his claim that *Jerusalem* was dictated to him, here Blake reads his own prophecy and is surprised at it.[30] The move from 'Is it a Truth . . .?' to 'If it is true . . .' to 'it is True, and cannot be controverted' is an enactment of the process of reading in which we, the audience, should also engage. Rather than taking the title as the grounding authority of the poem, Blake works backwards from a position of scepticism; the bulk of the poem does not assume the truth of its title, but instead works to prove or disprove its claim. Appropriately, the remainder of Blake's address to the Jews focuses on this supposedly 'incontrovertible' truth – that Jerusalem was, is, and always will be England – in order to replace it with an alternative story of development:

> The fields from Islington to Marybone,
> To Primrose Hill and Saint Johns Wood:
> Were builded over with pillars of gold,
> And there Jerusalems pillar stood. (27: 1–4)

Here Blake upends the familiar narrative in which the 'green and pleasant land' of England exists prior to its being 'built over' by the city, and offers instead an account in which Jerusalem, the original city, comes first. It is only later that its pillars fall, to be overgrown with English fields.[31] Primrose Hill and Saint John's Wood, both located near Blake's childhood home, were once Jerusalem, demonstrating the falseness not only of national borders but of national histories which chart the supposed progress from east to west, from country to city.[32]

But elsewhere, the alternate vision Blake poses depends far less on these familiar narratives.[33] Even the more precise of Blake's geographical descriptions are boggling; his account of *Jerusalem*'s great city, for example, confuses more than it clarifies:

> Around Golgonooza lies the land of death eternal . . .
> From the blue Mundane Shell, reaching to the Vegetative Earth.
> The Vegetative Universe, opens like a flower from the Earths center:
> In which is Eternity. It expands from the Stars to the Mundane Shell
> And there it meets Eternity again, both within and without. (13: 30–6)

Even Blake's own illuminations cannot begin to capture the delicious impossibility of this image: a universe which opens from eternity into eternity, where it again meets eternity.[34] The city of Golgonooza sits at the centre of this Klein-bottle universe, and its own orientations are as complex as eternity's: 'West, the Circumference: South, the Zenith: North,/ The Nadir: East, the Center, unapproachable for ever' but also 'the North is Breadth, the South is Heighth & Depth: / The East is Inwards: & the West is Outwards in every way' (1: 12.56–7; 1: 14.29–30). Cardinal directions are made three-dimensional, just as three dimensions become four for Blake; such directions are no more or less aligned with our own points than British geographies are with apocalyptic ones. Golgonooza, though modelled on Ezekiel's Jerusalem, turns Jerusalem's four gates into four dimensions; the city itself is eternity:

> [Los] views the City of Golgonooza, & its smaller Cities [. . .]
> And all that has existed in the space of six thousand years:
> Permanent, & not lost nor vanishd, & every little act,
> Word, work, & wish, that has existed, all remaining still [. . .]
> Shadowy to those who dwell not in them, meer possibilities:
> But to those who enter into them they seem the only substances
> For every thing exists & not one sigh nor smile nor tear,
> One hair nor particle of dust, nor one can pass away. (1. 13. 56–14: 1)[f]

Golgonooza is prophecy made spatial, time collapsed into the eternal city where past, present and future are indistinguishable from one another. ('I see the Past, Present & Future, existing all at once', insists Los [15: 8]). The division between those for whom eternity is 'shadowy' and those for whom the 'meer possibilities' are substance is the division between two kinds of readers – here, readers of space. The question of *Jerusalem* is how to be a reader who can 'enter into' that city, that eternity, that poem.

From the very beginning we are, after all, asked to enter the poem; Los pauses on the frontispiece so that the reader might follow him into the body of Albion.[36] Blake erased his own explanation of the scene 'both by incised lines emphasizing the texture and mortar-lines of the stonework and by solid inking of the plate'; it appears only on a proof Blake removed before the final printings (see Figures 4.2 and 4.3).³⁷ Inscribed above the archway into which Los has ventured one foot, the excised lines read, in part: 'There is a Void, outside of Existence, which if enterd into/ Englobes itself & becomes a Womb, such was Albions Couch/ A pleasant Shadow of Repose calld Albions lovely Land' (1: 1).³⁸ As so often in Blake, the void is about potential rather than absence – here a potential that, like the eternal city, can only be realised once it has been entered into. The pairing of this text with a depiction of Los's journey into Albion's body suggests that Los's act might be the very thing that can produce the 'lovely land' of England. Blake's account of Los's travels is worth quoting at length:

> Los took his globe of fire to search the interiors of Albions
> Bosom, in all the terrors of friendship, entering the caves
> Of despair & death, to search the tempters out, walking among
> Albion's rocks & precipices, caves of solitude & dark despair,
> . . . and there they take up
> The articulations of a mans soul, and laughing throw it down
> Into the frame, then knock it out upon the plank, & souls are bak'd
> In bricks to build the pyramids of Heber & Terah . . .
> [Los] came down from Highgate thro Hackney & Holloway towards London
> Till he came to old Stratford & thence to Stepney & the Isle
> Of Leuthas Dogs, thence thro the narrows of the Rivers side . . .
> To where the Tower of London frownd dreadful over Jerusalem:
> A building of Luvah builded in Jerusalems eastern gate to be
> His secluded Court: thence to Bethlehem where was builded
> Dens of despair in the house of bread . . .
> And he beheld Jerusalem in Westminster & Marybone,
> Among the ruins of the Temple . . . (45: 3–41)

Here the Tower of London looks over Jerusalem, Hackney and Holloway lie along the path to Bethlehem, and the ruins of the Temple can be found just outside of Westminster – and all exist within the body of Albion.³⁹ It is tempting to understand Albion's body and the worlds it contains as a symbolic spatiality, but Blake's precision suggests that his account is more than metaphorical. To locate the Tower of London in Jerusalem is one thing; to plot it along an exact course that Los has travelled is quite another. If, in fact, Blake imagines for us an impossible scenario, a mere literary

Figure 4.2 *Jerusalem: The Emanation of the Giant Albion*, frontispiece (proof), 1804–1820. © The Fitzwilliam Museum, Cambridge

Figure 4.3 *Jerusalem: The Emanation of the Giant Albion*, frontispiece (Copy E), 1804–1820. Yale Center for British Art, Paul Mellon Collection

device, he has taken pains to make it *seem* possible: he has given us directions. His carving out of 'caves of solitude & dark despair' and his construction of 'mountains of moral virtue' a few lines later ask us to read what sound like metaphors as, instead, a trajectory we can map; in Blake's imagination, caves of despair are built in the same way as pyramids of stone. He simply carries his metaphors too far for these distinctions to hold.

I would like to suggest here that the distinction Los's trip requires us to make is another one entirely, not between physical and metaphorical space, but between found and produced space. The 'interiors of Albion's bosom' are not static; they appear and shift as Los makes his way – from London to Jerusalem and back again. Los, in other words, literally *makes* his way, buildings 'builded' around him as he goes. Moreover, his experience of Albion, his ability to 'behold Jerusalem in Westminster & Marybone' while still in Albion's body, runs counter to nationalised accounts of space. Los is no more 'in' England than he is 'in' Palestine; his travels point up the inadequacy of such orientations. What the poem offers instead is an account of space as created rather than found, put to use rather than lived in. Consider the pyramids of Heber and Terah, which Los encounters somewhere near Highgate. As so often in *Jerusalem*, the mechanics of labour are fronted, but his decision to make this labour the work of the ancient Egyptians or Israelites – not only, then, from another place, but also from another time – does double work. If we think of *Jerusalem* as it deals with the problem of space and nation, then the insertion of the moment *just before* the exodus of the Jews from Egypt – which is to say, the beginning of the end of their exile from Israel – is prophetic as much as it is historical.[40] To build Jerusalem in England is to replace the slave labour of the Israelites in Egypt with the apocalyptic labour of building a new Jerusalem.[41]

But this is not just Los's itinerary. It is a map for us as well, if we can learn to read it: directions for finding Jerusalem in London, learning to properly inhabit 'here' so that we might see 'there'. How would you even begin to read such a map? Happily, Blake's *Vision of the Last Judgement*, which explains to the viewer how to approach his painting, offers some direction:

> If the Spectator could Enter into these Images in his Imagination Approaching them on the Fiery Chariot of his Contemplative Thought

if he could Enter into Noahs Rainbow or into his bosom or could make a Friend & Companion of one of these Images of wonder which always intreats him to leave mortal things as he must know then he would arise from his Grave and then would he meet the Lord in the Air & then he would be happy . . .[42]

This is Blake's account of what it would mean to move from real space to the space of art, an account of the extent to which one can literally occupy space through Imagination. We learn from this passage that if you can make that movement, you will 'meet the Lord in the Air'; if you occupy imagination in the same way you might occupy London, you can see the Eternal. This conception of dwelling *in* imagination disregards the distinctions usually at play in geographic understandings (here/there, within/without, city/nation); in exceeding mortal, vegetated vision, we might see that people inhabit, use, and share space in ways that cannot be contained by national divisions.

Having Passed the Polypus

The danger of such divisions is demonstrated most starkly in the problem that opens *Jerusalem*: 'Jerusalem is scatterd abroad like a cloud of smoke thro' non-entity' (5: 13). Certainly the city of Jerusalem was, in literal terms, scattered *abroad*; its ruined Judeo-Christian monuments were not scattered across England's green and pleasant landscape but were – to the constant frustration of millenarian Christians – built over by Muslims in the middle of Ottoman territory. But in the terms of Blake's poem, the scattering of Jerusalem is also the scattering of its future or rightful residents; the rebuilding of Jerusalem depends therefore not on scratching borders in the desert, but on creating a global community of the people who are Jerusalem.[43] Blake's four(fold) chapters seem to delineate these rightful inheritors: the Public, the Christians, the Jews, and the Deists.[44] The glaring omission? There are no Muslims in Blake's *Jerusalem*. In light of the seeming redundancy of *Jerusalem's* address to the Public, which effectively doubles the addresses to the Christians, Jews and Deists, the absence of an address to those who form the largest percentage of the actual population of nineteenth-century Jerusalem is striking.⁴⁵ With this omission, Blake runs the risk of erasing, into the future, an Islamic presence that has already been retrospectively erased by the contemporary travel accounts. In the same way that Chateaubriand finds 'no one in the streets' of his Jerusalem – which is to say no *Christian* in the streets – Blake hints in advance at the absence of Muslims from his city and his poem.

In fact, Muslims are absent from most of Blake's work. The closest he comes to an account of Islam is in *Vision of the Last Judgement*:

> Beneath the Cloud on which Abel kneels is Abraham with Sarah & Isaac [&] also Hagar & Ishmael . . . [Beneath] <Ishmael is Mahomet> & <on the left> beneath the falling figure of Cain is Moses casting his tables of stone into the Deeps. it ought to be understood that the Persons Moses & Abraham are not here meant but the States Signified by those Names the Individuals being representatives or Visions of those States as they were reveald to Mortal Man in the Series of Divine Revelations. as they are written in the Bible these various States I have seen in my Imagination when distant they appear as One Man but as you approach they appear Multitudes of Nations. Abraham hovers above his posterity which appear as Multitudes of Children ascending form the Earth . . .⁴⁶

Each 'state' is a permanent position that individuals temporarily inhabit, rather than the eternal essence of any individual. 'Man Passes on', Blake says, 'but States remain for Ever.'⁴⁷ Elsewhere he explains that states exist for the salvation of humanity; it is the permanence of states that allows human imperfection to be fleeting, with individuals to 'pass[ing] on' through any given state.⁴⁸ The multitude that exists in every apparently singular state – 'when distant they appear as One Man but as you approach they appear Multitudes of Nations' – is evidence not only of the inadequacy of human perception but also of the proximity of all the children of Abraham; Ishmael and Mahomet are indistinguishable from Isaac and Moses in the state of Abraham.

In fact, Blake's division of his audience into the Public, the Christians, the Jews, and the Deists should surprise us. We know that for Blake these separations are artificial – 'all religions are one', he tells us – and the addresses themselves will insist upon the falseness of the distinctions they make. The address 'To the Public' tells of 'that God from whom all books are given', a line reminiscent of *The Song of Los*'s account of how Poetic Genius became restrictive law:

'Rintrah gave Abstract Philosophy to Brama in the East', 'Moses beheld upon Mount Sinai forms of dark delusion', Jesus 'received/ a Gospel from wretched Theotormon', and Antamon 'to Mahomet a loose Bible gave'.[49] This reminder of the equivalence of all religions, in the midst of addresses that sound as if they wish to deny precisely that equivalence, is a gesture to how things are in Eternity. Here Blake addresses us not as we truly are, but as we see ourselves, having naturalised the earthly divisions between us. The whole of *Jerusalem* – even the content of the addresses themselves – makes plain that we have erred by accepting the distinctions its addresses establish.[50]

Blake is not, however, unaware of the risk in erasing distinctions, or of how fine the line is between imagining a global community and imagining a *British* global community. Late in *Jerusalem*, Los describes the 'sinful nation' of Albion, a Britain that has, by its expansion, assimilated all difference:

> What do I see? The Briton Saxon Roman Norman amalgamating
> In my Furnaces into One Nation the English; & taking refuge
> In the Loins of Albion. The Canaanite united with the fugitive
> Hebrew, whom she divided into Twelve, & sold into Egypt
> Then scatterd the Egyptian Hebrew to the four Winds,
> The sinful Nation Created in our Furnaces & Looms is Albion. (92: 1–5)

The compressing force of industry and trade, Los's furnaces and looms, reduces to equivalence the Briton and Roman, the Hebrew and the Canaanite. This is universalism gone wrong: the potentially unifying conditions of an industrial society result not in a cooperative network, but in the complete commodification of workers' bodies and the erasure of individual difference. Most often in Blake, the dangerous force of a homogenising imperialism is represented in the figure of the polypus,[51] first described in Los's account of what he has unknowingly built:

> ... Hand & Hyle rooted into Jerusalem by a fibre
> Of strong revenge & Skofeld Vegetated by Reubens Gate
> In every Nation of the Earth till the Twelve Sons of Albion
> Enrooted into every Nation: a mighty Polypus growing
> From Albion over the whole earth: such is my awful vision. (15: 1–5)

This mighty sea creature, a serpentine embodiment of imperial desire, originates in Albion and roots itself in every nation. But if the Polypus can be said to be distinctly British, he nevertheless exceeds Britain in import, length and width, as the ambitions of Albion-as-Polypus magnify to fill the globe. 'Like those science-fiction films which enlarge a lizard to a dinosaur', writes Morton Paley, Blake's Polypus is a creature whose body extends along the circumference of the planet, entwining himself from west to east: [52]

> In Verulam the Polypus's Head, winding around his bulk
> Thro Rochester, and Chichester, & Exeter & Salisbury,
> To Bristol: & his Heart beat strong on Salisbury Plain
> Shooting out Fibres round the Earth, thro Gaul & Italy
> And Greece, & along the Sea of Rephaim into Judea
> To Sodom & Gomorrha: thence to India, China, & Japan. (67: 35–40)

Mimicking the imperial ambitions of England, the Polypus expands into India and the Far East by way of Palestine and the Near East. And like the intellectual origins of those ambitions, he has his roots in Verulam. But this Polypus has a head and a heart, and with his 'fibers' and 'bulk' is too much an organism: too fleshy, too stringy and too big. The hyper-organisation of this creature should remind us of our implication in the destruction he brings – imperialism, like its practitioners, has a heart and a brain – but it should also emphasise the mutability of his condition, and therefore of our own. We can trace a negative evolution from the Divine Vision of Jerusalem's first plate to the Polypus in the fifteenth; this mighty Polypus is the obverse of the Divine Vision, a reversal as completely correspondent as Blake's copper plates to their printed pages. Whereas the Divine Vision is a recognition that 'I am in you and you in me, mutual in love divine: / Fibres of love from man to man thro Albions pleasant land', the Polypus conversely shows the world to be 'By Invisible Hatreds adjoind, they seem remote and separate/ From each other; and yet are a Mighty Polypus in the Deep' (1: 7–8, 66: 53–4). These two connections, 'fibres of love' and bonds of 'invisible hatreds', are the two possible manifestations of an internal and immutable relation, for 'As the Misletoe grows on the Oak, so Albions Tree on Eternity: Lo /He who will not comingle in Love, must be adjoind by Hate' (66: 53–6). As the Polypus's alternative association with cancerous growth would suggest, he is evidence of all the worst and uncontrollable aspects of civilisation. But the network of connections that the Polypus incarnates is also suggestive of an alternative: a global system of revolution and resistance based, like the Divine Vision, on a broad recognition of individuals' connections to one another.[53]

In political and literary accounts, this revolutionary alternative has frequently been represented as another kind of polyp: the many-headed hydra of the Hercules myth which, having lost a head, grows back two in its place. As a force that originates 'from below', the hydra has come to represent precisely that possibility of which Blake's polypus is a tantalising mirror image: a revolutionary, organised, global connection between oppressed people. Peter Linebaugh and Marcus Rediker recount:

> From the beginning of English colonial expansion in the early seventeenth century through the metropolitan industrialization of the early nineteenth, rulers referred to the Hercules-hydra myth to describe the difficulty of imposing order on increasingly global systems of labour.[54]

In literature, too, the hydra comes to represent the persistence of revolutionary ideas in spite, or because of, attempts to quell them; this hydra is all the imaginative possibilities of the Polypus made good. The primary lesson of Blake's *Jerusalem* is how to move from a connection built of the strands of 'invisible hatreds' to one woven from 'fibres of love' – how, in other words, to move from the Polypus to the Hydra.[55]

It is in this sense that *Jerusalem* is prophetic. Not prophetic in what Blake calls the 'modern' definition of the word – a prediction of an inevitable future – but in its clear diagnosis of cause and effect:

> Prophets in the modern sense of the word have never existed Jonah was no prophet in the modern sense for his prophecy of Nineveh failed Every honest man is a Prophet he utters his opinion both of private & public matters/Thus/If you go on So/the result is So/He never says such a thing shall happen let you do what you will. a Prophet is a Seer not an Arbitrary Dictator. ('Annotations to *An Apology for the Bible* by R. Watson, Bishop of Landaff. London, 1797', E 617)

This is a prophecy that looks as much to the past and present as to the future, an interpretation and diagnosis rather than a prediction.[56]

Jerusalem offers just such a prophecy, illuminating how it is that, with the potential for a planetary connection based on the inter-connectivity of all life, we instead have a dangerous and homogenising proliferation of the Polypus. The Polypus, Blake suggests in the second chapter of *Jerusalem*, is produced and enabled by our own flawed perspective, a misapprehension of time and space by our bound senses:[57]

> In one night the Atlantic Continent was caught up with the Moon,
> And became an Opake Globe far distant clad with moony beams.
> The visions of Eternity, by reason of narrowed perceptions,
> Are become weak Visions of Time & Space, fix'd into furrows of death...
> O Polypus of Death O Spectre over Europe and Asia... (49: 19–24)

The effect of our limited imaginations is to make the space in which we dwell – which is, in fact, eternity – unfamiliar, as if distant from us; we understand eternity only insofar as we can see it. The Polypus, here a 'Spectre over Europe and Asia', is evidence of our limited senses, rooted always in our vegetative proximity to death. Our failure is particularly a failure to understand space: our 'weak Visions of Time & Space', reasoned out by Newton and his followers, substitute an abstraction of physical knowledge for the imaginative certainty of global relations.[58] Far better would be the perspective offered in the *Vision of the Last Judgement* passage cited earlier. It seems that the difference between seeing the Polypus and seeing the hydra might be a matter of learning how to read: to read art, to read space, to receive Blake's prophecy.

What this prophecy requires, then, is a layering of imaginative and material space. Blake's building of Jerusalem in 'England's green and pleasant land' is an imaginative project; the labour required to build Jerusalem in part a mental labour. Though the result is, crucially, a material city, the process requires a re-apprehension of global relations, and so is imaginative as well as physical.[59] *Jerusalem*'s address 'To the Christians' declares that 'to Labour in Knowledge is to Build up Jerusalem: and to Despise Knowledge, is to Despise Jerusalem & her Builders' (77). To 'Labour in Knowledge' is to knowledgeably engage in labour but also to engage in the labour of knowledge, of Imagination – to recognise that Golgonooza is both tangible and, like eternity, literally a matter of perception. *Milton* is explicit on this point in a way that *Jerusalem* is not: 'Golgonooza cannot be seen till having passed the Polypus/ It is viewed on all sides round by a Four-fold Vision' (35: 22–3). In order to see Golgonooza, we must imagine precisely those connections that bind us to all others. To see the Polypus with a 'Four-fold Vision' is to see it not only as it is but as it can be: to see, in the Polypus, the potential of the hydra.

Notes

1. Quotations from *Jerusalem* and *Milton* are cited in text by plate and line number, and are from William Blake, *The Complete Poetry and Prose of William Blake*, ed. David V. Erdman (Berkeley: University of California Press, 1982).
2. Morton Paley calls *Milton* a 'preface' to Jerusalem, citing also Northrop Frye's assertion that '*Milton* describes the attainment by the poet of the vision that Jerusalem expounds in terms of all humanity.' [Morton D. Paley, *The Continuing City: William Blake's Jerusalem* (Oxford: Clarendon Press, 1983); Northrop Frye, *Fearful Symmetry: A Study of William Blake* (Boston: Beacon Press, 1962), 356.]
3. Julia M. Wright, *Blake, Nationalism, and the Politics of Alienation* (Athens: Ohio University Press, 2004), 155.
4. Saree Makdisi, *William Blake and the Impossible History of the 1790s* (Chicago: University of Chicago Press, 2003), 172–3.
5. Mark S. Ferrara, 'Blake's Jerusalem as Perennial Utopia', *Utopian Studies: Journal of the Society for Utopian Studies* 22, no. 1 (2011): 24.
6. See David Worrall, *Radical Culture: Discourse, Resistance and Surveillance, 1790–1820* (Detroit: Wayne State University Press, 1992) and Iain McCalman, *Radical Underworld: Prophets, Revolutionaries, and Pornographers in London, 1795–1840* (Oxford: Clarendon, 1993).
7. Steven Goldsmith, *Blake's Agitation Criticism and the Emotions* (Baltimore: The Johns Hopkins University Press, 2013), 344, 8.
8. Joseph Shadur, *Young Travelers to Jerusalem: An Annotated Survey of American and English Juvenile Literature on the Holy Land, 1785–1940* (South Deerfield, MA: Schoen Books, 1999), xiv.
9. John James Moscrop (New York: Leicester University Press, 2000), 10.
10. François-René de Chateaubriand, *Travels in Greece, Palestine, Egypt, and Barbary, During the Years 1806 and 1807* (Philadelphia, 1813), 1124.
11. William Rae Wilson, *Travels in Egypt and the Holy Land* (London, 1823), 198.
12. C. F. Volney, *Travels Through Egypt and Syria, in the Years 1783, 1784 &1785 Containing the Present Natural and Political State of Those*

Countries, Their Productions, Arts, Manufactures and Commerce; with Observations on the Manners, Customs and Government of the Turks & Arabs. By M. C-F. Volney. Translated from the French. In Two Volumes. Vol. I[-II] (New York: 1798), 548.

13. De Chateaubriand, *Travels in Greece, Palestine, Egypt, and Barbary, During the Years 1806 and 1807*, 536.
14. Barbara Tuchman writes of Burckhardt's account, which seems to have no 'consecutive plan': '[O]ne consistent theme – the relevance of each day's journey, each fallen pillar and abandoned well, to some incident of the Bible – holds the whole together.' Jerusalem was, moreover, not only the site of biblical events, but also the evidence of them. Maria Hack's 1829 *Oriental Fragments* is only one of many attempts, as her preface suggests, to 'illustrate the accuracy of Scripture by reference to the customs and peculiarities' of contemporary Palestine. Using the travel narratives of other writers, Hack offers everything from the 'dress of the Arabs in the vicinity of Nazareth', to the 'pleasantness of the [Palestinian] spring', to the size of Eastern doorways to prove the truth of the Bible. Weather, architecture and fashion are merged and decontextualised, refigured as evidence of the divine. In *Uncle Austin and His Nephews; Or, The Scripture Guide: A Familiar Introduction to the Study of the Bible*, an 1838 American Sunday School text, Uncle Austin begins a Bible lesson to his nephews by producing a pocket handkerchief, on which is printed a (Hebrew) map of the Holy Land 'for the convenience of Jews travelling to Palestine.' It – along with the 'better' map of contemporary Palestine published by the American Sunday School Union – becomes the occasion for biblical study. 'Impress this point on your mind', teaches Uncle Austin, 'that *Sacred Geography* is of the utmost importance, in order to render the Scriptures either plain or profitable . . . Many persons read the Bible, year after year, without ever taking the trouble to inquire whereabout the places mentioned in it are situated. Yet there are numerous passages which have little meaning to one who does not attend to the geography; and other passages which have peculiar beauty when we have the whole position of the scene in our minds.' Again, we have a refusal to distinguish the landmarks and streets of contemporary Palestine from the geography of Palestine more than 2000 years earlier. [Barbara Wertheim Tuchman, *Bible and Sword: England and Palestine from the Bronze Age to Balfour* (New York: New York University Press, 1956), 108; Maria Hack, *Oriental Fragments* (Philadelphia, 1829), 28, 37, 52; James W. Alexander, *Uncle Austin and His Newphews; Or, the Scripture Guide: Being a Familiar Introduction to the Study of the Bible* (New York: American Sunday School Union, 1838), 23 and 177].

15. Moscrop, *Measuring Jerusalem*, 6.
16. For more about the millet and related tai'ifa designations, see: Bruce Alan Masters, *Christians and Jews in the Ottoman Arab World: The Roots of Sectarianism*, Cambridge Studies in Islamic Civilization (New York: Cambridge University Press, 2001), 61, 99.
17. Moscrop, *Measuring Jerusalem*, 8.
18. By 1831, explains Moscrop, 'weakened Turkey couldn't prohibit foreign states from using the capitulations as an excuse for interfering in internal affairs. The problems raised by the capitulations was particularly great in the Holy Land where a multiplicity of religious groups gave Russia and France in particular an excuse for intervention.' (Ibid.)
19. Michael Ragussis, *Figures of Conversion: 'The Jewish Question' and English National Identity*, Post-Contemporary Interventions (Durham: Duke University Press, 1995), 4.
20. Eitan Bar-Yosef, 'Christian Zionism and Victorian Culture', *Israel Studies* 8, no. 2 (2003): 18–44.
21. Ibid., 28. The plans to repopulate Palestine with Jews continued through the century. In 1840, Lord Anthony Ashley Cooper, later seventh Earl of Shaftesbury, would write to Palmertson: 'If we consider [the Jews'] return in the light of a new establishment or colonization of Palestine, we shall find it to be the cheapest and the safest mode of supplying the wastes of these depopulated Regions – they will return at their own expense, and with no hazard but to themselves; they will submit to the existing form of Government, having no preconceived theories to gratify, and having been, almost everywhere, trained in implicit obedience to autocratical Rule – they will acknowledge the present appropriation of the soil, in the hands of its actual Possessors, being content to obtain an Interest in its Produce by the legitimate means of rent or purchase. Disconnected, as they are, from all the People of the Earth, they could appeal to no national or political sympathies for assistance in the path of wrong . . .' [Isaiah Friedman, *The Rise of Israel: Germany, Turkey, and Zionism, 1914–1918* (New York: Garland, 1987), 49.] The Jews – having no nation and no nation to which they might appeal – were the perfect settlers of these 'depopulated' lands. The lands were of course far from depopulated, and slippage in this passage from the 'rule' which the Jews are meant to obey (presumably British) and the 'actual Possessors' of the land (Ottoman) conceals even as it betrays the purpose of this Jewish settlement: a settlement on Ottoman soil by a 'disconnected' people whose only obedience would be to the nation that can best protect them from the real and imagined dangers of the Turkish 'wasteland'.
22. Bar-Yosef, 'Christian Zionism', 18.

23. In the eighteenth century, according to Colley, it was 'captivity, commerce, and Christian scholarship together, far more than any urge to conquest, that informed British curiosity about and reactions to the matter of Islam'. The paradox of Barbary captive-taking, she argues, is that it 'exacerbated pre-existing hostility to Islam and also increased the volume and variety of information available about it to Britain' thereby transforming 'both the extent and the complexity of Muslim-British contacts'. [Linda Colley, *Captives: Britain, Empire and the World, 1600–1850* (New York: Pantheon, 2002), 105, 112.]

24. Muslim powers were aware of that threat as well; in the backhanded compliment of Andrei Italiniski, Russian ambassador in Istanbul, 'The Turks are really ignorant, for sure, but when it comes to neighborly relations, they know their interests as clearly as the most diligent of governments.' The British knew their interests too, and it was in those interests to stay on the right side of what was still the most powerful empire in the world. [Andrei Italinski to Russian Foreign Minister Prince Adam Czartoryski, 4 February 1805, in *Ottoman Borderlands: Issues, Personalities, and Political Changes* (Madison: University of Wisconsin Press, 2003), 199.]

25. Colley, *Captives*, 133–4. The London Jews society never succeeded in sending any settlements to Palestine, caught out in this case by public opinion that knew better.

26. Sir William Sidney Smith, *The Life and Correspondence of Admiral Sir William Sidney Smith* (R. Bentley, 1848), 290.

27. Philip Guedalla, *Napoleon and Palestine*, ed. David Lloyd George (London: G. Allen & Unwin, 1925), 20.

28. There was a corresponding linguistic argument that what was passing for the Hebrew language was in fact not the authentic Hebrew at all. Anglo–Israelites believed that the British were the direct descendants of Japhet, who had, they claimed, settled in England after the flood. James Parson suggests that 'those who speak the dialects of the Japhetan language to this day, which are the . . . Scottish languages; and yet these are the only unmixed remains of the children of Japhet, upon the Globe; and the King of Great Britain, the only monarch upon the earth who rules the remains of that original people.' Sheila Spector shows that, though Parson's position is extreme, there is a long history of relating Hebrew and English (dating back at least until John Sadler's 1649 *Rights of the Kingdom*). [James Parson, *Remains of Japhet: Being Historical Enquiries into the Affinity and Origin of the European Languages* (London, 1767); Sheila Spector, *'Wonders Divine': The Development of Blake's Kabbalistic Myth* (Lewisburg: Bucknell University Press, 2001); Sheila Spector,

'Sources and Etymologies of Blake's "Tirzah"', *Blake: An Illustrated Quarterly* 23, no. 4 (June 1990): 176–83.]
29. Tuchman, *Bible and Sword; England and Palestine from the Bronze Age to Balfour*, 82.
30. Ian Balfour suggests that 'to write of Blake as a prophet conforms to a mythology and a tradition that he himself set in motion'. [Ian Balfour, *The Rhetoric of Romantic Prophecy*, Cultural Memory in the Present (Stanford: Stanford University Press, 2002), 127.]
31. Kathleen Raine understands Golgonooza as the physical instantiation of the 'heavenly archetype' of Jerusalem: 'Blake's London is ... the never-realized attempt of the collective life of its inhabitants to build the holy city of Jerusalem. Jerusalem can never, in the very nature of time and change be fully realized on earth, yet Jerusalem has, in Golgonooza, her refuges, her "secret chambers" in the houses of London's inhabitants ...' Here, as elsewhere in Raine, the slippage between Golgonooza and London suggests that Golgonooza (as the 'spiritual Four-fold London eternal') is one imaginative possibility of Jerusalem's Brittanic ties. [Kathleen Raine, *Blake and the New Age* (London; Boston: G. Allen & Unwin, 1979), 103.]
32. For a discussion of Blake's incorporation of his surroundings, see David V. Erdman, *Blake: Prophet Against Empire, a Poet's Interpretation of the History of His Own Times* (Princeton: Princeton University Press, 1969), 473.
33. This has led many critics to conclude that Blake's geographies, and even his cities, are merely metaphorical; Paul Miner, for example, glosses 'Jerusalem' simply as 'peace'. [Paul Miner, 'Blake: Milton Inside Milton', *Studies in Romanticism* 51, no. 2 (Summer 2012), 234.]
34. Also see S. Foster Damon's diagram of Golgonooza in *A Blake Dictionary*. He captions his diagram with an apologetic note: 'Golgonooza, being four-dimensional, cannot be reduced to a chart of two dimensions.'[S. Foster Damon, *A Blake Dictionary: The Ideas and Symbols of William Blake* (Hanover: University Press of New England, 1988), 163.]
35. Los's Halls are described in similar terms a few plates later: 'All things acted on Earth are seen in the bright Sculptures of/ Los's Halls & every Age renews its powers from these Works' (16: 61–2).
36. Steven Goldsmith describes the frontispiece: '. . . Los looks like he has been caught in an act of transgression. Sneaking about in the dark, with one foot on either side of a threshold someone doesn't want him to cross, making little effort to conceal an explosive device . . . Los is on a self-appointed guerrilla mission to agitate.' [Goldsmith, 44.]
37. Blake, *The Complete Poetry and Prose of William Blake*, 809.

38. These lines are echoed in *Milton*: 'Is this the Void Outside of Existence, which if enterd into/ Becomes a Womb? & is this the Death Couch of Albion' (2: 41.36–2: 42.1). Blake's voids are often not only productive but themselves an object of creation; consider the opening to *The Book of Urizen*: 'what Demon/ Hath form'd this abominable void/ This soul-shudd'ring vacuum?' (I: 1.3–4).
39. The play on the London Temple, foundation of the Knights Templar, brings both law and finance into this mix.
40. This is in keeping with Blake's own sense of prophecy. As Makdisi writes, 'In Blake's oppositional form of prophecy, the present is simultaneously projected as a future and renarrated as a past, but in such a way that the present, future, and past intermingle in an unresolved radical heterogeneity of time.' [Saree Makdisi, *Romantic Imperialism: Universal Empire and the Culture of Modernity* (Cambridge University Press, 1998), 3.]
41. Blake's 'eternal' city is eternal in the sense of being eternally incomplete, and thus always in the process of being built. Paley describes Blake's Jerusalem: 'Blake's continuing city, unlike Paul's, is "here" – but it is also "there", continually in the act of being formed. It takes its bricks and mortar from London ('Oxford Street is in Jerusalem'), but as a city of the imagination it is a transformation of the idea of Jerusalem deeply embedded in our cultural history and developed by writers from the time of Old Testament to Blake's own day.' Steven Goldsmith summarises neatly: '[W]e sometimes seem caught within one wheel-spinning problem: Is Blake's work the building or the unbuilding of Jerusalem?' [Paley, *The Continuing City*, 136; Goldsmith, *Unbuilding Jerusalem: Apocalypse and Romantic Representation*. Ithaca: Cornell University Press, 1993), 135.]
42. Blake, *The Complete Poetry and Prose of William Blake*, 560.
43. Many critics, including Nicholas Williams and Julia M. Wright, have cited Jerusalem as the most social of Blake's prophecies. Williams calls the move from *Milton* to *Jerusalem* 'the move from an individualistic psychological mode to a social communicative mode', and Wright argues that community is the 'dominant concern' of Jerusalem. [Nicholas M. Williams, *Ideology and Utopia in the Poetry of William Blake*, Cambridge Studies in Romanticism 28 (New York: Cambridge University Press, 1998), 173; Wright, *Blake, Nationalism, and the Politics of Alienation* (Athens: Ohio University Press, 2004), xiv.]
44. Again, Wright calls Blake on the charges against which I would like to defend him: 'For Blake's Christian, nationally specific utopia to prevail, the Jews and Deists must convert, and the Public and Christians must acknowledge that Britishness is a product of national interminglings that

can contain the global erasure of national difference as well as submit to Blake's definitions of a true public and a legitimate Christianity ... By dividing Jerusalem into four prefaces and four chapters ... Blake submits his readership to an administrative taxonomy. This taxonomy facilitates his management of the differences that he would erase in plotting the return of a metanational Jerusalem.' Nicholas Williams also suggests that the four chapters are an 'extension of [Blake's] artistic theory of the "bounding Line" to the construction of Jerusalem'. [Wright, *Blake, Nationalism, and the Politics of Alienation*, 166; Williams, *Ideology and Utopia in the Poetry of William Blake*, 189.]

45. The 'public' of Blake's address is first and foremost the British reading public. But as John Mee and Nicholas Williams have recently noted, *Jerusalem* is hardly reader-friendly. How, asks Williams, 'are we to deal with a poem which so consciously addresses itself to its audiences ... but which makes that address in a language which has driven away all but the most persistent readers?' The answer, for Williams, is that *Jerusalem* in fact 'concerns itself with those features of language which prevent it from being an ideally communicative medium, and thus suggests, by means of critique, what such a utopian language might look like'. This public is, in any case, a suspect category. Blake's address famously, in the mode of what Williams calls the 'amiable eighteenth century author', refers to the kind reception of his previous work, but as Williams points out, 'only by the most imaginative standard could Blake's previous work be described as "kindly received", only by a standard that would not normally occur to any reader not "in" the know.' [Williams, *Ideology and Utopia in the Poetry of William Blake*, 173, 188; Jon Mee, *Dangerous Enthusiasm: William Blake and the Culture of Radicalism in the 1790s* (New York: Clarendon Press, 1992), 214.]

46. Blake, *The Complete Poetry and Prose of William Blake*, 555.

47. Ibid., 556.

48. In *The Four Zoas: Night the Eighth*, Los instructs Rahab: 'There is a State namd Satan learn distinct to know O Rahab/ The Difference between States & Individuals of those States/ The State namd Satan never can be redeemd in all Eternity' (115.23–5).

49. 'Song of Los', 3. The choice of 'loose' in particular to describe the Muslim 'Bible' may come from a contemporary theory, referenced and dismissed in Sale's famous 1734 translation of the Qur'an, that the origin of the term Qur'an (from the root k-r-a, to recite or to read; the imperative that the angel Gabriel gave the prophet Muhammad at each scene of revelation was 'Iqra', 'Read/recite') could also mean to gather or collect. George Sale disagrees with, but nevertheless elaborates on,

the theory that the Qur'an is so named because it is 'a collection of the loose chapters or sheets which compose it'. Jon Mee argues that Blake's dismissal of the Qur'an nevertheless puts it on equal footing to the Bible (owing in part to Blake's use of the capital letter in 'loose Bible'). Both texts, Mee suggests, 'are represented negatively as reified and corrupted versions of stupendous originals'. [*The Koran, Commonly Called the Alcoran of Mohammed, Translated into English Immediately from the Original Arabic; with Explanatory Notes, Taken from the Most Approved Commentators. To Which Is Prefixed a Preliminary Discourse. By George Sale, Gent* (London: C. Ackers, 1734), 40; Mee, *Dangerous Enthusiasm*, 128.]

50. Keep in mind, also, the hyper-controlled publication and distribution of this text; by Blake's own account, only one copy was ever completed; the other six copies printed during his lifetime were either incomplete or uncoloured. Blake did not find a buyer for his finished copy of *Jerusalem*. His famous violence against the address 'To the Public' – in which he gouged out the words 'love', 'friendship', and 'blessed' – suggests at least a temporary inability to imagine an audience for his work at all. If Blake had found a buyer for his single copy of *Jerusalem*, we can safely assume that that buyer would have been of the British Christian public. All four of *Jerusalem*'s addresses, then, are in a sense addressed to the same audience. Rather than choosing the ideal inhabitants for his city, Blake is asking his readers to imagine themselves in the address to the other; the Christian public is addressed not only as 'Christian' and 'Public' but as 'Jew' and 'Deist'. Saree Makdisi argues that, in fact, there is *no* audience for Blake's work, insofar, at least, as there is an 'incommensurability' between his poems and our world. Blake, he argues, 'was making art for an audience that literally did not exist, that no longer existed – or that does not yet exist.' (Makdisi, *William Blake and the Impossible History of the 1790s*, 324.)

51. For a discussion of the 'massive sensation' of the polypus in the eighteenth-century scientific community, see Denise Gigante's *Life: Organic Form and Romanticism* (New Haven: Yale University Press, 2009), 126–7. 'The polyp,' she writes, 'by providing empirical evidence for the generation of new life forms beyond the traditional coupling of the sexes, decentralized God's creative power, spreading it through all the fibers of nature and shattering those structures (preformed parts and germs) supposed to contain it' (127).

52. Paley, *The Continuing City*, 214.

53. Denise Gigante also reads a revolutionary potential in the polypus, though backwards, through *Milton*, where 'every Man born is joined/

Within to One mighty Polypus. And this Polypus is Orc' (*Milton* 28). 'Although it goes somewhat against the grain to propose,' she writes, 'Blake ultimately reappropriates the "mighty Polypus" as a symbol of revolutionary power.' (*Life*, 129).

54. Linebaugh and Rediker, *The Many-Headed Hydra: The Hidden History of the Revolutionary Atlantic* (Boston: Beacon Press, 2000), 3.
55. Morton Paley and Karl Kroeber suggest that the actual sea-creature to which Blake's Polypus refers is in fact the Hydra, a green freshwater polyp discovered by Abraham Trembley in 1740, named by Linnaeus in 1758. [Paley, *The Continuing City*, 214; Stuart Curran, ed., *Blake's Sublime Allegory; Essays on The Four Zoas, Milton, Jerusalem* (Madison: University of Wisconsin Press, 1973), 360.]
56. 'Prophecy is a call and a claim much more than it is a prediction,' writes Ian Balfour, 'a call oriented toward a present that is not present.' (Balfour, *The Rhetoric of Romantic Prophecy*, 18.)
57. Though the focus of this chapter is primarily on the spatiality of Eternity (though a spatiality that is, in a sense, collapsed into time), our realisation that we dwell in Eternity requires a reimagining of the temporal as much of the spatial. This reimagining might be provoked by the poems themselves; as Makdisi concludes *William Blake and the Impossible History of the 1790s* by arguing that 'Blake's texts . . . rarely move either "backward" or "forward", and open up instead into a kind of eternal time of repetition.' (Makdisi, *William Blake and the Impossible History of the 1790s*, 12.)
58. Consider Principle 4 of Blake's *All Religions are One*: 'As none by traveling over known lands can find out the unknown. So from already acquired knowledge Man could not acquire more. therefore an universal Poetic Genius exists[.]' The argument that new knowledge can only come from the 'Poetic Genius' rather than the experiments of a certain kind of practical science – or, as the example would have, of practices of geography – shows the importance of the imagination in any true understanding of space.
59. Belief, as for Joanna Southcott, is itself a kind of labour. There is a precedent for this in Milton's Eden as well. Kevis Goodman suggests that Adam and Eve's 'Miltonic labor of restitution' is a labour of sympathy (first extended from Eve to Adam); their reparation of the 'ruins of our first parents' comes of the labour of relating to God. Joanna Picciotto writes: 'Literally imperfect, [Milton's] Eden is an unfinished, fermenting space of growth with "unsightly" as well as beautiful features, which, like any objects of reforming efforts, "mock[s]" and "derides" attempts to improve it . . .' Picciotto persuasively argues for reading the poem as itself an instrument for the

recovery of paradise, a 'lens' through which we might see (and see through) the 'veils of custom and fallen perception'. In this way, Milton offers us the means by which we might (continue to) build and unbuild paradise through mental labour. [Kevis Goodman, '"Wasted Labor"? Milton's Eve, the Poet's Work, and the Challenge of Sympathy', *English Literary History* 64, no. 2 (1997): 433; Joanna Picciotto, 'Reforming the Garden: The Experimentalist Eden and *Paradise Lost*', *English Literary History* 72, no. 1 (2005): 46.]

Chapter 5

From Here to Timbuktu

> So geographers, in *Afric*-maps,
> With Savage-Pictures fill their Gaps,
> And o'er unhabitable Downs
> Place Elephants for want of Towns.
> Jonathan Swift, 'On Poetry: A Rhapsody'

In 1815, a man named Robert Adams declared to Britain's African Company that he was the first white man ever to have been to Timbuktu. Neither part of that claim was true. But a story about something that did not happen and the person who did not do it might be the best way to talk about a city that is so persistently unreal to most people.[1] Timbuktu has, for centuries now, been simultaneously the mythical city of wealth and learning, and a primitive town at the edge of the earth; in both cases, Timbuktu is wholly inscribed in a Western perspective that deems it, whether real or imaginary, a destination.

In the late eighteenth century, Timbuktu – and the interior of Africa more generally – was a destination still tantalisingly out of reach; maps of the region were a mixture of errors and empty space. As Henry Beaufoy described in 1790, 'the map of its Interior is still but a wide extended blank, on which the Geographer ... has traced, with a hesitating hand, a few names of unexplored rivers and of uncertain nations.'[2] Explorations to the interior were rare, in part because of their difficulty. Prominent African geographer James Rennell lamented:

> Africa stands alone in a geographical view! Penetrated by no inland seas, like the Mediterranean, Baltic or Hudson's Bay; nor overspread with extensive lakes, like those of North America; nor having, in common with the other continents, rivers running from the centre to the

extremities: but, on the contrary, its regions separated from each other by the least practicable of boundaries, arid deserts of such formidable extent, as to threaten those who traverse them, with the most horrible of all deaths, that arising from thirst! Placed in such circumstances, can we be surprised either at our ignorance of its interior parts, or of the tardy progress of civilization in it?[3]

But it was in fact the hope of 'rivers running from the centre to the extremities' that drove Europeans towards Africa's interior. Explorers had been unable to determine the course of the Niger, knowledge which they ardently pursued in the hopes that it met up with the Nile – a happy intersection which would provide a transcontinental route to the Mediterranean, facilitating trade with central Africa. With the decline of the slave trade, Britain and France in particular began to shift their African ambitions from the trade of humans to the trade of goods; Africa was increasingly imagined as a potential market. The interior of Africa also held out the possibility of a more refined population; some Europeans even believed that remnants of ancient Egyptian and Carthaginian civilisations survived there. In 1782, the editor of Ignatius Sancho's letters insisted that 'he who could penetrate the interior of Africa might not improbably discover negro arts and polity . . .'[4] A decade later, physician Paul Isert argued that proponents of slavery, who believed Africans to be full of vices, would be 'cured of their prejudices' if they were to travel in the interior of the continent.[5]

It was therefore with both economic and academic aims that the Association for Promoting the Discovery of the Interior Parts of Africa (known as the African Association) was founded in 1788.[6] Its founders were members of the Saturday's Club dining club, including Sir Joseph Banks, President of the Royal Society. The record of the proceedings of their 9 June meeting begins:

> *Resolved,* That as no species of information is more ardently desired, or more generally useful, than that which improves the science of Geography; and as the vast Continent of Africa, notwithstanding the efforts of the Antients, and the wishes of Moderns, is still in a great measure unexplored, the Members of this Club do form themselves into an Association for Promoting the Discovery of the Inland Parts of that Quarter of the World.[7]

The general 'usefulness' of geographic knowledge to which the Association's founding statement refers is, of course, as much about trade as it is about science. In 1792, the Association codified economics as an official aim, proposing that a consul be appointed to Senegambia: 'as there is reason to believe that an extensive and lucrative Trade from Great Britain may be opened by way of the Gambia and the Niger . . . [which] would equally promote the Interests of the Public and facilitate the Geographical Improvements that are the peculiar objects of this Association.'[8] The government agreed to the proposal and appointed James Willis as consul in 1794; with this move, the Association was rapidly reconceived as a national project.[9] The government was motivated in part, as we will see shortly, by competition with the French, who had a far more significant presence in the Senegambia region and were therefore poised to make the geographic discoveries that were the aims of the Association. Not unaware of the conflict, the Association baldly claimed that they were the 'origin, head, and model of every succeeding [European] plan of discovery in Africa' – an implicit comparison to the French Société de Géographie de l'Afrique.[10] They intended to prove their superiority by going to Timbuktu.

What Europe knew of the fabled city at this point came from a 1510 account by Leo Africanus, a Grenadan Moor who had travelled to Timbuktu on a diplomatic mission for the Sharif of Fez. His account describes the city of gold and learning that Europeans had come to expect. 'The inhabitants, and especially strangers there residing, are exceedingly rich', he writes, and the king 'hath many plates and scepters of gold, some whereof weigh 1,300 pounds.' His account also supports the idea of Timbuktu as a city of learning, reporting 'great store of doctors, judges, priests, and other learned men, that are bountifully maintained at the king's cost and charges'.[11] This vision of the city lingered and fuelled, over 250 years later, the African Association's Timbuktu dreams. Association member John Sinclair rhapsodised: 'gold is there so plentiful as to adorn even the slaves . . . If we could get our manufactures into that country we should soon have gold enough.'[12] They would need new intelligence, new explorers to map the territory, both physically and culturally. The Association was 'in the business of producing knowledge', suggests Philip J. Stern, but also, 'if things went right, national heroes'.[13] Mungo Park was that hero, and he was to go to Timbuktu.

It should be noted from the start that Park never made it to Timbuktu, nor did he discover the termination of the Niger. After volunteering to make the trip, he set out from the Gambia River in 1795, accompanied by a guide, a slave, and an ex-slave. He was captured during his first encounter with Muslims, but managed to escape after four months. Though he insisted on continuing his journey, he eventually returned to Britain without reaching Timbuktu. Despite his failure, Park was hailed as a hero, and his discoveries – such as they were – were declared a scientific triumph. In particular, his discovery of the eastward course of the Niger renewed the hope of its meeting the Nile (though it does not), and his success in this regard, at least, encouraged the Association's conviction that the interior of Africa might indeed become a site of manufacture and trade. In what Robin Hallet calls 'one of the most significant utterances of the age', Joseph Banks declared at a 1799 meeting of the Association that Park's first exploration had 'opened a Gate into the Interior of Africa, into which it is easy for every Nation to enter and to extend its commerce and Discovery from the West to the Eastern side of that immense Continent'.[14] Banks' confidence may have been less based on Park's geographical information than on his confirmation of the backwardness of Africans. In a by now recognisable move, Banks collapsed the enlightenment of natives with the riches to be won: 'If Science should teach these ignorant Savages,' he insisted, 'is it not probable that the Golden harvest they are already in the habit of gathering might be increased an hundred fold?'[15] The Association rushed to assist Park in the publication of his *Travels in the Interior Districts of Africa*. In 1799, Bryan Edwards, who helped Park with his writing, declared – with hyperbole exceeding even Banks' – that 'some parts [of *Travels*], which he was lately sent to me, are equal to anything in the English language'.[16] The first 1,500 copies, printed in 1799, sold out within a month. Two more editions were printed the same year, and by 1800 it had been published in France, Germany and America.[17] In 1805, Park returned to Ségou to complete his mission of finding the Niger's end, this time accompanied by 50 men, but he and his party were mistaken for Muslim raiders and killed 500 miles from the Niger's termination.

Fuelled in part by an increased concern about French presence in the region, the Association would continue their quest to reach Timbuktu in the decades following Park's second, fatal attempt.[18] In 1821, Hugh Clapperton made the journey but found neither the Niger nor Timbuktu. He returned to Britain in 1825 and was insulted to learn that the Association had sent Gordon Laing to Timbuktu in his stead. Clapperton returned to Africa just three months later, determined to beat Laing to the city, but again failed to reach the Niger and died of disease and malnutrition.[19] It was finally Laing who reached Timbuktu, where he stayed for a month before the Foulahs descended on the city and demanded his execution – in order, it was reported, to 'prevent Christian nations from receiving such information as might enable them, at some future period, to penetrate into, and enslave, the countries of Africa'.[20] Laing escaped but was murdered just days later; his notes were never recovered. The Foulahs had, for a moment, held off the Christian nations.

Gigantic Schemes

The African Association was not the only group intent on reaching Timbuktu. They had competition from the rival Company of Merchants Trading to Africa, known as the African Company, and this is where Robert Adams enters the story. The African Company was established by the government in 1750, with the dissolution of the Royal African Company of England, and it controlled British trade along the 7,000 miles of coastline between the Port of Sallee in South Barbary and the Cape of Good Hope.[21] Though they traded in other commodities, the primary business of the Company had been slavery: between 1690 and 1800, the African Company (and the Royal African Company before it) accounted for 20 per cent of the British slave trade to the New World. It was formed, argues James Walvin, to 'trade in Africans more efficiently, more nimbly – and more profitably'.[22] The Company was, for the time being, unapologetically dedicated to this cause; in 1788 it sponsored the pro-slavery tract *Slavery No Oppression: or, Some New Arguments and Opinions Against the Idea of African Liberty*. Surprisingly, though *Slavery No Oppression* makes all of the predicable arguments for slavery (slavery brings the gift of Christianity to savages, employs the indolent, etc.), it also diagnoses the drive for abolition as coming from a particularly *British* weakness:

> A very fine moralist remarks, that it is the height of Tyranny to remind any afflicted person of an evil, of which he himself may not complain. A misadvised and unseasonable benevolence is the characteristic of

> Great Britain. [. . .] This national infirmity exposes us to much prejudice and illusion, and I am suspicious, that our enemies, both exterior and domestic, are not a little zealous to improve this failing to their own availment.[23]

The claim that slaves do not complain about their treatment is unsurprising in a text that insists there *is* no mistreatment. What is more surprising is the suggestion that abolition is both quintessentially British and self-destructive; the British are vulnerable when they are too much like themselves. From the church to the university to the 'amusive chit-chat' of the ladies' tea table, the author argues, British sensitivity indulges itself in misdirected empathy.[24] As in the Association's arguments for African exploration, the French are the primary villains in this scenario:

> But, above all, the people of the closest artifice and deepest design, the French Emissaries, who busily swarm in this Metropolis, are ever ready to avail themselves of this country's characteristical weakness; and whilst these Insinuators are dropping gentle hints into the ears of our half-witted politicians, to this effect, that we should exhibit a bright example of public philanthropy to Europe, as the first abolishers of this traffic, are known at the present moment to be tampering with many English Factors and Merchants, and are industriously plotting to undermine and supplant us in the Negro trade.[25]

The rhetoric of enlightening the African natives is always a double-edged sword, at once the argument of abolitionists and of slavery's proponents. But the 'bright example' that the British might set is ironised here into the naïveté of politicians; the author moves enlightenment to the centre of a conspiracy theory.

It was not the swarming French, though, but the British government itself that would undermine the slave trade. When Britain abolished the trade in 1807, the Company found itself with a significant public relations problem – not to mention a government relations problem. Despite the Company's promise that trade in different commodities would replace the trade in humans, the House of Commons censured the Company for its lack of interest in promoting education and religious instruction, as well as for its failure to take 'measures for civilizing the natives . . . since the abolition of the Slave Trade'.

The Company was also found to have illegally aided those who were still engaged in the trade by selling fresh water to slave ships.[26] The African Institution, an abolitionist organisation with great influence on parliament, recommended the replacement of current members of the Committee:

> Whilst the great business of the Gold Coast was the Slave Trade, the choice of the Committee [members] . . . might [have been] very suitable; but now that a total change has taken place in the trade of that coast, some change also might with propriety be made in the direction of its concerns. London, Liverpool, and Bristol, might be limited to a small number; and the deficiency be supplied by other Gentlemen, whose long and public hostility to the Slave Trade had clearly proved their sincere desire to ameliorate the state of Africa.[27]

The 'deficiency' the African Institution references is their own proposed decrease in the number of Company representatives, but the choice of words implies a more fundamental deficiency of the Company: their failure to undertake serious projects of research and improvement. The Company was, as Charles Hansford Adams sums up, an 'embarrassing contrast' to the African Association. They were therefore in desperate need of something – anything – to indicate their sincere interest in improving the African people and to re-establish their scientific credibility.

Robert Adams was that something. In 1814, London was the 'hub of the Black Atlantic', as W. Jeffrey Bolster puts it,[28] and Adams was just one of many African American sailors begging on the docks. But Simon Cock, secretary of the African Company, recognised him as the sailor well known in Spanish ports for his fantastic stories of the time he spent in Timbuktu. The timing was right, as interest in reaching the great city had not subsided. In the years surrounding the publication of Adams' *Narrative*, letters about the importance of a successful British expedition to Timbuktu proliferated in British periodicals. A letter from someone calling himself Vasco da Gama, for example, appeared in the May 1812 edition of *Gentleman's Magazine*, warning that:

> our ancient Rivals and Enemies are exerting all their power to destroy the British Commerce, and have nearly affected their gigantic schemes of cutting off all communication between Great Britain, and the various

Ports, States, and Kingdoms; at such a time when we are in imminent danger of losing the markets of a quarter of the globe, it becomes essentially important to discover . . . other markets for our manufactures.[29]

Like members of the African Association, Vasco da Gama articulates Britain's competition with other nations – and African exploration more explicitly – in terms of its commercial endeavours; the various 'ports, states, and kingdoms' which Britain might lose amount to the loss of markets; they are, therefore, replaceable. And so, da Gama argues, information about Timbuktu should be 'highly interesting to the Statesman as well as to the Merchant'; the two, here, are hardly distinguishable.[30] In another letter to *Blackwood's Edinburgh Magazine* in 1819, da Gama calls the efforts of the African Association a 'disaster', and suggests using the East India Company as a model for a new African Company. Unlike the natives of India, he argues, the natives of Africa are 'in want of our manufactured goods, and give immense sums for them', therefore making an African Trading Company even more profitable than the East India Company.[31] The real Vasco da Gama might have had something to say about this plan; he was, after all, the first to discover an ocean route from Europe to India, and he made frequent stops in Africa along the way (even posing as a Muslim in Mozambique). The reversal, 300 years later, of da Gama's focus – now Africa over India, then India over Africa – highlights the idea of African trade as progress; Africa was to replace India as the new frontier. If the African Company was able to conquer that frontier, it might shed the stigma of its association with the slave trade by demonstrating its interest in culture and science – and, more immediately, publically dedicating itself to the improvement of a poor African American's conditions. The African Company therefore needed Adams' story, and Adams needed money, food, clothes and passage back to America: there was a deal to be made. And so the Company bought, in both sense of the word, Adams' narrative.

In 1816, John Murray published *The Narrative of Robert Adams, a Sailor, who was Wrecked on the Western Coast of Africa . . . and Resided Several Months in the City of Tombuctoo*. It was written by one or more members of the African Company (attributed to S. Cock) and ostensibly based on Adams' own narrative. The Timbuktu that it describes is nothing like the Timbuktu of Leo Africanus' account, not a city of gold, but a town of mud huts in the middle of the desert.

Adams' editor, however, is convinced by his 'plain and unpretending answers' which, he argues, gives 'a strong impression in favour of his veracity'.[32] Not everyone was persuaded. The *Narrative*'s editor admits:

> [Adams'] answers disclosed so extraordinary a series of adventures and sufferings, as first to excited a suspicion that his story was an invention; and the gentleman by whom he was accompanied to the office, and who were present at his first examination, were decidedly of that opinion, when they considered how widely his account of Tombuctoo differed from the notions generally entertained of the magnificence of that city, and of the civilization of its inhabitants.[33]

His editors manage this difficulty by padding the *Narrative* with their own commentary. In fact, only one quarter of the *Narrative of Robert Adams, a Sailor*, is a narrative of Robert Adams, a sailor. The remainder is anxious evidence and analysis of the doth-protest-too-much variety: Adams' story, his biographers and benefactors spend 'his' *Narrative* insisting, is true. One hundred and ten pages of explanation, apology, correction, documentation.

Certainly, for practical reasons, someone needed to vouch for Adams and his story; as a homeless African American, Adams was hardly in possession of sufficient cultural capital to persuade, or even acquire, a large audience. But there was another issue besides credibility at stake. The African Company needed its presentation of Adams' tale to seem a benefit to the British public, as well as to Africans; it therefore needed his journey to Timbuktu to be read as a collective achievement for Britain. That meant that Adams had to appear representative enough of the white, British, Christian, literate public that his achievement would be an achievement for them as well. But Adams was not white, not British, barely Christian, and illiterate. And so the members of the Company do their best to gloss over these shortcomings and, in particular, to muddle Adams' race and nationality. Joseph Dupuis, in a letter that introduces Adam's *Narrative*, writes:

> The appearance, features and dress of this man upon his arrival at Mogadore, so perfectly resembled those of an Arab, or rather of a Shilluh, his head being shaved, and his beard scanty and black, that

> I had difficulty at first in believing him to be a Christian. When I spoke to him in English, he answered me in a mixture of Arabic and broken English, and sometimes in Arabic only. At this early period I could not help remarking that his pronunciation of Arabic resembled that of a Negro...[34]

After leaving this confused impression for several paragraphs, Dupuis goes on to explain that he 'learnt, either from himself or from some other of the Charles' crew, that [Adams'] mother was a Mulatto' and agrees – despite being unsure about the identity of his source – that Adams' 'features and complexion' seemed to confirm this.[35] Adams is later described as a 'very dark man, with short curly black hair'; remarkably, he repeatedly identifies himself as a white man.[36] Paul Baepler, in an introduction to an anthology of Barbary captivity narratives, describes Adams as a racial 'chameleon' who changes colour in contrast to the colour of those who surround him.[37] To the Moors he is white, to the blacks he is Moorish; in Timbuktu he is white compared to both Moors and blacks, but in an 1824 account of Adams he appears as 'Arab, Negro, and Berber all at once'.[38] At the same time, the *Narrative* manages to muddle Adams' origins just enough to obfuscate his American roots. It begins 'Robert Adams, aged 25, born at Hudson, about one hundred miles up the North River from New York, where his father was a sail maker, was brought up to the seafaring line, and made several voyages to Lisbon, Cadiz, Seville, and Liverpool.'[39] Here Adams' birthplace is described in terms of movement – not 100 miles *from* New York but 100 miles *up* the river from New York – and even the relative definitiveness of this location is undone by the description of his mobile upbringing. In backpedalling from Adams' American origins, his narrators present a hero who is as much from Lisbon, Cadiz, Seville, and Liverpool as he is from New York. Nationality, like race, is unstable.

It is this fluidity of identity that both participates in and disrupts the book's status as a Barbary captivity narrative, a genre which generally articulates two significant dangers. The first, and most obvious, is that white Europeans might themselves become the objects of slavery – that, as Linda Colley puts it, 'those non-European peoples whom the British sought to invade or exploit sometimes proved able to resist and punish them, and even find their own uses for them'.[40] Captivity narratives represent the inverse of the African slave trade, depicting Africans as masters over whites. In Adams' narrative, the account of Barbary captivity (and also of slavery within Africa) becomes suggestive of the eclipsed narrative of the British and American slave trade.[41] When Adams 'after much reflection on this miserable state in which he had been so long kept, and was likely to pass the remainder of his life, determined to remonstrate upon the subject', the reader already knows that Adams will in fact not 'pass the remainder of his life' in slavery. The reader also knows who *will*: most victims of the American and European slave trade. Adams' remonstration (not reproduced in the text) is therefore more appropriately read as a commentary on the interminability of the West Indian or American slave's sentence than on Adams' own (ultimately finite) captivity. In this, his tale potentially rewrites the captivity narrative to critique Europe's enslavement of Africans, rather than the reverse.

The second threat typically elucidated by Barbary captivity narratives is both more explicit and more subtle: the risk of Christian captives converting to Islam.[42] Adams' tale is no exception. When Adams is taken to Wadinoon (or Wed-Noon) on the African coast, he is reunited with three members of his ship's crew. One is killed, and the two who survive are lost to their faith:

> As the Moors were constantly urging them to become Mohamedans, and they were unceasingly treated with the greatest brutality, the fortitude of Williams and Vaison being exhausted, they at last unhappily consented to renounce their religion, and were circumcised, and thus obtained their liberty; after which they were presented with a horse, a musket, and a blanket each, and permitted to marry . . .
>
> As Adams was the only remaining Christian at Wadinoon, he became in a more especial manner an object of the derision and persecution of the Moors, who were constantly upbraiding him and reviling him, and telling him that his soul would be lost unless he became a Mohammedan, insomuch that his life was becoming intolerable.[43]

Conveniently, it is a mere three days later that a letter arrives from Joseph Dupuis, the British Consul at Mogadore, addressed to the Christian prisoners of Wadinoon. The letter 'exhort[s] them most earnestly not to give up their religion, whatever might befall them', and promises to emancipate them within the month.[44] Adams is the only one rescued. But despite this heavy-handed Christian lesson, the divide between Christian and Muslim is significantly disrupted in

Adams' tale. The natives of Hilla Gibla, where Adams is held shortly before Wadinoon, refer to him as a 'Christian who never prayed', and they hold both his Christianity and his impiety against him.[45] His status as Christian is not evident in his behaviour, not based on Christian beliefs; he is Christian only insofar as he is not Muslim. Christianity, here, is an absence. This undercuts the *Narrative*'s seeming insistence on Adams' fidelity to his religion, thus complicating the Barbary captivity narrative's function as a pitting of Islam against Christianity. Furthermore, Adams' account goes on to divorce Islam from the barbarity with which it is typically associated in captivity narratives. When Adams arrives at Agadeer after being freed, the governor apologises for the poor treatment he received at Wadinoon, saying he 'well knew their manner of treating Christians' and insisting that 'they were savages, and not subjects of the Emperor'.[46] The governor's reference to the emperor is the *Narrative*'s first suggestion of a cohesive Ottoman territory – a cohesiveness undone in the very moment that it is asserted. If this is a Barbary captivity narrative, it is one about a Christian who is not really Christian, who resists the temptation to convert to an Islam that is not necessarily savage, within an empire that is not really an empire.

And indeed for the French and Americans who challenge the truth of Adams' claims, the *Narrative* is not about Barbary. In fact, it is not about Adams' tale at all, but about the British gentlemen of the African Company. Jared Sparks, for example, writes in the *North American Review*:

> It was sent into the world under the sanction of some of the most distinguished men in England . . . [T]he narrative gained credit every where, and made an article in almost every periodical publication in the British dominions. It was gravely and elaborately reviewed in the Edinburgh and Quarterly Reviews, and the latter in particular entered into a manful defence of its most glaring absurdities. Considered in this light, it assumes an importance, and deserves a notice, to which it would not otherwise be entitled.[47]

For Sparks, the book's importance lies not in the information it conveys about the people or land of Africa, but in what it indicates about the Britons – and especially the 'distinguished men' – who believe it. As Charles Hansford Adams points out in his introduction to the 2005 edition of the *Narrative*, these gentlemen were 'irresistible targets' for Sparks, 'a man whose entire career was devoted to establishing American cultural independence from Britain'. The *North American Review*, Adams explains,

> stood for a nascent national culture and offered an excellent platform on which to display the spectacle of an illiterate sailor hoodwinking some of Britain's brightest minds. Especially gratifying, from Sparks's perspective, would have been the fact that these 'distinguished men' were obviously connected with the London *Quarterly Review*, a Tory publication mentioned with approbation in the *Narrative*.[48]

On the surface, theirs is an amusing, if damning, mistake: these British gentlemen, greedy for information about the legendary city, are too anxious to believe any story they hear. But the incompetence of the African Company – evidenced in a basic ignorance about the land they intended to trade with and eventually colonise – suggests to some a broader incompetence, one that might mean the Company was finally not up to the task of civilising the primitive world. The *North American Review* and other American critics were happy to read the African Company as a synecdoche for British colonial power; the Company's failure, therefore, to manage intelligence on a backward African city suggested that they had little claim – and posed little threat – to the young America.

There were also plenty of people in Britain who found Adams' tale preposterous. In 1824, for example, London's *New Monthly Magazine and Literary Journal* published a spoof of Adams' *Narrative* entitled 'Specimens of a Timbuctoo Anthology'. It stars Captain Jonathan Washington Muggs, a fictional American of mixed race whose account of Timbuktu is dismissed 'merely because it contains facts that may startle the narrow intellects of Europe'.[49] The Timbuktu in Muggs' tale, as in Adams', is not a city of gold but of mud huts (though the mud of the huts, he reports, is 'of a finer texture', and 'the architecture approached in several instances the ingenuity displayed in the nidification of birds').[50] Muggs also translates Timbuktu's poetry, ostensibly to illustrate the 'refined and delicate sentiments' of the citizens. The poem 'To Tambooshie' is representative:

> O wert thou mine, Tambooshie I would make
> Suet and soot pomatum for thy head
> Then powder it with bukcu dust, and take
> Cowdung cosmetics o'er thy face to spread.[51]

Captain Muggs, the uncultured mulatto, is no literary critic. 'The imputation', writes Charles Hansford Adams, is that 'Muggs, like [Robert] Adams, is unqualified to judge what he sees in Timbuctoo, and that whatever valuable information he possesses must be culled by those of a broader knowledge . . . Black civilization *and* its hapless chronicler are both mocked . . .'[52] The further implication is that the chroniclers of the chronicler – that is, the Britons of the African Company – are hapless as well. The story of Muggs aligns Adams with the Timbuktuvians, the African Company aligns itself with Adams, and in the end these British gentlemen come out looking like they have taken Timbuktu a little too seriously. Muggs' fictional editor manages one final and crucial dig at the African Company's good intentions: he concludes his narrative with the warning that any attempt by Europeans to reach Timbuktu would be 'hopeless and desperate', an unnecessary risk to European life. This is a direct refutation of the aim of Adams' own editors; Adams' *Narrative* is meant to prove the *necessity* of European colonisation of Timbuktu. Muggs' editors argue that there is no reason to go to a goldless, unlearned Timbuktu; Adams' editors, on the other hand, argue that the goldlessness and unlearnedness of Timbuktu are precisely the reasons to go there. It is the job of Europeans to bring the gold, literally or figuratively, to turn Timbuktu back into a city of culture. Timbuktu's wealthless ignorance is actually ideal for their purposes, because it confirms what the Europeans have known all along: the Africans are not capable of preserving a great city. Muggs' editor's insistence that exploration of Timbuktu is a waste of resources is therefore more broadly a mockery of the rationale for colonisation. The message: these potential colonisers are no smarter than the potentially colonised. The people of Timbuktu don't have God or literary taste, but the African Company doesn't have sense enough to know a fiction when they read one.

Impressions Exclusively National

But what, exactly, was at stake in these fights over physical and intellectual control of Timbuktu? To help distill the political, social, and racial tensions that structured the debates about Timbuktu, it might be helpful to turn briefly to another (equally false) narrative of Timbuktu, written four years after Adams'. Asseed El Hage Abd Salam Shabeeny was a native of Tetuan, who claimed to have spent ten years in Timbuktu. His story is relayed in James Grey Jackson's 1820 *Account of Timbuctoo and Housa*, which is very much in dialogue with Adams' narrative; Jackson frequently cites Adams as evidence that Shabeeny's details are correct. Shabeeny is 'a Muselman', Jackson writes, 'whose father and mother are personally known to Mr. Lucas, the British counsul'.[53] There is an implied 'but' here (he is Muslim but he is known to those with credibility), but there is also an implication that Shabeeny has authority *because* he is a Muslim – as opposed, for example, to the Christian Robert Adams. He is also opposed to the African-American Robert Adams, as Jackson makes a point of demonstrating Shabeeny's construction of his own identity against the black Africans. Jackson writes that Shabeeny 'made great profit by his traffic at Timbuctoo and Housa, but *he says* money gained among the Negroes has not the blessing of God on it, but vanishes away without benefit to the owner; but, acquired in a journey to Mecca, proves fortunate, and becomes a permanent acquisition' (italics are Jackson's).[54] Shabeeny, through Jackson, establishes an opposition between Muslim and black African – between himself and the other kind of African – but he also aligns himself with the European by stressing his primary interest in profit; Shabeeny was a merchant by profession, travelling to Germany, Belgium and England, as well as within Africa. Because he claims that Timbuktu is black *rather than* Muslim, he sets himself up as able to give the kind of objective account that an outsider – a Westerner – would give.

Though Jackson is anxious to establish Shabeeny's credibility, he is far more anxious to establish his own. In response to those 'fire-side critics' and the 'desultory intelligence of other travellers, who certainly did not possess those opportunities of procuring information that I did', he asserts that his accounts 'continue daily to receive ... confirmation from all the African travellers themselves'.[55] This claim falls in the middle of a litany of Jackson's qualifications: he spent sixteen years in West and South Barbary, and he was diplomatic agent to several maritime nations of Europe, which, he says, 'familiarized [him] with all ranks of society in those countries'. He has 'perfect knowledge of the commercial and travelling language of Africa', and brags: 'I corresponded *myself* with the Emperors, Princes, and

Bashas in this very language; my commercial connections were *very* extensive, amongst all the most respectable merchants who traded with Timbuctoo ...' This long residence in the country has enabled him, he claims, to 'ascertain who were competent and who were not competent' to give information, and he has had opportunities to investigate their motives and moral character. 'Possessed of all these sources of information,' he concludes, 'how could I fail of procuring correct and authentic intelligence?' He is especially proud that the Europeans are beginning to adopt his orthography of African names, and in particular his spelling of 'Timbuctoo', to replace the 'barbarous orthography of *Tombuctoo*'.[56]

Jackson's fashioning of himself as a scientist who is a reliable interpreter rather than a mere scribe makes his *Account* a different genre from Robert Adams'. Though Adams' narrator asserts Adams' distance from the text by speaking of him in the third person, Adams is nevertheless always present in the narrative; it is at every moment clearly *his* story that is being told: an account of Adams going, Adams seeing. By contrast, just as soon as Jackson has finished insisting on Shabeeny's reliability, he abandons him. From this moment on, Jackson's account reads as if it is *Jackson's* account, with few signals that the information he relays has actually come from Shabeeny. Shabeeny only appears in the text at points where there is some uncertainty about the facts – 'he thinks', 'he recollects' – and even in these instances, he is never referred to by name. In keeping Adams present as a character in his own narrative, the members of the African Company open themselves up to criticism; Jackson may have learned from their mistake.[57]

It is possible, however, that in avoiding the image of the Muslim explorer, Jackson is not merely trying to pre-empt racially-based attacks of Shabeeny. It is possible, in fact, that the Arab-looking explorer is not too Eastern, but too *French* – that Jackson's acrobatics are inscribed in the larger debate between France and England. In 1824, the Société de Géographie in Paris offered a prize for the first non-Muslim to reach Timbuktu and report back. Though the non-Muslim stipulation was in part bigotry, it was also reflective of the belief that a Muslim who made it to Timbuktu was cheating by the mere fact of his ability to blend in and communicate. But Christians could cheat too. It was Jackson himself who wrote to Société member Edmé-François Jomard to express his hope that European travellers would not engage in the 'hypocrisy' of assuming African dress and presenting themselves as Muslim; he recommended that the contest stipulate that the prize would only be awarded to those who dressed in European clothing and publically professed their Christianity. The Société did no such thing, and in 1828 René Caillié successfully reached Timbuktu – dressed in African clothing and posing as Abd Allahi, a convert on his way to Egypt in search of his long-lost family.[58] When it was necessary for Caillié to take notes along his journey, he concealed himself under a bush or rock in order to avoid 'awaken[ing] the suspicion of the Moslems'; when he was forced to write in the open desert, he pretended that he was copying leaves of the Koran.[59] He includes in his *Travels to Central Africa to Timbuctoo* a portrait of himself carrying out this deception (Figure 5.1).

But Caillié's Muslim ruse was not the only objection British geographers had to his expedition. John Barrow, a protégé of Joseph Banks, dismissed Caillié's narrative more because of nationalistic pride than any commitment to accuracy. When Jomard declared Caillié to be the 'first European traveler who has accomplished such an enterprise', Barrow responded angrily:

> Far be it from me to conceive the idea of detracting from the merit of this bold and adventurous traveller . . . but the justice which is due to the memory of another traveler, who has perished by the barbarous hand of an assassin, calls upon me to show you, Sir, that M. Caillié is neither the only, nor the first European who has visited Timbuctoo.[60]

Barrow refers here to Gordon Laing, who had perished two years earlier. But Jomard and Barrow are quibbling over semantics; Jomard insists, in his response to Barrow, that the 'enterprise' in question is not *visiting* Timbuktu but *returning* from Timbuktu. He goes on, somewhat too enthusiastically, to declare the universality of Caillié's accomplishment, claiming it as a triumph not for France but for all the world: 'no one is less accessible than myself to impressions exclusively national', he writes, 'and it is on behalf of humanity in general that I am devoted to the cause.' He also assures Barrow that he himself has established as a principle of the Société de Géographie that 'travelers of all nations are equally entitled to its attention; that its rewards belong to all, whatever may be their nation'.[61] This echoes Banks' grandiose claims about the universal importance of Mungo Park's discoveries, but Jomard, like Banks, uses the supposed universality as evidence of his own nation's superiority. It is Caillié, and

Fig. 5.1 'Mr. Caillié meditating upon the Koran and taking notes', printed in *Travels Through Central Africa to Timbuctoo*, 1830

by extension the French, who have brought light to the European nations – nations who plan, in turn, to bring light to Africa. Jomard reads Barrow's letter for what it is and composes a twenty-five-page scathing critique of Caillié in *The Quarterly Review*:

> 'Here,' says some one, speaking of Caillié's travels in Africa, 'here we have a subject of glory for France, and jealousy for her eternal rival! That which England has not been able to accomplish, with the aid of a whole group of travelers, and at the expense of more than twenty millions (*bravo*!) a Frenchman has done with his scanty personal resources alone, and without putting his country to any expense.' Mortifying as it may be to be writer of this paragraph, we can assure him, with great truth, that, so far from being 'jealous,' a very small fraction of the 'eternal rival' will ever know or care whether M. Caillié has or has not visited Timbuctoo, and will concern themselves still less about the 'glory' which France imagines herself to have reaped from his travels. What does this eternal cant and whining about the 'jealousy' and 'rivalry' of England imply, but a constantly-recurring consciousness of the intellectual and physical superiority of our countrymen over theirs? [. . .] Frenchmen would seem to travel solely to boast of their feats, all for the honour and glory of France, however insignificant the feats really achieved may be.[62]

Though he will go on to declare Caillié's report so worthless that 'he might just as well have staid at home', Barrow's account of the French-British clash is the true crux of his critique.[63] Here is an explicit acknowledgement of what these expeditions are really about: the wrangling for economic and intellectual dominance. To this extent, the content of the narratives is unimportant, except insofar as it provides fodder for accusations of inaccuracy or plagiarism, as well as evidence for which nation is better suited to colonise central Africa. The accounts – like so many travel narratives – are more about the nations that produce them than they are about the lands the travellers visit: their geographies are symbolic.

A Bewildering Flux

And now it is time to return to Robert Adams, because to the extent that the struggle between France and England was over cultural and scientific authority, it was a fight over the conceptual rather than the material – and this was a fight that Robert Adams could win. The political uses to which Adams' Timbuktu narrative is put might make it appear that Adams is a pawn in some larger political game. But while the African Company was busy getting duped, Adams was busy duping, manipulating a national narrative to his own ends. I began this chapter by suggesting that Timbuktu is always a destination, and certainly the ostensible value of Adams' narrative was his having reached the city. And yet his account of Timbuktu is actually just a small part of what is, on the whole, a tale of travel and movement, not of place. Charles Hansford Adams summarises it in one stunning sentence: Robert Adams was

> shipwrecked along the Mauritanian coast, captured and enslaved by desert nomads, carried hundreds of miles across the Sahara into the interior of Africa, taken from his masters by black Africans who murdered the Moors and marched him into Timbuctoo, held there as human merchandise for six months, sold back into Moorish slavery and marched back across the Sahara, sold again and traded from one vicious master to another in southern Morocco . . . ransomed by Dupuis at Mogador, taken to Meknes and interviewed by the Emperor himself, conveyed under imperial guard to Tangier, and placed aboard a ship to Cadiz . . . before finally making his way via Holyhead to London and the office of the African Company.[64]

Shipwrecked, captured, enslaved, carried, taken, marched, held, sold, marched again, sold again, ransomed, taken again, conveyed, and placed, Adams is not moving but moved; it is only when he sets off for London that he has any agency attributed to him, 'making his way', bound for the African Company office. Of course, Adams didn't make his way at all, and certainly he wasn't headed toward the African Company; he was, rather, found loitering by the docks, homeless and without the means to make his way anywhere. But the fact is that Adams, in telling his story to the African Company, intends to exchange imaginary travel for actual travel: this fictional account of his movement around Africa is meant to secure the money that will allow him to move himself from England to America. Adams also recognises the uses to which a British self-conception might be put, because it is the African Company's national egotism that makes them so stunningly naïve. Adams' Timbuktu is easy for them to swallow because it is just the kind of place that the British love to imagine: an uncultivated land which nevertheless has potential (a potential that only the West could recognise) to be great again. The African Company's belief in the superiority of British ways can get Adams where he needs to go: straight out of Britain.

In other words, this story he tells – one that in every detail seems to prove Britons' superiority and give them the material means to colonise African land – is a lie that actually winds up helping the poor sailor and humiliating the British gentlemen. Ann Fabian writes of Adams and other beggars: 'Some participated in their country's first imperial adventures and described the beginnings of a world where claims of national identity could give order to a bewildering flux of experience.'[65] And Adams makes use of that 'bewildering flux'. When he gives the African Company exactly the vision of a backwards Timbuktu that they need, he participates in the country's 'imperial adventures' *and* challenges precisely the kind of national identity that justifies those adventures. In deploying his story as he does, he subverts the very power that the facts of that story seem to enforce. These 'facts' – that Africa is primitive and lesser – are part of what Edward Said and others have termed the 'imaginative geographies' upon which colonialism is dependent. But in quite literally imagining – inventing outright – its imaginative geographies, Adams' *Narrative* collapses the distance between 'us' and 'them' that such geographies are meant to enforce. The (fake) details of his tale might hold out the promise of more land to cultivate. But Adams' manipulation of the colonial imagination insinuates that from here to Africa – from here to Timbuktu – might not be quite as far as the British gentlemen of the African Association and the African Company would like to believe.

Notes

1. In a poll of young British people taken in 2006, thirty-four per cent did not believe that Timbuktu existed, and the remaining sixty-six per cent considered it to be a 'mythical place' or a made-up name. ['Search on for Timbuktu's Twin', *BBC*, 18 October 2006, http: //news.bbc.co.uk/2/hi/uk_news/6062360.stm.]
2. Jean Baptiste Bourguignon d'Anville was a notable exception to eighteenth century geographers' tendency to fill the map of Africa not only with savage creatures, but also with 'boundary lines and mountain

ranges, for which no authority could be quoted', as Hallett writes. [Robin Hallett, ed., *Records of the African Association 1788–1831* (New York: Thomas Nelson and Sons, 1964), 44, 4.]
3. Hallett, on the contrary, argues that the physical impediments to African exploration were not as great as they are made out to be, that the Sahara was 'like a sea: it divided but it also joined'. [Ibid., 247–8, 5.]
4. Ignatius Sancho, *Letters of the Late Ignatius Sancho, an African. In Two Volumes. To Which Are Prefixed, Memoirs of His Life* (London: J. Nichols,1782), 2.
5. Mary Louise Pratt, *Imperial Eyes: Travel Writing and Transculturation*, 2nd edn (Routledge, 2007), 68.
6. The almost immediate abbreviation of 'Association for Promoting the Discovery of the Interior Parts of Africa' to 'African Association' – a move made by the Association itself – is telling. Their full name was unwieldy, but the abbreviation produced convenient ambiguities. For one, in omitting the term 'interior', the Association erased the distinction between Africa as the site of slave trading, and Africa as an untapped market; Africa, in the mind of the British, was to become its potential rather than its past. But perhaps more importantly, their shortened name confused the relation between the Association and African peoples: an 'African Association' might just as easily be an association *of* Africans.
7. Hallett, *Records of the African Association 1788–1831*, 46.
8. Ibid., 143–4.
9. John Gascoigne argues explicitly that the Association became a means for Banks to 'advance his imperial ends'. [John Gascoigne, *Science in the Service of Empire: Joseph Banks, the British State and the Uses of Science in the Age of Revolution* (New York: Cambridge University Press, 1998), 178.]
10. Philip J. Stern, '"Rescuing the Age from a Charge of Ignorance": Gentility, Knowledge, and the British Exploration of Africa in the Later Eighteenth Century', in *A New Imperial History: Culture, Identity, and Modernity in Britain and the Empire, 1660–1840*, ed. Kathleen Wilson (Cambridge; New York: Cambridge University Press, 2004), 125.
11. Leo Africanus, *The History and Description of Africa and of the Notable Things Therein Contained*, ed. Robert Brown, trans. John Pory, vol. 3 (London: Hakluyt Society, 1896), 824–5. There were, they explain, other reports received by Europe through the next two hundred years, including reports of 'unicorns' horns . . . eunuchs, dwarfs, and women and men slaves, besides fifteen virgins'. [Brian Gardner, *The Quest for Timbuctoo* (New York: Harcourt, Brace & World, 1968); Robert Adams, *The Narrative of Robert Adams, a Barbary*

Captive, ed. Charles Hansford Adams (New York: Cambridge University Press, 2005), xxxv–xxxvi.]
12. Adams, *The Narrative of Robert Adams, a Barbary Captive*, xxxvi.
13. Stern, '"Rescuing the Age from a Charge of Ignorance": Gentility, Knowledge, and the British Exploration of Africa in the Later Eighteenth Century', 124.
14. Ibid., 129.
15. Hallett, *Records of the African Association 1788–1831*, 168–9.
16. Ibid., 165.
17. Park was more modest – or at least feigned modesty – regarding his own success and, therefore, the appeal of his story: 'I should deliver this volume to the world, with that confidence of a favourable reception, which no merits of my own could authorize me to claim; were I not apprehensive that expectations have been formed by some of my subscribers, of discoveries to be unfolded, which I have not made, and of wonders to be related, of which I am utterly ignorant.' [Mungo Park, *Travels in the Interior Districts of Africa: Performed Under the Direction and Patronage of the African Association, in the Years 1795, 1796, and 1797*, vol. 1 (London, 1799), ix–x.]
18. In 1802, Banks wrote to John Sullivan at the colonial office to report that he had 'met with a book written with the clear intention to induce the French to colonize the whole of the Senegambia Country'. Golberry, in turn, believed Park's narrative an affront to France: 'It was not, therefore, without great regret that I beheld the voyages and discoveries of Mungo Park published in 1799, and which yet awarded to the English the merit of having made the first successful advances in this path, which I had considered as particularly belonging to us.' [S.M.X. Golberry, *Fragments D'un Voyage En Afrique Pendant Les Aneés 1785, 86, 87* (Paris, 1802).]
19. Jamie Bruce Lockhart and Paul E. Lovejoy, eds, *Hugh Clapperton into the Interior of Africa: Records of the Second Expedition, 1825–1827* (Boston: Brill, 2005).
20. *The New Monthly Magazine and Literary Journal*, vol. 24, Part III (London: Henry Colburn, 1828), 210.
21. In fact, this amounted to only nine 'humble African trading posts' (Adams, *The Narrative of Robert Adams, a Barbary Captive*, xxiii.
22. James Walvin, *Black Ivory: Slavery in the British Empire* (Oxford: Blackwell, 2001), 31.
23. *Slavery No Oppression; or, Some New Arguments and Opinions Against the Idea of African Liberty. Dedicated To the Committee of the Company That Trade to Africa* (London, 1788), 6–7.

24. The author devotes significant attention to the role of the university in abolition: 'A very learned and enlightened University has not been behindhand in pushing this subject [of abolition]. But, I presume, her meekness and Christianity had drowned every political concern of interest, or perhaps she may flatter herself, that she may still lounge over a cup of tea in uninterrupted ease and quite, and that the sweet produce of the cane will be still had with equal facility and cheapness. But various Merchants, Traders, Manufacturers in London, Bristol, Liverpool, Lancaster, Whitehaven, have professionally a deeper insight into the ruinous event of this project, than the academical Seat of Literature—our *Alma Mater*. The Student, secluded within the silence and tranquility of Classic Cloisters, is ready enough, in that happy security, to indulge a credulous, or a luxuriant imagination with scenes of pictured woe; as the prattling Mariner, when safe in his social chimney-corner delights to magnify his escapes, and to amplify storms and shipwrecks. But the Learned makes inquietude only for his own breast, and either feels, or affects to feel adversity, which is unfelt by the African himself . . .' (Ibid., 8–9).
25. Ibid., 9.
26. Adams, *The Narrative of Robert Adams, a Barbary Captive*, xxvii–xxviii.
27. Joseph Marryat, *Thoughts on the Abolition of the Slave Trade: And Civilization of Africa, with Remarks on the African Institution, and an Examination of the Report of Their Committee Recommending a General Registry of Slaves in the British West India Islands* (J. M. Richardson and J. Ridgway, 1816), 79–80.
28. W. Jeffrey Bolster, *Black Jacks: African American Seamen in the Age of Sail* (Cambridge, MA: Harvard University Press, 1997), 19.
29. Vasco da Gama, 'Commercial Intercourse with Africa', *The Gentleman's Magazine*, May 1812, 404.
30. Ibid.
31. Vasco da Gama, 'Hints Concerning the Colonization of Africa', *Blackwood's Edinburgh Magazine* 4, no. 24 (March 1819): 653–4.
32. Adams, *The Narrative of Robert Adams, a Barbary Captive*, 9.
33. Ibid.
34. Ibid., 15.
35. Ibid., 17.
36. Ibid., 32, 47, 49, 55.
37. *White Slaves, African Masters: An Anthology of American Barbary Captivity Narratives* (Chicago: University of Chicago Press, 1999), 21.
38. Joseph Dupuis, *Journal of a Residence in Ashantee*, 2nd edn (London: Cass, 1966).
39. Adams, *The Narrative of Robert Adams, a Barbary Captive*, 26.

40. Linda Colley, *Captives: Britain, Empire and the World, 1600–1850* (New York: Pantheon, 2002), 12.
41. As George Hansford Adams writes, 'Moslem slavery is Adams's interest, and that of his London editors. Christian slavery, though, informs the book at every turn and is the unwritten story behind the production of the *Narrative*' (Adams, *The Narrative of Robert Adams, a Barbary Captive*, xiv).
42. See Chapter 1 for more on the fear of captives 'turning Turk', as it was called.
43. Cock's ironic note to this section insists that, despite the disproportionately poor treatment of Christian captives (who are 'looked upon as hardened infidels, and as deliberate despisers of the Prophet's call', as opposed to the innocently 'ignorant' pagans), owners often did not desire their slaves' conversion. On the contrary, suggests Cock, they 'often encourage the Christians to resist the importunities of those who wish to convert them: for, by embracing Islamism the Christian slave obtains his freedom; and however ardent may be the zeal of the Arab to make proselytes, it seldom blinds him to the calculations of self-interest' (Adams, *The Narrative of Robert Adams, a Barbary Captive*, 99).
44. Ibid., 63.
45. Ibid., 57.
46. Ibid., 65.
47. Jared Sparks, 'Review of *The Narrative of Robert Adams, a Sailor* . . .', in *The North American Review and Miscellaneous Journal*, 1817, 204–5.
48. Adams, *The Narrative of Robert Adams, a Barbary Captive*, xvii.
49. 'Specimens of a Timbuctoo Anthology', *The New Monthly Magazine* 11, no. 43 (January 1824): 23.
50. Ibid., 25.
51. Ibid., 26.
52. Adams, *The Narrative of Robert Adams, a Barbary Captive*, xliv.
53. James Grey Jackson, *An Account of Timbuctoo and Housa, Territories in the Interior of Africa: By El Hage Abd Salam Shabeeny, with Notes, Critical and Explanatory* (London: Frank Cass & Co., 1967), 5.
54. Ibid., vii.
55. Ibid., xi–xii.
56. Ibid.
57. In assigning the narrative voice to a more seemingly reliable witness than Shabeeny – that is, to himself – Jackson may have avoided the problem of his audience picturing a visibly other and therefore unreliable narrator, but his approach had its own risks. By setting himself up as insurance of the story's veracity, he stood to lose even more than the

African Company if it turned out that the story was not true – which, of course, is exactly what happened.
58. Initially, Caillié felt only triumph at reaching Timbuktu. 'On entering this mysterious city, which is an object of curiosity and research to the civilized nations of Europe, I experienced an indescribable satisfaction', he writes. 'I never before felt a similar emotion and my transport was extreme.' But his initial excitement is short-lived; he quickly sees a city not unlike the city that Shabeeny and Adams describe: 'I looked around and found that the sight before me, did not answer my expectations. I had formed a totally different idea of the grandeur and wealth of Timbuktu. The city presented, at first view, nothing but a mass of ill-looking houses, built of earth. Nothing to be seen in all directions but immense plains of quicksand of a yellowish white colour. The sky was a pale red as far as the horizon: all nature wore a dreary aspect, and the most profound silence prevailed; not even the warbling of a bird was to be heard. Still, though I cannot account for the impression, there was something imposing in the aspect of a great city, raised in the midst of sands, and the difficulties surmounted by its founders cannot fail to excite admiration . . .' It is the emptiness of Timbuktu that makes it great, and the 'difficulties surmounted by its founders' suggest possibility of Europeans accomplishing the similarly daunting task of reviving the city. [René Caillié, *Travels Through Central Africa to Timbuctoo; and Across the Great Desert, to Morocco, Performed in the Years 1824–1828*, vol. 2 (London: H. Colburn and R. Bentley), 71.]
59. Ibid.
60. Ibid., 2: 483–4.
61. Ibid., 2: 486–7.
62. John Barrow, 'Art VI: *Journal D'un Voyage à Temboctoo Et à Jenné, Dans l'Afrique Centrale, &c*', Quarterly Review 42 (1830): 450–1.
63. Ibid., 464.
64. Adams, *The Narrative of Robert Adams, a Barbary Captive*, xii.
65. Ann Fabian, *The Unvarnished Truth: Personal Narratives in Nineteenth-Century America* (Berkeley: University of California Press, 2000), 11–12.

Conclusion:
Land Pirates and Republican Ragamuffins

In conclusion I offer four brief readings, gestures towards places one might venture. The subjects are neither prophets nor pirates, but they are prophetic and piratic, practising a collective resistance both on land and at sea. This resistance is produced by and productive of mobility; it is a resistance that comes out of necessity and – by necessity – imagines a new system of power.

The first is Haitian maroon François Mackandal, who was referred to as a prophet by his followers. He pillaged and plundered and killed; he and his gang threatened the plantation system in Haiti as surely as pirates threatened the slave trade, and they paved the way for the Haitian Revolution. Next is ex-slave Olaudah Equiano, who took to the sea, after having been taken to the sea, to use the space where his oppression began in order to resist and undermine that very system. As an abolitionist he trod fairly gently, allowing his *Narrative* to speak for itself and appealing to his audience's investment in trade as much as to any absolute ideal of freedom or the rights of man. But what Equiano *did* was more complex; it was a material resistance as much as a rhetorical one. Following Equiano's *Narrative* are two British accounts of two (very different) alternative black societies. Anna Maria Falconbridge was the wife of a Sierra Leone agent whose epistolary *Narrative of Two Voyages to the River Sierra Leone* told of her time in the Colony between 1791 and 1792. The colony her husband managed was a mistake, but it was nevertheless one test of what an alternate society might look like. Though it was not a happy experiment, the mistakes of Sierra Leone pointed to what it might have been at its best: a site of common resistance to the oppression of the slave trade. William Earle's novel *Obi: Or the History of Three-Fingered Jack* was, likewise, a British treatment of a black society that might have gone otherwise, a society that failed and yet gestured towards revolution. Three-Fingered Jack, inspired by the violent death of his father on board a slave ship, was a 'daring freebooter', as a Jamaican newspaper put it, committing land piracy against those whose property was humans. Earle's fictionalised account of Jack, like Equiano's *Narrative*, leaves unspoken the possibility of a mass slave revolt, while identifying the forces against which such a revolt would battle. And so this conclusion ends not with Sierra Leone or Jamaica, but where it began – in St Domingo. The birth of Haiti was Sierra Leone's inverse: a black society of ex-slaves built from the bottom up. This was the revolution that worked. In Haiti is the legacy of the pirates, Mackandal, Equiano, and Three-Fingered Jack. The pirates were exterminated, Mackandal and Jack were executed, and Equiano could escape slavery only by purchasing himself. But in St Domingo, the spirit of resistance that finally persevered resulted in everything that the Sierra Leone colony had promised and everything that Mackandal, Equiano and Earle had implicitly prophesied: a free nation of ex-slaves.

Those Who Will Remain Masters of the Island

As the Golden Age of piracy drew to a close, pirates headed to the hills and re-emerged – both literally and figuratively – as maroons. The term *maroon* comes from the Spanish *cimarron*, 'mountain-dwellers', because maroons inhabited the supposedly uninhabitable mountains surrounding slave plantations. Maroons were generally escaped slaves who often, like many pirates, formed alternative societies, based on a communal lifestyle otherwise unavailable to them. And, like pirates, maroons fought violently against their oppressors, pillaging and stealing from slave-holders, and even from free mulattos and creoles who chose to be complicit with slave-owners and government officials. Though maroons had been living in Jamaica and St Domingo for at least 200 years, the narratives of maroons that emerged in the mid- to late eighteenth century were far more attentive to the broader Atlantic roots of maroon societies, possibly because maroons were increasingly engaged with Atlantic revolutionary culture. Pirates and maroons had encountered one another in earlier decades and had sometimes formed alliances, which is unsurprising given the similarity of their social and economic positions. Erin Skye Mackie writes that piracy and marronage 'both constitute sustained and organized refusals of participation in the two central institutions of the colonial machine: plantation slavery and the vastly expanded merchant navy . . .'[1] Nevertheless, Mackie argues, piracy and marronage are not a departure from so much as a reproduction of the systems against which they form:

> But while pirates refused the economic and social conditions of the merchant navy, they were, in the main, trained in that institution, and their cultural situation is significantly similar to that of any ship society. Just as the Maroons share many features of the Afro-creole slave society that they refused, yet with which they were in constant, if sometimes oppositional, contact, so the pirates' demographic identity, language, way of life, and, to some degree, ethos, is contiguous with that of the general body of seamen.[2]

I would disagree that pirate societies were 'contiguous' with institutionalised maritime society and would argue that, on the contrary, they were inversions of it. Though superficially the demographics of pirates may have been similar to the demographics of merchant sailors, the social, political and economic *structure* of their society was its opposite; pirate society was founded on a rejection of the economic system upon which merchant sailing was based. Maroons, however, are a more complicated matter. Structurally and ideologically, their societies seemed to share with the pirate ship a communal mentality that stood in stark opposition to the hierarchical (and slave-holding) society that they operated outside of. But in both Jamaica and St Domingo, maroons frequently cut deals with the government; in exchange for their own freedom, maroons would capture and turn in escaped slaves. In this respect, maroons were fake pirates, merely mimicking an alternate society.

François Mackandal, however, was a maroon squared, practising a marronage distilled: a rejection of the maroon society which was dependent on the slave trade from which maroons had themselves escaped. Like other maroons, he escaped and lived physically outside the plantation. Unlike other maroons, however, he set himself outside the system ideologically as well. Mackandal was truly piratic in his ability to not only function as an outlaw, but to deftly manipulate revolutionary networks.[3] Mackandal was born in Guinea and was well-educated there. He spoke Arabic; this, and rumours of his occasional pleas to Allah, lead some historians to believe he was Muslim. He was captured at age twelve as a prisoner of war and was sold to European slave-traders who transported him to St Domingo. After his escape, Mackandal spent eighteen years as leader of a band of 'considerable number', possibly around fifty members. Like most maroons, Mackandal and his band lived at the top of a 'nearly inaccessible mountain retreat', from which they sometimes descended to 'spread terror and ravage the plantations of the neighboring plains, or to extinguish those who had disobeyed the prophet [Mackandal]'.[4] Their mountain retreat was a community of families and farms; in this respect, too, it was similar to other maroon settlements in its coherence as an independent society.

But Mackandal's maroon band differed in substance from other maroon communities. Despite its coherence as a settlement, it did not, Carolyn Fick explains, participate in the 'restorationist' movement of other maroon bands, who were primarily engaged in the re-creation of an Afro-Caribbean community. Mackandal instead established what Laurent Dubois calls a 'cross-plantation network of resistance', widely disseminating information (primarily about the use of poisons) to slaves on different plantations.[5] This interchange enacted the distributed quality of Mackandal's movement, rendering him an embodiment of what was actually a network of revolutionary violence on the island. His society was, as Fick writes, an

> organizational vehicle ... for building a resistance movement aimed at nothing less than the destruction of the white masters and of slavery ... Here, then, was a case of a maroon band... operating in a permanent state of marronage, but one that extended itself, at the same time, to set afoot a vast movement of resistance ... It was the first real attempt in the long history of slave resistance at disciplined, organized revolt aiming not only at the destruction of the white masters and of slavery, but at the political notion of independence ... .[6]

Mackandal's maroon band's distinguishing quality was its engagement with (or against) slave-society; it sought not to form an alternative world of its own but to re-order the broader society. It was literally revolutionary.

And Mackandal was explicit about his revolutionary intentions, explicit about his plan for black slaves to assume power of the island. There is a well-circulated story of Mackandal as a revolutionary prophet, standing before a group of slaves with three scarves – one yellow, one white and one black – which he put in a vase and then removed one at a time. The first was the yellow scarf, representing, he said, the original rulers of the island. The second was the white, symbolising the present rulers. Removing the last scarf, Mackandal declared: 'Here, finally, are those who remain masters of the island: it is the black scarf.'[7] His prophecy was correct, if premature: the slaves would eventually rule the island, fuelled by precisely the sort of revolutionary network that Mackandal established.

An Almost-Englishman

Olaudah Equiano – aka Gustavas Vassa, aka The African, aka Himself – embodies a revolutionary network, one that spans from Equiano in Esaka to Vassa in England to himself at sea, in motion. Having originally refused to be called 'Gustavus Vassa', Equiano adopts it, for much of his life, as his primary name. He is at least nominally an Englishman, then; here identity is emergent rather than determined, adopted by choice rather than produced by origin. The title of Equiano's *Narrative* is not merely an equation of identities but is, rather, a proliferation of identities: a narrative of Olaudah Equiano who is also Gustavus Vassa, who is also the African, who is also Himself, whoever that might be. It is not surprising, Paul Youngquist argues, that Equiano has so many names:

> As a member of the maritime proletariat of the Black Atlantic, he has lost the simple sequence of links that would trace identity once and always back to Africa, to Carolina, or even to England, the land where he longs to be and belong in freedom. His identity is diasporic, routed, multiple, motley, hybridized. He shares with many sailors of the Black Atlantic the inability to be in any authentic way African, or American, or British, or whatever.[8]

It would be a mistake to trace Equiano's identity back to any particular place, to root his identity territorially or nationally; no place, national or otherwise, can account for the spatial practices of the exile. What is interesting about the *Interesting Narrative* is the futility of any attempt to track down the 'himself' that wrote the thing. 'The life' his *Narrative* depicts is a life not rooted to any place – not to Africa, where he was born, and not to England, where he winds up.

And not to South Carolina, either – though according to Vincent Carretta, that is where Equiano was born. Relying on ship registers and baptismal records he uncovered, Carretta claims that Equiano was not African at all, as his title and story insist; the *Narrative*, Carretta concludes, is (however well-informed) a fiction. But Carretta seems to have missed the point of Equiano's story – a story which defies precisely the ideas of place and origin upon which Carretta's 'discovery' relies. Michael Wiley suggests that Carretta's terms are inadequate to account for Equiano's narrative, arguing that Equiano's life 'presents serious problems mostly for interpretations that essentialise geographical identity in a way that the *Narrative* actively resists.'[9] Paul Youngquist raises a similar objection:

> I was bothered by the possibility that the protocols he invoked, institutional memory, historical citation, national origin, and territorial sovereignty, might not be appropriate to a life so miraculously mobile and entrepreneurial as Equiano's. Maybe Carretta had done little more than illustrate the way identity gets produced in the West . . .[10]

For Equiano, identity gets produced on a boat. Before his capture, Equiano was Igbo, identifying with a community, not a continent. Until he was taken to sea, Equiano had no sense of Africa as a coherent or defining space; the continent as a continent only came to matter when 'Africans', based on their colour, became potential property. Africans, in other words, only became Africans outside of Africa – once they were taken on board a slave ship.

But Equiano also became English on board. Almost, anyway. 'I soon grew a stranger to terror of every kind', Equiano writes, 'and was, in that respect at least, almost an Englishman.'[11] The absent terror in question might be read one of two ways: either Equiano is a stranger to *feeling* terror, or he is a stranger to being terror*ised*. The play between the two as definitions of (almost-) Britishness is a play between an idealised national identity, the fearless Britons, and the reality of an Afro-British identity, where the best possible life is one absent of terror. Equiano settles for the latter during his time in the West Indies. 'Going about the different estates on the island', he writes, 'I had all the opportunity I could wish for to see the dreadful usage of the poor men – usage that reconciled me to my situation, and made me bless God for the hands into which I had fallen.'[12] Here is another kind of terror that Equiano is a stranger to. He is *almost* English because he does not get beaten, and the West Indian slaves are African because they do: identity is about the proximity of terror. Moreover, Equiano's exposure to the 'usage' of the West Indian slaves is, more broadly, an exposure to the idea that, as Wiley puts it, 'other physical and cultural spaces – the nations of Europe, for instance . . . might consume and digest Africa.'[13] To be African in the West Indies is to be defined in the context of whiteness and white oppression; the Africans' usage is the terms of their identity. To be African in England, on the other hand, is to layer identities, to allow each to consume the other and be digested into a new whole.

And it is worth keeping in mind that the sort of nation with which Equiano is otherwise imagined to identify is not a universal concept. In fact, the idea of a nation (in either territorial or political terms) was new to Equiano, learned – like the idea of Africa – only once he was captured as a slave. Equiano was born in Essaka, 'one of the most remote and fertile' provinces of Benin, but due to its distance from the capital, Essaka's 'subjection to the king . . . was little more than nominal'.[14] All governmental transactions, Equiano reports, were carried out by the elders of Essaka. They had no commerce with other nations, no notion of Europe or the sea or even a greater 'Africa'. It is no wonder that when he first encountered European slave-traders, Equiano believed they 'had no country, but lived in this hollow place, the ship'.[15] It is a place he would himself later claim to have come from; he was, he writes, 'bred to [the sea]'.[16] Outside the nation in the most literal terms, Equiano is also outside the nation in figurative terms: first as a slave, then as a free sailor, Equiano's spatial experience is circulatory.

Furthermore, it is Equiano's circulation that buys his freedom. Sent to sea as a servant for his master's friend, a captain, Equiano 'endeavoured to try [his] luck and commence merchant'.[17] Despite trouble with locals on shore, Equiano manages fairly well, and hopes, 'by these voyages', to purchase his freedom. Which, eventually, he does. Travel for Equiano is not merely a metaphor for freedom or some expression of it. He does not travel because he is free; rather, he is free because he travels. After finally obtaining his freedom, Equiano meets his former master Captain Pascal in London. 'When he saw me', Equiano writes, 'he appeared a good deal surprised, and asked me how I came back. I answered, "In a ship."'[18] Equiano's answer correct in a larger sense: he returned to London a free man because of what he was able to do at sea.

And yet the freedom of Equiano's travel is unavoidably complicated by the fact that it depends upon and then reproduces, symbolically but also literally, the routes of the Atlantic slave trade. The travel that produces his freedom is the travel of a merchant. He first earns his keep by overseeing slaves in the West Indies; he then participates in the slave trade in the most ironic way, by purchasing himself. His self-purchase, however necessary, is the act of a slaveholder: like any other master, he buys and therefore owns a slave. His *Narrative* is the enacting of that ownership; he is, as his title suggests, literally selling 'the life' of Olaudah Equiano/ Gustavus Vassa/ the African. And he travels the world to do it. Retracing one third of that infamous triangle, Equiano sails to Great Britain – from America to London, London to Liverpool, Liverpool to Dublin, Dublin to Cork, Cork to Belfast, Belfast to Clyde, Clyde to London, London to Soham – and back again. Along the way, Equiano learns that his book travelled even further than he; he 'found persons of note from Holland and Germany, who requested [him] to go there', and reported that his *Narrative* had been 'printed in both places, also in New York'.[19] Equiano's celebration of his own capitalist ventures is seemingly without irony. 'Himself the object of commerce and trade', writes Ross J. Pudaloff,

> Equiano does not, against expectations, caution against the spread of market capitalism that commodifies and alienates people, leading to slavery as its inevitable conclusion. On the contrary, despite his own enslavement, Equiano celebrates commerce and exchange because they make the self a product of exchange. He gains his freedom by purchasing himself and implies that the exchange of money for self can lead to a new and better identity.[20]

That 'new and better' identity is, again, one that is constructed in the terms of a European subjectivity, one that, as Pudaloff suggests, is explicitly based on the exchange of capital. But this is just a stopgap measure, swapping the traded subject for the trading subject. Equiano's best option is to carve out a choice between being commodified and participating in the market economy.

Finally, Equiano takes this measure to its inevitable conclusion, and suggests that, instead of trading in African people, Europe might trade in African goods:

> ... I doubt not, if a system of commerce was established in Africa, the demand for manufactures will most rapidly augment, as the native inhabitants will insensibly adopt the British fashions, manners, customs, &c. In proportion to the civilization, so will be the consumption of British manufactures.[21]

This is a simple substitution – material goods for people – but it is also a substitution of British for African. The assumption is that British ways are universally desirable: who, given the choice, wouldn't want to wear British clothes, adopt British customs? Who wouldn't recognise the superiority of British manners over the savage ways of the African? It is, writes Equiano, 'trading on safe grounds'.[22] He documents the potential economic benefits with precision, offers unquestionable evidence that England will profit: a ship bound for Sierra Leone carried 1,330 pairs of shoes, 'an article hitherto scarcely known to be exported to that country'.[23] From this detail alone one could imagine the prospects of a continent 10,000 miles in circumference – as Equiano points out, 'nearly twice as large as Europe'. Furthermore, he concludes,

> if the blacks were permitted to remain in their own country, they would double themselves every fifteen years. In proportion to such increase will be the demand for manufactures. Cotton and indigo grow spontaneously in most parts of Africa; a consideration this of no small consequence to the manufacturing towns of Great Britain. It opens a most immense, glorious, and happy prospect . . .[24]

This is a logic we know well from the plantation: it is in the economic interests of Britain to let Africans reproduce; 'trading on safe ground', indeed. But the ground is also safe for trading because it is, or at least will be, British; the importation of British goods, and the Africans' adopting of British customs – in short, Britain's economic takeover of Africa – renders Africa effectively a British colony. It will be safe ground, in other words, because it will be British ground.

But Equiano's plans read differently when we remember that Equiano is not just a merchant and a consumer, but a traveller. We might think this in terms of W. Jeffrey Bolster's *Black Jacks*, which broadens our conception of the black seafaring world from the limited movement of slaves through the middle passage, to a network of black travellers that united the entire black Atlantic world. Picture, as Bolster asks us to do, a graphic rendition of the sea, mapping not the exchange of commodities but 'currents of black people in motion carrying and exchanging ideas, information, and style'.[25] These currents, argues Bolster, enabled black sailors and enslaved seamen to 'observe the Atlantic political economy from a variety of vantage points, to subvert their master's discipline, and to open plantation society to outside influence'.[26] In this context, we can see how Equiano's unsettling suggestion about trading with Africa is actually a means of subverting the discipline of the white trading world. To replace the slave trade with the trade of commodities in Africa is actually to reroute trade *to* Africa *from* other places. It is no wonder, then, that Peter Linebaugh and Marcus Rediker cite Equiano as the member of a select group who represent 'the grandest possibility of both their age and ours.'[27] What they call the 'grandest possibility' is, put simply, a knowledge of how to do the most with what already is. Equiano's is a prophecy not unlike Mackandal's, a vision of how what is could be otherwise. He is trying to work the system – and his knowledge of how to do that is a knowledge born of travel, of being always in-between.

Equiano's between-ness, his paradoxical identification as both/neither African and/nor English, manifests itself most clearly in his witnessing, first-hand, the disaster of the first Sierra Leone colony. The colony was an attempt by prominent abolitionists to establish a society in Sierra Leone for free blacks; though fairly well-intentioned, the 1787 endeavour was disastrous. There was a shortage of food and supplies, and the settlers were ravaged by disease; after struggling for a few years, the city was burned to the ground by the indigenous Koya tribe. Equiano had been assigned to the project as its sole black representative, but quickly became disillusioned; as the situation in Sierra Leone deteriorated, Equiano, 'struck with the flagrant abuses committed by the agent, endeavoured to remedy them.'[28] Of this attempted 'remedy', Thomas Boulden Thompson, commander of a ship assigned to transport settlers to Africa, wrote to the Navy Board:

> the conduct of Mr Gustavus Vasa [Equiano], which has been, since he held the situation of Commissary, turbulent and discontented, taking every means to actuate the minds of the Blacks to discord: and I am convinced that unless some means are taken to quell his spirit of sedition, it will be fatal to the peace of the settlement and dangerous to those intrusted with the guiding [of] it.[29]

Thompson's warning is hardly subtle: Equiano could start a slave revolt. Equiano was, unsurprisingly, quickly dismissed from his post. He in turn fought back, publicly claiming that Irwin, agent conductor of the project, had defrauded the government to secure his dismissal, calling Irwin a 'villain' and charging him with the intention of using the Sierra Leone settlers 'the same as they do in the West Indies'.[30] Sierra Leone had been billed as a corrective to the horrors of slavery and the problem of 'misplaced' Africans (ex-slaves and otherwise); Equiano's accusation is that it in fact perpetuates rather than counters the institution of slavery. In this light, Thompson's fear of revolt was not unfounded, grounded as it was in the ubiquitous possibility of a slave uprising. There was, finally, no revolt in Sierra Leone. But it is a specter always hinted at by Equiano's mobility, a mobility that itself highlights the interconnectedness of Atlantic spaces and, therefore, the potential of revolution to erupt at any moment.

A Savage-Looking Set

The second Sierra Leone colony was a site ripe for just such a revolution. After the failure of the first colony in 1789, John Clarkson (brother of abolitionist Thomas Clarkson) tried again, recruiting over 1,000 blacks from Nova Scotia. This was, perhaps, the first problem, since the number of people who volunteered was over twice the number that the Sierra Leone Company had planned for. After a tragic voyage, with 60 people dead from illness, the settlers arrived in Freetown (as their settlement was named) to find no structure in place. Rations grew short, promises of land and care were broken or never kept at all.[31] A. M. Falconbridge was the wife of Sierra Leone agent Alexander Falconbridge, and she relays her story of the settlement in her 1802 *Narrative of Two Voyages to the River Sierra Leone During the Years 1791-2-3*. The book is a collection of letters which, Falconbridge claims, were 'written without any design or intention of sending them into the world'. But encouraged by friends, she decided to publish them because she believed the Sierra Leone settlement to be 'a Colony, whose success or *downfall* ... the Inhabitants, at least the thinking part, of almost every civilized country, must feel more or less interested about'.[32] This is a surprising declaration: Sierra Leone was a black colony in a distant land with no clear impact on the economics or politics of Europe. But it was also a society that started from scratch; in this respect, the struggle of the Briton who desired its 'improvement' is the struggle to tame Sierra Leone into a British colony. The question of Falconbridge's *Narrative* becomes a question of how to keep a society of oppressed people from revolting.

In the blank-slate outpost of the nation, order, above all else, had to be guarded. It is for this reason that Falconbridge agreed with a decision by Clarkson to arrest fleeing slave-ship sailors. Seamen had begun to take refuge in Freetown, which despite terrible conditions was nevertheless preferable to the poor treatment to which sailors on slave ships were subjected. Threatened with lawsuits by angry shipmasters, Clarkson found himself, as Falconbridge puts it, in an 'awkward situation', as 'his orders [were] to *protect every man*'. He was, she reports, 'at a loss of what to do'. But with a little compromise he found his way, issuing a declaration to be posted around the Colony:

> This is to give Notice, that I will not on any account, permit Seamen, who may leave their respective Vessels, to take shelter in this Colony; and I shall give orders in the future, that the Constables seize every man who cannot give a good account of himself, or whom they may suspect to have deserted from their employ.[33]

His only concession to the fleeing sailors was that he would 'be always ready to listen to the complaints of every injured man ...

provided they make application in a proper manner.'³⁴ The settlement was intended as a semi-revolutionary haven for the oppressed, but its top-down organisation meant it could not, in the end, 'protect every man'. Falconbridge insists that, however 'desirable' abolition may be, it is nevertheless 'much to be lamented' that 'property of individuals in that trade should be harassed and annoyed by want of order and regularity in this Colony, or by the fanatical prejudices of any set of men'.³⁵ The possibility that the colony will lack 'order and regularity' is, for Falconbridge, the primary risk. The Sierra Leone colony finally can go one of two ways: the way of the French and Haitians, or the way of the British.

The 'renegade seamen' Clarkson was so desperate to control were the spectre of what could happen in the colony, just as the French and Haitian Revolutions were a model of how the black settlers might finally take over. Falconbridge never mentions Haiti, but she does relay the report of a captain who encountered some French corsairs – 'republican ragamuffins', she calls them – who had taken their revolution to the sea. The captain 'never saw such a savage looking set in his life', he says:

> They all had on horsemen's caps (having a tin plate in front, with the emblem of *Death's head and marrow bones*, and underneath inscribed, 'Liberty, or Death)', a leather belt round their waist, with a brace of pistols, and a sabre, and they looked so dreadfully ferocious, that one would suppose them capable of eating every Englishman they met with, *without salt or gravy*.³⁶

The French revolutionary slogan, *Liberté, Egalité, Fraternité*, has morphed into the call of the American Revolutionary war, Patrick Henry's 'Give me liberty or give me death'. The conflation of these two revolutions suggests that the death the corsairs swear to choose over enslavement is not only their own but the death of the English, modelled by the success of American republicanism in the Revolutionary War and the symbolic triumph of the republic over the monarchy in France. These 'republican ragamuffins' are an embodiment of the kind of government that results when common people seize control, a narrative of the oppressed defeating the powerful: those who have no cake defeating those with plenty, or, unspoken here, slaves defeating their masters. Certainly, as was the case with other Atlantic pirates, these corsairs were a threat not only to British social order but also to its materialisation in the form of British commerce. Falconbridge mourns that the Orpheus, a ship sent out to protect British trade on the coast of Africa, missed the French corsairs by a few days; the corsairs were therefore able to 'considerably annoy' British trading. To revolt militarily, economically, or politically against a legitimate government, Falconbridge and the captain seem to suggest, is necessarily to turn pirate.

Falconbridge's use of the term 'corsair' here is telling as well. Corsairs were similar to privateers, but they were authorised by religious rather than national authority. Though there were Christian corsairs, most eighteenth- and nineteenth-century corsairs were Barbary corsairs whose targets were Christian European ships trading in the Mediterranean and along the western coast of Africa. To call these French revolutionaries 'corsairs', then, is to align them with Muslims; these corsairs might finally devour British religion, order, and commerce.[37] The danger of the Sierra Leone colonists following in the way of the French revolutionaries was very real (though the potential for revolution was more aptly demonstrated by the revolts in St Domingo than by the storming of the Bastille). After the controversial dismissal of Clarkson from his post as director, the colonists, still lacking food and the most basic supplies, wrote to Clarkson's successor, William Dawes, 'harass[ing him] with insults, in hopes he may take it in his head to be disgusted and march off', says Falconbridge.[38] Among these 'harassments' was an articulated threat of revolution: after receiving news of the death of King Louis XVI, settlers wrote to Dawes hinting that he might come to a similar end.[39] But Falconbridge maintained hope that the British might yet make proper Britons of the Africans:

> ... I am sure they thirst for literature; therefore, if seminaries were established on different parts of the coast, and due attention paid to the morals and manners of the rising generation, I do not question but their geniuses would ripen into ideas congenial with our own; and that posterity would behold them, emerged from that vortex of disgrace, in which they have been overwhelmed since time immemorial, establishing social, political, and commercial connections throughout the globe, and even see them *blazing* among the *literati* of their age.[40]

To develop as a nation is to develop into something decidedly British – geniuses 'ripen into ideas congenial with our own' – and so to imagine a global network is, for Falconbridge, to imagine multiple Britains linked to one another across oceans. Here is the alternative to that other global network within which Sierra Leone was inscribed: Gilroy's Black Atlantic, which brought news of France to Haiti, and news of Haiti to Sierra Leone. This is why Sierra Leone should matter to the citizens of 'almost every civilized nation': its 'success or downfall' was less a marker of the viability of European charity than of the extent to which oppressed peoples could be controlled. It turns out that they could not.

A Three-Fingered Toussaint

'A sooty African *can* become a Toussaint L'Ouverture, a murderous Three-Fingered Jack', warned Thomas Carlyle in 1839.[41] At its most innocent, this equation is just bad math. Touissant led a revolution that resulted in a free nation of former slaves; 'Three-Fingered' Jack Mansong failed in his own attempted slave revolt, before escaping to the hills to terrorise passers-by for less than a year before he was captured and murdered. But Carlyle wasn't the first or the last to elevate Three-Fingered Jack to the level of Toussaint; Jack was, and continues to be, a hero of epic proportions. The question is why.

The first historical document we have about Jack is a Jamaican newspaper article from August 1780, shortly after he had escaped from his plantation. The article tells of a 'gang of runaway Negroes of above 40 men, and about 18 women', who were stealing sheep, goats, poultry, and 'particularly a large herd of hogs from Mr. Rial'; it warns that 'these banditti may soon become dangerous to the Public'.[42] In December of that year, Jack became the first Jamaican fugitive to have a bounty placed on his head, when the governor of Jamaica offered £100 for his capture, and the House Assembly added another £200 to that and promised freedom to any slave who killed Three-Fingered Jack. Jack was tracked down shortly after by maroon bounty hunters, but he didn't go easily: he was shot three times and threw himself down a forty-foot precipice before he was finally decapitated by one of the maroons. They carried his head and his three-fingered hand back to Kingston in a bucket of rum to claim the reward.

William Earle's epistolary novel *Obi, or the History of Three-Fingered Jack* was written nine years after Jack's death, while the most successful slave revolt of all time was raging in soon-to-be Haiti. Earle's fictionalised account of Jack is a collection of letters from an Englishman named George Stanford, who is residing in Jamaica, written to a friend back in England. It is primarily a domestic tale, beginning with Jack's father's violent death aboard a slave ship and his mother's vow to 'curse the European race forever' and to 'nurture the baneful passion of revenge' in her only son Jack.[43] Srinivas Aravamudan argues in his introduction to the novel that 'Earle's decision to opt for the genre of family romance rather than describe Jack more overtly as a precursor to full-fledged political rebellion produces definite limitations.'[44] We can imagine several such limitations, not least among them a trivialisation of Jack's role as a revolutionary. And yet it might also be that, despite the primacy of the family narrative, Earle is raising – without actually raising – the possibility of an independent nation of former slaves. I would suggest that he accomplishes this in part by drawing a stark distinction between true Britishness and what passes for Britishness in the West Indies, a distinction which makes it possible to criticise the British without criticising the imagined essence of Britishness. But perhaps most crucially, Earle employs the rhetoric of European heroism in order to celebrate the heroism of the slave; this is a delicate manoeuvre, aligning Jack's promise to destroy the British with the British whom he has sworn to destroy.

I am therefore more interested here in the language of Earle and his narrator than I am in the novel's plot. The epistolary framing of the narrative is itself framed by Earle's brief opening advertisement, which concludes by dedicating the book 'to him who shall applaud Jack through the varied scenes of his life; to him, whose heart shall sympathize in his misfortunes, who shall smile upon his deeds, at the same time that he laments their cause'.[45] This is not, at least as Earle presents it, a narrative intended to convert anyone: the intended readers of *Obi* already despise the slave trade enough that they will celebrate Jack's murders. Naturally, Stanford will echo Earle's – and Earle's imagined audience's – sentiments. His first letter home recounts an argument which Stanford claims he will have with 'every cruel, hard-hearted planter' – 'until the last hour of [his] life':

- Man cannot be slave to Man.
- He is my property.
- How did you acquire that property?
- By paying for it.
- Paying! Paying whom?
- Him who brought him from Africa.
- How did he get possession of him?
- He caught him there.
- And what became of that robber?[46]

It is notable that Stanford, like Equiano, traffics in the capitalist terms of the slave-trade: the African is property. The twist here is that the African, as a sovereign subject, is his *own* property; strangely, then, he might well be stolen from himself. Stanford goes on to compare the crime of the slave-trader to the crime of the starving man who, in an attempt to provide for his children, 'goes on the highway and frightens the traveler out of a few pieces of gold'. This man, he says, is hanged, while the slave-trader, that 'daring ruffian, who is openly guilty of a crime more heinous in its nature and baneful in its effects, goes respected by every body and pass[es] his days in the peaceable enjoyment of riches acquired by such infamous means'.[47] But Jack is not a desperate father out to secure food for his children; in making this comparison, Stanford defangs the very real threat of Jack and of slave violence more generally.

To the extent that Stanford is himself a character in the novel, he occupies a middle ground between the planters and the slaves, between two kinds of West Indians. When Stanford tells the story of Jack's mother's capture, he claims that its purpose is to 'delineate the character of a European West-Indian'.[48] The character of the European West Indian is the character of the slave-trader, but it is this notion of a *European* West Indian – within the colonial system, not at all a contradiction – that Earle's novel puts pressure on. Stanford, after all, is a European West Indian too. When, overcome with emotion, he must break off a letter, he resumes his next by bidding, 'Adieu to the impulse of the moment, to the feeling tear! I am a West-Indian again, and can proceed.'[49] While this is clearly an indictment of the heartlessness of the planters, it is also an acknowledgment of Stanford's own complicated identity: West Indian when he sympathises with Jack and European West Indian when he can tell the violent tale without weeping. This fluidity of identity is much at play in *Obi*, most evident in the frequent and vexed use of the term 'countrymen'. Early in his tale, Stanford writes, 'Think not that I mean to revile my countrymen; those are not my countrymen, whose inhumanity is the subject of my page. They may be Britons born, but not Britons at heart.'[50] Stanford assumes, here, an ideal of Britishness that is at odds with the British practices that make Jack's depredations necessary.

Also in question is Jack's own identity, his own relationship to a 'country'; Earle frames Jack's tale in national terms. He writes in the advertisement:

> I have published these letters . . . with a view to commemorate the name of Jack, and place upon the list of heroes, one who, had he shown in a higher sphere, would have proved as bright a luminary as ever graced the Roman annals, or ever boldly asserted the rights of a Briton. His cause was great and noble, for to private wrongs he added the liberty of his countrymen, and stood alone a bold and daring defender of the rights of Man.[51]

Here Jack's cause is situated in a tradition of resistance that has antiquity as its origin and Jamaica as its end. Collapsing the Roman hero with the British hero with Jack, Earle re-situates the domestic tale as a collective one: Jack's avenging of his father's death becomes an avenging of the wrongs committed against all slaves. But he also, and most crucially, figures slave revolution in European terms – a little British, a little French, and a lot Roman. Benjamin Mosley's 1799 *Treatise on Sugar* (a source text for Earle's novel) makes a similar gesture, claiming that Jack had 'ascended above Spartacus'.[52] Despite Jack's heroics, it is difficult to imagine in what sense he might have outshone Spartacus, that great slave leader who conquered at least seven Roman armies before his death. This hyperbole is not unlike Carlyle's comparison of Jack to Toussaint; the scale is off. But the comparatively small scale of Jack's tale is precisely the point: Jack's revolution is no less a revolution for not having existed in that 'higher sphere'. This, more than any litany of crimes, is why Jack is such a force of terror and heroism. Earle's novel is not a story about one man's rebellion or one gang's attacks; it is about where revolution comes from: not only what directly produces it – here, the mistreatment of slaves – but even more, the fact of a broader revolutionary tradition in which any individual eruption takes part. In Stanford's first description of Jack, he writes:

> Jack was every thing in soul and person requisite for the hero. Give me now a short pause. Sketch the man as you would wish—a bold and daring fellow, ready to undertake any thing for the *good of his country*, inspired by a rooted revenge, on the strongest foundation villainy can fabricate, Jack's the man to a point.[53] (italics mine)

The term 'country' functions here in several ways. It seems in part to bear an implied 'men', in that Jack fights for his countrymen in the West Indies; more symbolically, Jack fights for his country in that he fights for its honour. But it is also the case that Jack fights for 'his country' that does not exist: the as-yet unrealised nation of free Africans in Jamaica. The Jack who is fighting for his country is Jack as Toussaint; his bravery is tied to defence of one's country rather than defence of one's person. Carlyle fears the 'sooty African's' potential; and the threat (and promise) of Jack's story is that that potential is always and everywhere present.

Prophets of Revolution

In the same year Falconbridge arrived in Sierra Leone, St Domingo started on the path to become what Sierra Leone and Jamaica could not: a free black nation. On the night of 14 August 1791, Maroon leader and voodoo priest Dutty Boukman gathered slaves in Bois Caïman and delivered a prayer that doubled as a call-to-arms; a week later, on 21 August, the revolution began. Within a few weeks, the revolting slaves numbered 100,000; by 1792, slaves controlled a third of the island. Finally, on the first of January 1804, Haiti became an independent nation.

The Haitian Revolution is a chapter that is frequently omitted from British history; even in eighteenth-century abolitionist texts, the Haitian Revolution was often invisible.[54] But while Britain was at war with France, it was also deeply invested – ideologically and militarily – in the revolution in St Domingo. And despite its elision from current accounts of British history, as well as from most abolitionist texts of the period, the Haitian Revolution remains perhaps the greatest revolutionary success of the era. I do not mean here to idealise the nation that emerged, but rather to reassert the importance and pervasiveness of a spirit of resistance that had concrete effects. Carlyle's equation of Toussaint and Jack Mansong, a collapse of both time and place, connects revolution to revolution and marks an anxiety about revolutionary potential more generally. The fear, racialised and implicitly classed, is that revolution might emerge anywhere and that it might succeed; Carlyle's warning echoes the warnings of the maroons and revolutionaries themselves. The Haitian Revolution was promised by both word and action: Mackandal, Jack, and even Equiano were its prophets. They created a network of resistance which spanned, as Carlyle's warning accidentally implied, both time and space.

Notes

1. Erin Skye Mackie, *Rakes, Highwaymen, and Pirates: The Making of the Modern Gentleman in the Eighteenth Century* (Baltimore: Johns Hopkins University Press, 2009), 128.
2. Erin Mackie, 'Welcome the Outlaw: Pirates, Maroons, and Caribbean Countercultures', *Cultural Critique*, no. 59 (1 January 2005): 47.
3. Though in the early eighteenth century, there were nearly 3,000 French slaves living in marronage in the Spanish colony of Santa Domingo alone, Mackandal was, argues Carolyn E. Fick, 'by far the most extraordinary and awesome' of the pre-revolutionary maroon leaders. [Carolyn E Fick, *The Making of Haiti: The Saint Domingue Revolution from Below*, 1st edn (Knoxville: University of Tennessee Press, 1990), 59.]
4. There are two differing stories of the impetus for his escape from his master. In one version, he escaped after he lost his hand in a sugar-mill accident. The other version has him in a dispute with his master over 'a young and beautiful negress'; after refusing the fifty lashes with which he was to be punished, he escaped to the woods. [Fick, *The Making of Haiti*, 60; Laurent Dubois, *Avengers of the New World: The Story of the Haitian Revolution* (Cambridge, MA: Belknap Press of Harvard University Press, 2004).]
5. Fick, *The Making of Haiti*, 61; Dubois, *Avengers of the New World*, 55.
6. Fick, *The Making of Haiti*, 61.
7. Ibid., 495; Dubois, *Avengers of the New World*, 56.

8. Paul Youngquist, 'The Afro Futurism of DJ Vassa', *European Romantic Review* 16, no. 9, Literature Online (2005): 188.
9. Michael Wiley, *Romantic Migrations: Local, National, and Transnational Dispositions* (New York: Macmillan, 2008), 137.
10. Marcus Rediker argues that even if Carretta is correct, Equiano merely 'becomes the oral historian, the keeper of the common story, the griot of sorts, of the slave trade, which means that his account is no less faithful to the original experience, only different in its sources or genesis.' [Youngquist, 'The Afro Futurism of DJ Vassa.', 183; Marcus Buford Rediker, *The Slave Ship: A Human History* (New York: Viking, 2007), 109.]
11. Olaudah Equiano, *The Interesting Narrative and Other Writings* (New York: Penguin Books, 2003), 77.
12. Ibid., 103.
13. Michael Wiley, 'Consuming Africa: Geography and Identity in Olaudah Equiano's "Interesting Narrative"', *Studies in Romanticism* 44, no. 2 (1 July 2005): 165.
14. Equiano, *The Interesting Narrative and Other Writings*, 32.
15. Ibid., 57.
16. Ibid., 166.
17. Ibid., 116.
18. Ibid., 165.
19. Ibid., 235.
20. Ross J. Pudaloff, 'No Change Without Purchase: Olaudah Equiano and the Economics of Self a Market', *Early American Literature* 40, no. 3 (2005): 2.
21. Equiano, *The Interesting Narrative and Other Writings*, 233.
22. Ibid., 234.
23. Ibid., 305.
24. Ibid., 233, 235.
25. W. Jeffrey Bolster, *Black Jacks: African American Seamen in the Age of Sail* (Cambridge, MA: Harvard University Press, 1997), 21.
26. Ibid., 26.
27. Peter Linebaugh, *The Many-Headed Hydra: The Hidden History of the Revolutionary Atlantic* (Boston: Beacon Press, 2000), 333.
28. Equiano had reservations from the beginning: 'I pointed out to [the committee] many objections to my going', he writes, 'and particularly I expressed some difficulties on the account of the slave-dealers, as I would certainly oppose their traffic in the human species by every means in my power.' He was persuaded, though, and became the only black representative on the committee; 'as a black man', writes Vincent Carretta, 'he was probably presumed to be a more welcome emissary to African

leaders from the British government than a European would be.' And Equiano, Carretta continues 'took his charge as the government's representative very seriously – perhaps too seriously.' Equiano also made some serious mistakes, reports Carretta, administrative and practical oversights – enough, judges Caretta, to justify his dismissal. Carretta argues that 'despite the opinion of some historians, little evidence supports the contention that Equiano's dismissal was racially motivated'. [Gates, *The Classic Slave Narratives: The Life of Olaudah Equiano / The History of Mary Prince / Narrative of the Life of Frederick Douglass* (Prentice Hall, 2000), 171; Vincent Carretta, *Equiano, the African: Biography of a Self-Made Man* (Athens: University of Georgia Press, 2005), 226–30; Olaudah Equiano, 'For the Public Advertiser', in *The Interesting Narrative and Other Writings*, 327–8.]

29. Carretta, *Equiano, the African*, 229.
30. Ibid., 230.
31. Settlers were given a fifth of the land they had been promised, and they were – despite promises to the contrary – charged land tax. Later, Clarkson's replacement William Dawes would force the settlers to relinquish their land (moving them away from the waterfront and reassigning those desirable lots to white Company officials). Dawes informed the settlers that Clarkson was in the habit of making 'prodigal and extraordinary promises without thinking of them afterwards,' and that he 'more than probable *was drunk* when he made them.' [A. M. Falconbridge, *Narrative of Two Voyages to the River Sierra Leone During the Years 1791–1792–1793* (Liverpool: Liverpool University Press, 2000), 70.]
32. Ibid., vii.
33. Ibid., 171.
34. Ibid., 171–2.
35. Ibid., 172.
36. Ibid., 221.
37. That the revolutionaries look like cannibals is reminiscent of European (most often spurious) accounts of the cannibalism of African natives. Equiano turns this trope on its head, describing how newly captured black slaves feared that the white slave traders would eat them.
38. Falconbridge writes, 'This cannot in any way be rationally accounted for, but it is universally supposed the directors have been betrayed into an act of prejudicial to their interests, and the welfare of their Colony, by listening to some malicious, and cowardly representations, sent home by certain persons here, who are fully capable of assassinating the most immaculate character, if thereby they can acquire latitude for their boundless ambition, or, for a moment, quench their

unconscionable thirst for power. No language can perfectly describe how much the generality of people are chagrined on this occasion; they have added to their petition the most earnest solicitation for Mr. Clarkson to be sent out again.' [Falconbridge, *Narrative of Two Voyages to the River Sierra Leone During the Years 1791–1792–1793*, 224–5.]

39. Ibid., 225.
40. Ibid., 239.
41. Thomas Carlyle, *Chartism* (James Frases, 1840), 60.
42. William Earle, *Obi, Or, The History of Three-fingered Jack*, ed. Srinivas Aravamudan (Broadview Press, 2005), 10.
43. Ibid., 71.
44. Ibid., 51.
45. Ibid., 68.
46. Ibid., 70.
47. Ibid.
48. Ibid., 82.
49. Ibid., 96.
50. Ibid., 82.
51. Ibid., 17.
52. Benjamin Mosley, Treatise on Sugar (1799), in *Obi, Or, The History of Three-fingered Jack*, ed. Srinivas Aravamudan, 65.
53. Earle, *Obi, Or, The History of Three-fingered Jack*, 73.
54. Marcus Rainsford's 1805 *An Historical Account of the Black Empire of Hayti* is a notable exception. [Marcus Rainsford, *An Historical Account of the Black Empire of Hayti*, ed. Gregory Pierrot and Paul Youngquist (Durham: Duke University Press, 2013).]

Index

References to illustrations indicated by *italics*.

abstract space, 16n15
Account of Timbuctoo and Housa (Jackson), 137–9
Adams, Charles Hansford
  on *The Narrative of Robert Adams*, 134–5
  Robert Adams' travel, 142–3
Adams, Robert, 123
  Account of Timbuctoo and Housa (Jackson), 137
  African Company, 127, 129–30, 131–2
  Barbary captivity, 132–3, 134
  British colonialism and, 143
  conversion attempts, 133–4
  Dupuis on, 132
  The Narrative of Robert Adams, 14, 130–6
  racial identity, 132–3
  travel, 142–3
African Association, 124–5, 144n6
  African Company comparison, 129
  Clapperton, Hugh, 126–7
  de Gama on, 130
  Laing, Gordon, 127
  Park, Mungo, 125–6
  Timbuktu descriptions, 125
  Willis, James, 125
African Company, 127
  Adams, Robert, 129–30, 131–2
  African Association comparison, 129
  British colonial power and, 135–6
  slave trade and, 127–8
African Institution, 130
African interior, 123–4
  African Association, 124–5
  Clapperton, Hugh, 126–7
  descriptions, 144n11
  exploration, 124–7, 143n2, 144n3
  Laing, Gordon, 127
  Park, Mungo, 125–6
  see also Timbuktu
Africanus, Leo, 125
Albion, Blake and, 91
Anderson, Benedict, *Imagined Communities: Reflections on the Origin and Spread of Nationalism*, 9
Aravamudan, Srinivas, *Tropicopolitans: Colonialsm and Agency, 1688-1804*, 9
Association for Promoting the Discovery of the Interior Parts of Africa *see* African Association

Baker, Samuel, *Written on the Water*, 8
Banks, Joseph, 124–5
　on Park's exploration, 126
Barbary captivity narratives, 132–4
　fear of conversion, 147n43
Barbary pirates, 36n5
Barrow, John, on Caillié, 139, 141
Battle of Bossenden, 85
Beaufoy, Henry, 123
belief as labour, 121n59
Benton, Lauren, *A Search for Sovereignty*, 5
Black Bart, 19
Black Jacks (Bolster), 158
black pirates, 22–4
　Captain Mission and, 31
Black Romanticism, 9
　British national identity and, 9
black sailors, 158
Blackbeard, 10–11, 20
　description, 21, 22
　early accounts, 19
　symbolism of beard, 22
Blake, William
　Anglocentrism, 91–2
　England as Jerusalem, 100–2
　Golgonooza, 92–3
　Jerusalem, 91–3, 100–9
　Jerusalem imagined, 13, 14, 91
　as prophet, 117n30
　'To the Jews', 100–1
　universalism, 109–10
　Vision of the Last Judgement, 106–7, 108
Bolster, W. Jeffrey, *Black Jacks*, 158
Bonny, Anne, 19
Borges, Jorges Luis, maps scale, 15n2

Boukman, Dutty, 167–8
Brenner, Neil, *State/Space: A Reader*, 7
The Bride of Abydos (Byron), 11, 12, 42–8
　'No Land Beyond My Saber's Length', 45
British Romanticism, 9
Britons: Forging the Nation, 1701–1837 (Colley), 9
Brothers, Richard, 12, 13, 67–8
　arrest, 76
　attempt to flee the Lord, 76
　A Correct Account of the Invasion and Conquest . . ., 81
　as descendent of Jesus' brother, 76, 80
　A Description of Jerusalem, Its Houses and Streets, Squares, Colleges, Markets, and Cathedrals, the Royal and Private Places, 76–85
　donations to Jerusalem, 83–4
　Holy Land's population, 82
　imperialism and new Jerusalem, 84–5
　labour, 78–9
　Letter to Miss Cott, 83
　London as spiritual Babylon, 82–3
　one from sea, 78–9
Byron, George Gordon, Lord
　The Bride of Abydos, 11, 12, 42, 43–4, 46–8
　Childe Harold, 41
　The Corsair, 11, 12, 42, 43–4, 49–52
　corsairs, 45
　Don Juan, 12, 56–61
　French Revolution and, 42–4
　Katsonis, Lambro, 43–4, 47

Byron (*Cont.*)
   'No Land Beyond my Saber's Length', 45
   pirate poems, 11, 42
   quitting poetry, 44–5
   travel, 65n34, 65n35
Byronic Philhellenism, 62n12

Caillié, René, 140
   Travels to Central Africa to Timbuctoo, 139, 148n58
cannibalism fears of slaves, 170n37
capitalism, piracy and, 26
Captain Avery, 19
Captain Kidd, 19
Captain Mission, 29
   Captain Tew and, 33–4
   Caraccioli and, 29–32
   Libertalia, 32–4
   rights for Africans, 31
Captain Teach *see* Blackbeard
Captain Tew, 33–4
Captives (Colley), 98–9
Caraccioli, Captain Mission and, 29–32
Carlyle, Thomas, Three-Fingered Jack as Toussaint, 163
Carretta, Vincent, on Equiano, 154
cartographer's mad project, 2
cartography, war and, 3
Childe Harold (Byron), 41
Christian Zionists, 98
Clapperton, Hugh, 126–7
Clarkson, John
   settlement plans, 160
   Sierra Leone Company, 159–60
   slave-ship sailors, 160–1
coastal fraternity of pirates, 24
Cohen, Margaret, *The Novel and the Sea*, 8

Colley, Linda
   Britons: Forging the Nation, 1701–1837, 9
   Captives, 98–9
colonialism
   African Company and, 135–6
   ocean's resistance, 41
colonisation
   Eden and, 68
   maps and, 4
Company of Merchants Trading to Africa *see* African Company
A Correct Account of the Invasion and Conquest . . . (Brothers), 81
The Corsair (Byron), 11, 12, 42–4, 49–52
   Lafitte, Jean, 52–4
corsairs, 162
Courtenay, William Percy Honeywood, 85–6
creole negros, 22
cultural geographers, 6–7
cultural mixing, Blackbeard and, 22

da Gama, Vasco, 129–30
d'Anville, Jean Baptiste Bourguignon, 15n1
Dawes, William, settlement plans, 162–3, 170n31
A Description of Jerusalem, Its Houses and Streets, Squares, Colleges, Markets, and Cathedrals, the Royal and Private Places (Brothers), 76–85
Don Juan (Byron), 12, 56–61
Dupuis, Joseph, 131–2
   on Adams, 132

Earle, William, *Obi: Or the History of Three-Fingered Jack*, 150, 164–5
the East, 67–8
economic system
  piracy and, 24–6
  traitor, term use, 25
Eden, colonisation and, 68
England, as historical site of Jerusalem, 100–2, 103
Equiano, Olaudah, 149, 169n28
  Gustavus Vassa, 153–4
  identities, 154–5, 156–7
  The Interesting Narrative and Other Writings, 149, 150, 153–4
  origins, 154
  purchase of self, 156–8
  Sierra Leone, 158–9
  trading on safe grounds, 157–8
  travels, 156
Europe, pirate's defiance, 28–34

Falconbridge, Alexander, 160
Falconbridge, Anna Maria, 149
  corsairs, 162
  Narrative of Two Voyages to the River Sierra Leone, 149–50, 160
  republican ragamuffins, 161–2
  slave trade, 160–1
Ferrara, Mark, on *Jerusalem* (Blake), 91–3
The First Book of Wonders (Southcott), 74–5
Fly, William, 28
Foulahs in Timbuktu, 127
The Fourth Book of Wonders (Southcott), 72–3
French Revolution
  Byron and, 42–4

Sierra Leone and, 161–2
space, power of, 6

A General History of the Pirates (Johnson), 10–11
  authorship questions, 36n1
  Blackbeard, 20: description, 21–2
  causes of piracy, 28
  post-piratical piracy, 29–30
A General History of the Pyrates (Johnson), 19
geography
  beginnings, 3
  cultural geographers, 6–7
geometrical space, 17n20
Gillray, James, *The plumb-pudding in danger: – or – state epicures taking un petit souper*, x, 3–4
Golgonooza, 92–3, 100–2, 117n31, 117n34

Haitian Revolution, 167–8
heteronormativity, pirates and, 37n13
The Holy Land
  population plans, 99, 115n21
  Protestants' absence, 96–7
Hone, William
  Hone's Lord Byron's Corsair Contrade, The Corsair: or, The Pirate's Isle, 54–6
  Lord Byron's The Corsair, 11, 12, 42
  piracy of Byron's work, 54–6, 62n21, 62n22
Hopkins, James, *A Woman to Deliver Her People: Joanna Southcott and English Millenarianism in an Era of Revolution*, 69–70
Hydra, 111–12

Imagined Communities: Reflections on the Origin and Spread of Nationalism (Anderson), 9
imperialism
   Jerusalem and, 13
   maps and, 6
inhabited space, 17n20
The Interesting Narrative and Other Writings (Equiano), 149, 150, 153–4
Islam, conversion fears in Barbary captivity narratives, 133–4, 147n43; see also Muslims

Jackson, James Grey, *Account of Timbuctoo and Housa*, 137, 138, 139
Japhet as British ancestor, 116n28
Jerusalem
   Brothers and, 12–13
   Chateaubriand, François-René de, 95
   Christian Zionists, 98
   colonial interests of Britain, 95
   descriptions countering Biblical one, 95–6, 114n14
   England as historical site, 100–2, 103
   versus literary representation, 13–14
   Southcott and, 12–13
   Volney, Constantin François, 96
   Wilson, William Rae, 95–6
   see also New Jerusalem
Jerusalem (Blake), 91–3
   Britain and, 92–3
   city scattered abroad, 107–8
   copies, 120n50
   description of city, 100–2
   divisions of Christians, Jews and Deists, 107–9, 118n44
   eternal city, 118n41
   Ferrara on, 91–3
   Los's journey, 102–3, *104–5*, 106, 117n35, 117n36
   Muslims, 107–8
   nations, 93–4
   Negroland, 93, 94
   Polypus, 109–11, 112, 120n51, 120n53, 120n55
   readership, 119n45
   sinful nation of Albion, 109
Jerusalem: The Emanation of the Giant Albion, 104–5
Johnson, Charles, *A General History of the Pyrates*, 10–11, 19
Jomard, Edmé-François, Barrow, and, 139, 141
Journey in Egypt and in Syria (Volney), 96

Katsonis, Lambro, 43–4, 47

Lafitte, Jean, 52–4
   Byron's Conrad and, 62n15
Laing, Gordon, 127
Lefebvre, Henri, 7
   The Production of Space, 5
Letter to Miss Cott (Brothers), 83
Libertailia of Captain Mission, 32–4
Linebaugh, Peter, *The Many-Headed Hydra: Sailors, Slaves, Commoners, and the Hidden History of the Revolutionary Atlantic*, 8, 24, 111, 158
London Jews Society, 98, 99, 116n25

The London Society for Promoting Christianity Among the Jews, 98, 99
Lord Byron *see* Byron, George Gordon, Lord
Lord Byron's The Corsair (Hone), 11, 12, 42

Mackandal, François, 149
  maroon society, 151–3
Mackie, Erin Skye, 151
Mansong, Jack *see* Three-Fingered Jack
The Many-Headed Hydra: Sailors, Slaves, Commoners, and the Hidden History of the Revolutionary Atlantic (Linebaugh and Rediker), 8, 24, 111, 158
maps, 2
  class distinctions and, 16n10
  colonisation and, 4
  d'Anville's map of Africa, 15n1
  empire and, 3
  imperial power, 6
  ordering directives, 6
  scale, 15n2
  sovereignty and, 5, 6
maroons, 150–1
  Mackandal, François, 151–3
  see also pirates
Mather, Cotton, pirates' final words, 28–9, 38n28
mental space, 17n20
Mosley, Benjamin, *Treatise on Sugar*, 164–7
mulatto, racial fears, 22
Murray, John, and *The Narrative of Robert Adams*, 130–1
Muslims
  absence from Blake's work, 108
  Barbary captive-taking, 116n23
  Caillié, René, posing as, 139
  Qur'an, naming of, 119n49
  Shabeeny in Timbuktu, 137
  Société de Géographie and, 138–9
  see also Islam

Napoleon
  Palestine invasion, 95
  plum-pudding world, 3–4
  Siege of Acre, 99–100
The Narrative of Robert Adams a Barbary Captive (Adams), 14, 130–1, 132
  Adams, Charles Hansford and, 134–5
  Britons and, 134–5
  spoofs, 135–6
Narrative of Two Voyages to the River Sierra Leone (Falconbridge), 149–50, 160
nation
  pirates and national law, 27
  pirates' disaffiliation, 10–12, 27
  see also state
national identity, pirate crews and, 24
Negroland in Blake's Jerusalem, 93, 94
New Jerusalem
  Brothers, 76–84
  Southcott's, 69
Nineteenth Century Transatlantic Studies series (Ashgate), 8–9
The Novel and the Sea (Cohen), 8

Obi: Or the History of Three-Fingered Jack (Earle), 150, 164–5

Olsson, Gunnar, 6
Ottoman Empire
    pirate poems of Byron, 42, 50, 64n26
    Protestants' absence, 97

Park, Mungo, 125–6, 145n17
    Travels in the Interior Districts of Africa, 126
physical space, 17n20
piracy
    capitalism and, 26
    economic system and, 24–6
    revolution and, 162
    as service industry, 26
    socio-economic causes, 28
    war on, 27–36
    wealth redistribution and, 26
pirate crews
    cultural mixing and, 22–3
    national identity, ideas of, 24
    social organisation, 24
pirate poems of Lord Byron, 11, 42
pirates
    Barbary pirates, 36n5
    black, 22–3
    Blackbeard, 10–11
    Captain Avery, 19
    Captain Kidd, 19
    Captain Mission, 29–34
    Captain Teach *see* Blackbeard
    Captain Tew, 33–4
    as coastal fraternity, 24
    colonists as, 40n47
    cultural definition *versus* legal, 27
    defiance of Europe, 28–34
    disaffiliation with nation, 27
    effects, 10
    flag, 14
    heteronormativity and, 37n13
    last words, 28–9
    legal status, 21
    maritime society and, 151
    maroons, 150–1
    modern conception, 19, 21
    national law and, 27
    radicalism and, 2
    rejection of nation, 10–12
    revolutionary spirit and, 1
    social structure, 21, 37n15, 151
    territorial origins, 38n25
The plumb-pudding in danger: – or – state epicures taking un petit souper (Gillray), x, 3–4
privateers, 27
The Production of Space (Lefebvre), 5
prophecy, 67
    Golgonooza, 102
    see also Brothers, Richard; Southcott, Joanna
prophets, 12
    radicalism and, 2
    of revolution, 167–8
Protestants
    absence from Holy Land, 98
    London Jews Society, 98

Qur'an, naming of, 119n49

radicalism, 1
Read, Mary, 19
Rediker, Marcus, *The Many-Headed Hydra: Sailors, Slaves, Commoners, and the Hidden History of the Revolutionary Atlantic*, 8, 24, 111, 158
Rennell, James, 123–4
republican ragamuffins, 161–2
revolution
    Equiano and slave revolt, 159–61

Haitian, 167–8
as hydra, 8
Mansong, Jack, 163–4
mobility and, 8
piracy and, 162
Roberts, Bartholomew *see* Black Bart
Romanticism
Black Romanticism, 9
British Romanticism, 9
Royal Society, African Association, 124–5

St Domingo, 167–8
A Search for Sovereignty (Benton), 5
Shabeeny, Asseed El Hage Abd Salam, 14–15, 137, 138
Sierra Leone
Clarkson, John, 159–60
Equiano in, 158–9
French revolutionaries, 161–2
slave trade, 146n24
African Company and, 127–8
African Institution, 130
British government and, 128–9
cannibalism fears, 170n37
capitalist terminology, 165
enlightenment of natives rhetoric, 128–9
Equiano and, 158
Falconbridge, 160–1
slaves
Equiano and revolt fears, 159
maroons, 150–1
pirate-owned, 37n8
revolt fears, 160–1, 163–4
Smith, Sidney, 99–100
social organisation of pirate crews, 24, 37n15

Société de Géographie prize for non-Muslims to Timbuktu, 138–9
Sound an Alarm (Southcott), 69–70
Southcott, Joanna, 12, 13, 67–8
Britain's chosenness, 71–2
The First Book of Wonders, 74–5
first communication with God, 69
The Fourth Book of Wonders, 72–3
geography of prophecy, 72–3
labour, 70
Napoleon and, 74–5
New Jerusalem, 69
Ottoman Muslims, 73
the poor and, 69–70
pregnancy, 70–1
Reece's statement, 71
Satan's space, 74
Sound an Alarm, 69–70
The Strange Effects of Faith, 69
The Third Book of Wonders, 71
Woman clothed with the Sun, 74–5
A Woman to Deliver Her People (Hopkins), 69–70
sovereignty
maps and, 5, 6
state territories and, 17n24
space
abstract, 16n15
atopia, 6
geometrical, 17n20
inhabited, 17n20
interpenetrating, 7
mental, 17n20
physical, 17n20

space (*Cont.*)
  power of, 6
  as a priori condition, 7
  social, 6, 7
  spatiality, 17n20
spatiality, social construction, 17n20
Stanford, George, Three-Fingered Jack, 164–7
state
  dynamism, 7
  territorial, 17n24
  see also nation
State/Space: A Reader (Brenner et al.), 7
The Strange Effects of Faith (Southcott), 69
symbolic reading, 67

Taylor, Edward, 28
territorial origins of pirates, 38n25
The Third Book of Wonders (Southcott), 71
Thom, J. N. *see* Courtenay, William Percy Honeywood
Three-Fingered Jack (Jack Mansong), 163
  escape, 163–4
  Obi: Or the History of Three-Fingered Jack (Carlyle), 164–5
  slave revolt, 163–4
  Stanford's narrative, 164–7
  Treatise on Sugar (Mosley), 164–7
Timbuktu, 14–15
  Account of Timbuctoo and Housa (Jackson), 137
  Adams, Robert, 123
  African Company, 127
  Africanus, Leo, 125
  Beaufoy, Henry, 123
  Caillié, René, 139
  da Gama, Vasco, 129–30
  descriptions, 125
  false narratives, 14
  Foulahs, 127
  Laing, Gordon, 127
  as mythical place, 143n1
  The Narrative of Robert Adams and, 130–1
  Park, Mungo, 125–6
  Rennell, James, 123–4
  Shabeeny, Asseed El Hage Abd Salam, 137, 138
  spoofs on *The Narrative*, 135–6
  see also African interior
Touissant, 163
traitor, economic system and, 25
Travels in The Holy Land, Egypt, &c. &c (Wilson), 95–6
Travels in the Interior Districts of Africa (Park), 126
Travels to Central Africa to Timbuctoo (Caillié), 139, *140*, 148n58
Treatise on Sugar (Mosley), 164–7
Tropicopolitans: Colonialism and Agency, 1688–1804 (Aravamudan), 9

universalism, 109–10

Vassa, Gustavus *see* Equiano, Olaudah
Vision of the Last Judgement (Blake), 106–7
  Islam, 108

Volney, Constantin François, *Journey in Egypt and in Syria*, 96

war
  cartography and, 3
  on piracy, 27–36
wealth redistribution, piracy and, 26

Willis, James, 125
Wilson, William Rae, *Travels in The Holy Land, Egypt, &c. &c*, 95–6
A Woman to Deliver Her People: Joanna Southcott and English Millenarianism in an Era of Revolution (Hopkins), 69–70
Written on the Water (Baker), 8

EU representative:
Easy Access System Europe
Mustamäe tee 50, 10621 Tallinn, Estonia
Gpsr.requests@easproject.com

www.ingramcontent.com/pod-product-compliance
Lightning Source LLC
Chambersburg PA
CBHW051100230426
43667CB00013B/2385